THE ELECTRIC WOMAN

A MEMOIR IN DEATH-DEFYING ACTS

TESSA FONTAINE

SANDSTONE PRESS

First published in Great Britain by
Sandstone Press Ltd
Dochcarty Road
Dingwall
Ross-shire
IV15 9UG
Scotland

www.sandstonepress.com

The publisher acknowledges subsidy from Creative Scotland
towards publication of this volume.

ISBN: 978-1-912240-20-3
ISBNe: 978-1-912240-21-0

Cover design by Two Associates
Typeset by Iolaire Typography Ltd, Newtonmore
Printed and bound by CPI Group (UK) Ltd, Croydon, CR0 4YY

For Mom & Davy, and their courageous hearts

AUTHOR'S NOTE

I have tried to re-create events, locales, and conversations as accurately as possible from my memories and extensive notes. In a few instances I have changed the names or identifying details of individuals in order to preserve anonymity. There are no composite characters, though I had to omit some people and events in the interest of book length. If you want some juicy stories that were left out, send me a postcard and I'll see what I can do.

CONTENTS

PROLOGUE

The Trick Is There Is No Trick

We start by lighting ourselves on fire. Parts that are easier to put out than our faces. Hands, to begin. Arms outstretched, palms toward the darkening sky, I watch as a flaming torch is wiped across my hand from wrist to fingertips. For one, maybe two seconds, I am on fire. The flame trail is two inches high. My hand warms. It doesn't burn exactly, but it feels like touching black leather after it has baked in the sun, a heat I impulsively want to move away from. I close my fist around the flame and put myself out.

⚡

"What sorts of acts can you do?" the sideshow manager, Tommy, asked.

Before I wrote back, I googled "acts in a sideshow." I culled a list of what I saw on Wikipedia's sideshow page: "Juggling. Fire swallowing. Poi spinning. Magic." I started feeling more brazen. What couldn't I learn in a couple of months? "Bed of nails. Snake charming," I wrote. Then, "All animal charming. I'm good with animals."

"Terrific," Tommy wrote back. "See you in two months."

I decided to learn one of the many acts I'd claimed to know, so now I'm in an "Introduction to Fire Eating" class at a fire arts collective in Oakland, California, because, of course, these things exist in the Bay Area. The evening outside the fence does not notice me. Buses sigh, a kid across the street accuses another of a basketball foul, old women roll their groceries behind them. I smell slow-cooking meat and exhaust. This is not a time to pause, close my eyes, and try to remember all these sounds and smells, but I do anyway.

I'd hoped some magic was involved in learning to eat fire. Something that meant you didn't really have to do the thing it appeared you were doing. Maybe you spread a flame retardant solution in your mouth, like on hotel curtains. Perhaps there was a little machine you wore behind your ear that shot fire-squelching foam onto the flame as it approached your face. Maybe it was an illusion.

But the class is a total disappointment.

There is no trick.

You eat fire by eating fire.

On the first day, Shaina, our teacher, all smiles, says: "Look at my severe burns!" She rolls up her sleeves and points with delight to a series of scars on her arms, like she is identifying constellations for a child. "This was from Japan. This one Rio. Sometimes, you burn yourself really badly in a performance," she says.

"What do you do then?" I ask.

"You put yourself out and keep on smiling."

The class is in a massive warehouse full of fire artists. We trudge past the welders and blacksmiths and ceramicists into an outside yard full of huge gas canisters and no smoking, dangerous, and flammable signs. We light our torches. I try not to think about the waiver I signed detailing possible death and dismemberment.

The first lesson: how to put yourself out.

There is only one other student in the class, a video-game designer with small gauges in his ears. I ask him why he's in the fire-swallowing class and he tells me that he feels too ordinary at Burning Man as a stilt walker. He wants something special. To be special.

Shaina hands me a thick, damp kitchen towel, picks up a can of white gas—the kind you use to refill lanterns on a camping trip, the kind I was never allowed to touch as a kid—and shakes some down both legs of her jeans. There is too much. Whole, fat droplets land on the fabric and soak right in, hundreds of them, a rainstorm from a metal canister never meant for such an offhanded joggle. She flicks a lighter and ignites herself.

Her legs, from midthigh down to ankle, are on fire. She is looking at me, smiling. Waiting. I dive toward her legs with the wet towel outstretched between my hands as she's saying, with firm encouragement, "Smother, smother, smother." I'm sure my hands will go up in flames the moment they near the fire. I pat the towel against her legs, up and down, and though I feel a little bit of warmth on my hands, they do not melt or blister. As I bring the towel away, I realize I have, indeed, put Shaina out. "Nice," Shaina says, and I feel a greater sense of success than I have about anything in a long time. "But that was way too gentle. If I'd really been cooking, I'd be singed by now. You'll understand the kind of force that's needed once you have to put yourself out." It is hard not to picture self-immolation, a body barely an outline inside a small cosmos of flame.

We practice again, this time with Stilt Walker and me really smacking Shaina's legs with force. We're winded and flushed and ready for a break, but it's time for us to get lit on fire.

Shaina tells us to reach out our hands, palms up, like bad schoolchildren in old movies readied for the switch. My heart is starting to pump fast. I haven't felt any fear about running

3

away with the sideshow until this moment. But Shaina is approaching my skin with fire. Excuses for leaving build in my throat, and though every instinct in my body encourages me to bail, I do not withdraw my palm. It is shaking. My upper lip is coated in sweat.

"See yourself on fire," Shaina says. "Let the flame dance. And then squelch it."

She wipes a torch across my skin. My palm is alight. I immediately close my fist and kill the flame.

She hands me the torch.

I hold it in my right hand and dab it to my left palm, but it doesn't catch. "Longer, firmer," she says. I try again. I am okay getting the fire to my hand, but keeping it there, pressing it into the flesh, that's the hard part. It's also what distinguishes fire performers from children who run their fingers through candle flames. But watching fire rise from your own skin is distressing. Why shouldn't it be? Evolution has trained us to flee from fire threatening our bodies.

We move on quickly. The next step is to wipe the flame along the top of the arm. "Do not wipe against the underside of the arm," she tells us, rubbing the blue-veined underbelly of her scar-crossed arm.

Stilt Walker is short and very hairy. The moment he wipes the fire against his arm with a jerky, nervous spasm, a wide swath of hairs instantly coils and blackens, then disintegrates. "My hair!" he yells. "It's burning!"

"Yes," Shaina says calmly. "It is."

He is wide-eyed and trying his hardest to fake a smile. I look down at my blond arm hair and imagine it growing back in thick black tendrils, like poison fairy-tale vines. I take a deep breath and wipe the torch across the top of my arm. Heat spreads as all the hairs take flame and are quickly singed.

"Let it burn!" Shaina yells as I suffocate the flame too quickly. I wipe my hand across my arm. Smooth as a baby's.

"In Turkey," Shaina tells us, "a barber singes his customer's face after he shaves it for ultimate smoothness. They find it relaxing."

I touch my arm again. I would not say this is relaxing, but there is something satisfying about how quickly we're building intimacy with an element most people fear. With an element that, just twenty minutes before, I'd been scared of. But here I am. Letting it rise on me.

Next, it's time for the tongue. Because he is a human with naturally developed survival instincts, Stilt Walker does not get the flame all the way to his tongue the first several tries. His tongue is stuck as far out from his body as it can go. I can see the muscles at the base of it quivering with effort. His neck is taut and the thin tendons protrude with strain. He turns the torch toward his mouth and lowers the flame. It is a foot away, six inches, four, then moves swiftly away from his face with a flame trail like a comet. He laughs nervously, shakes out his neck, and resumes his pose, head tilted slightly back, tongue out, a lizard midcatch. He begins lowering the flame toward his tongue again. Somehow, he's trying to back his body away from the flame at the same time he is bringing the fire closer to his face. Again, it's five inches, three, one inch away, and a retreat.

It's not surprising. Shaina tells us nobody puts the fire right into her mouth, right onto her tongue. There are too many years of learned behavior in the way.

At the end of his turn, Stilt Walker has attempted five or six times and brought the flame very close. I'm impressed, though my stomach clenches a little each time, worried for his face.

"Your turn," Shaina says.

I dip the torch in fuel and shake it out, and Shaina lights it. I'm sure I won't get it all the way in. She has demonstrated the movements a few times. I replicate what she's done. I widen my legs into a triangle, arch my spine, tilt my head back ninety degrees, bring the torch up above my face a foot or so and, with a dramatic turn of the wrist, beeline it right into my mouth.

I touch the torch to my tongue for one second and then pull it back out toward the sky.

"Jesus Christ," Shaina says. My mouth tastes like camping. My lips tingle. "You just lit your tongue on fire!" she says, and this is the only time I can imagine that being a congratulatory exclamation. I bring the still-lit torch back above my head, angle my wrist, and bring it down straight into my mouth again.

"Wow," Shaina says, laughing. "You don't have many instincts for self-preservation."

I consider telling her the whole story, then think better of it. The back of my teeth feel a little sooty on my tongue.

Oxygen feeds fire. If you succumb to impulse and attempt to blow out the flame as it nears your lips, you have forgotten about chemistry. An hour later, when I learn to swallow two torches at once, my desperate attempt to blow out the fire does not, in fact, succeed in extinguishing the flame but instead collects more oxygen that grows the torches into a huge fireball that engulfs my hands. It hurts. It *burns*. Shaina describes the most common types of burns—the kinds you get no matter what, no matter how careful you are in this line of work—as bad sunburns. I am now in a tradition of performers and mystics and childhood pyromaniacs; I will honor them by burning myself as infrequently as possible.

As soon as the class is over, I can tell my mouth is burned. Shaina says this is normal. Patches of my face and arms are reddish and tender. And there is cracked skin, almost like little dried-out blisters, on the corners of my mouth. I have a blind date after my class. It looks like I have herpes.

I avoid remembering this while I'm in the fire-eating class, but I used to be a chicken. My childhood memories are haunted by feeling too scared to do anything—from taking out the garbage at night to striking a match for incense. I watched all the other kids act brazen and bold, as I stood at eight years old, twelve, seventeen, upset with how much I did not want to be the person I was becoming. Later, I told people that I willed myself to stop being a fraidy-cat, but I think, as these things go, we develop personality traits when we need them.

For my whole life, I have been scared, terrified, of losing my mom.

I am losing my mom.

While I'm standing among explosive containers on a quiet Oakland night, she is humming at a nurse in one of her daily therapy sessions, because she no longer has language. While I am running a flame along my palm, she is running her hand across the half of her body that can no longer move. She touches it a lot, the paralyzed side. Perhaps it doesn't feel like it belongs to her. She touches everything around her. *Kitchen table, fork, husband*, we say as she touches those things, to let her know they still belong to her, too. *Wound*, we say as she touches her head where it was opened after her brain would not stop bleeding.

She is a yes person, a woman of adventure. When I begin to doubt that I can pull this off, I stop and think of her.

The only way to do it is to do it.

There is no trick.

THE ARCHITECTURE OF A WAVE

One Day after the Stroke

OCTOBER 2010

Her arms were tucked against her sides. She had been arranged.

"Prepare yourself," my stepdad, Davy, whispered into my hair when he hugged me outside her hospital room. I'd just arrived from across the country after a night of emergency phone calls. I was not prepared. My mom was in a hospital bed, covered in machines. There were remnants of fluid, blood and yellow secretions, dried all along her head. A ventilator taped across her mouth pulled her skin taut.

I started to whisper something to Davy, but he stopped me. "She can't hear you," he said. "She won't wake up."

"Until when?" I asked.

He let out a sigh that caught in his throat halfway, the air turning into a sob that turned into a cough that turned into silence. We stood beside one another, not touching.

She was in an induced coma. They had filled her with barbiturates to knock her out. That's what a nurse told me, when I asked, after being in the room with my mom for ten minutes and then fleeing to find some goddamned information. I pinched and pinched and pinched myself.

"What is happening?" I asked another nurse. She squeezed my shoulder like a football coach.

An induced coma reduces the rate of cerebral blood flow.

After her blood slowed, they hauled out the chain saw. I do not know if they actually used a chain saw. Probably not. But it had to have been a big saw to cut away half of a human skull.

When I came back to her room, Davy, my aunt, and my uncle stepped outside.

"We'll give you a few minutes alone," they said. "To say what you need to say."

Two weeks before, a handwritten note had arrived from her that said, for no reason, she was proud of me.

I walked into the room. Sat in a chair beside her bed. I knew she would not open her eyes. She would not say *babygirl*, that high-pitched, delighted greeting that was all mine.

The bandage covering her head poofed out over the opened area because her brain was so swollen, because the bleeding would not stop. It looked like a piece of popcorn that had begun bursting from its kernel. Her head was shaved.

Her hospital-room window looked out onto the roof of another building, a large, flat rectangle coated with something like pressed gravel. There were seven seagulls standing on the roof. Fat, white bodies with bright orange beaks and spindly legs.

She had had a hemorrhagic stroke.

I needed to say the important stuff.

"Mom," I said, touching her arm. All my insides were aflame.

I kept my hand on her arm. The ventilator wheezed. Took my hand off to cover my mouth. I thought I'd scream. I thought I'd throw up every single thing I'd ever eaten. I needed to tell her the things I'd done such a shitty job telling her. Open. Your. Mouth. Speak.

The fire in my lungs turned to ash. Every word I'd ever known was burned.

Out the window, the seagulls were all facing the same

9

direction. Seven seagulls, evenly spaced, their faces pointed the same way. I stood up and looked where they were looking. A parking lot, scattered trees, a road. I didn't believe in omens.

Davy came in and sat beside me. He gave a few details. The very private specifics of an emergency.

The vomit and shit when he'd walked into their bedroom.

The eyes rolled back in the head.

The speed with which the paramedics came.

The unknowing at the hospital.

The chaplain assigned to him as he waited.

"When I saw the chaplain, I knew," he said. "That's when I knew how bad it was. I didn't know until then, but it was the chaplain that made me understand. The hospital assigns them to families who are losing someone. Even after I said no thanks to his counseling, no to prayers or hand-holding or any of that shit. He kept coming back, checking on me, asking how Teresa was doing. So I knew. They thought she'd die for sure."

His voice was steady this entire conversation—the shock of it, maybe. The up-all-night-at-the-hospital of it.

The gulls were not facing the window. That would be too obvious. An omen.

Outside, there were bay trees and beyond that the dried-out October hills and far beyond that, twelve miles at least, the Pacific, which is where those birds must have come from originally. And if that was true, if they'd left the salt and spray, taken wing from the smooth sand, found wind to ride and flapped and let their feathers carry them here, then were they here for her? Did they know? Did they come to guide her back to the ocean?

$$\pmb{\mathscr{f}}$$

The water is clear and the sand is warm and every morning, before going to work at the travel agency, she slices into an orange-pink papaya. She eats half for breakfast, spooning out the flesh in big hunks, wiping her chin with the back of her hand, because there is almost too much juice, too much perfume, because it spills over no matter how careful she is.

But she is not going to work.

She's nineteen and about to climb onto a surfer's shoulders out in the turquoise waters of a Hawaiian beach. Her name is Teresa.

There's a crowd gathering on the sand. She steps into the ocean beside the surfer, paying no attention to the small sharp shells beneath her feet.

Out into the water then, deeper, until it is time to paddle.

They climb onto the board belly-first, she below, the surfer on top of her, two sets of arms paddling in tandem. They must move with one another like oars along a canoe. Over the break, farther out to the point where the waves begin swelling enough to catch.

They are so far out, and then a little farther, and a little farther still. They turn their board toward the shore. She can feel her heart hammering against the wood. Waves pass beneath them, lifting the back and then the front in a gentle roll.

Mornings when they practice, gulls swoop nearby, small clear fish move in clouds. The pincushion sea stars wink and wave.

A big swell nears. Teresa looks over her shoulder a few times, checking to see how quickly the wave approaches, how it is rising. The audience holds their hands above their eyes to block the glare. They are ready to be amazed.

The wave catches hold of the board with a little tug and they begin to fly. She presses herself up, stands quickly, and the surfer behind her does as well. He grips her by the waist.

She springs up and he lifts her, one fluid motion, her body rising from the board and into the air, her feet at his knees and then she's nearly to the sky, touching the sun, her head and shoulders bent back as he lifts her waist above his head and then plants her on his shoulders. Her legs bent

11

around his chest, she lifts her arms in the air, sitting high above the water.

She smiles and waves for the audience. They cannot hear the blood roiling in her temples, the nerves, they cannot feel her hammering heart. She performs fearlessness. The board is unsteady atop the water and the surfer's legs shake with the effort of balance and she quivers as she flexes her muscles to stay upright, she must stay upright, and still, she keeps one arm up, up, up toward the sky, that kind of queen, pointing at the sun, that high.

THE SNAKE CHARMER

Day 7 of 150

I've just finished Windexing the glass in front of Queen Kong, our giant taxidermy gorilla, when Tommy pops his head into the tent. "You ready to meet the snakes?" he asks.

The night before, Tommy had gone to negotiate the purchase of two giant boa constrictors from some guy in town—I didn't know who, or where they came from, or how Tommy knew these snakes were safe to handle, but I knew they were being delivered to our show today.

It is the night before we open at our first fair. I've been with the sideshow for seven days. Our circus tent is up, taut and shining, the banner line is hung, stages built, curtains scrubbed, illusions bolted, ratchets oiled. Fireflies spark and fade. Men in yellow "Safety Is Non-Negotiable!" shirts straddle the metal arms of the scrambler beside our tent, cursing above the blaring pop country hits as they hinge and pin the little metal closures.

I follow Tommy into the bunkhouse/ backstage area, the back end of a semi where we all sleep and eat and live, just a curtain away from the audience when we'll be performing.

Tommy unlatches a plastic trunk and inside, coiled around one another, are two boa constrictors.

"Do you know how to pick them up?" he asks me.

13

"Maybe you could show me how you like it done," I say.

"Sure," he says, a half smile across his face that makes me wonder if he believes my e-mail bluff about the snakes at all. "You've gotta reach both your hands all the way inside the box, under the bodies of the snakes," he says, crouched low and elbow-deep in the snake box. I was hoping for some kind of net or gloves. But his hands are right on the scaly bodies. Not even the illusion of protection.

"The dude I got these beauties from said they'd been handled before, so they should be easy enough to manage. Use both hands to pick them up," he says, his nearly cartoonish New Jersey accent thick in his voice. "If you pick up a giant snake with one hand, it could kill it. Their backs break, they get paralyzed, and they can't eat. Last season, one of the snakes died after a performer accidentally picked him up that way."

Tommy stands and faces me. His arms are stretched out wide in front of him and the snake, a seven-footer, is draped between his hands, her body making a giant M.

It is my turn. I should hold out my arms and take the snake. But there is ringing in my ears. I can't stop swallowing and my heart is pounding and I can't move toward Tommy. I try to focus on what I see.

The snake has tan and chestnut diamonds down her back, the shapes outlined in black and cream. She is as big around as a grapefruit. Wrangling these snakes will be one of my primary jobs and one of the skills I listed on my qualifications. I can't let him know how scared I am. I stretch a smile across my face as wide as I can.

"What's her name?" I ask.

"No name yet."

"Hello, snake," I say. She does not blink.

Tommy steps toward me, and without meaning to I step backward. He steps toward me again. I involuntarily step back, trying to throw a casual laugh on top of my ducking and dodging like this little tango is just a joke. After a few

14

steps, though, I've come to the wall. My back is cold against the metal-and-wood paneling that runs inside the truck. I feel the film of dust slide against my palms. I try to come up with excuses that might explain why I'm trying to escape the snake, but my mind is nearly blank. I start to sweat.

"Will she bite?" I ask, desperate to stall.

"Boas don't bite," he says. "They squeeze their prey to death."

"Oh, right."

"But she won't do that to you. She knows you're too big to eat," he says. "Just make sure she doesn't get around your throat, of course," he says. I touch my neck, imagining her body tightening around me.

I had some idea that because I'd been through so many harder things, once this moment of reckoning arrived—once it was me and the snake, not the imagined fear, not the generic childhood phobia—I'd see she was just another beautiful creature on the earth trying to get by, and I'd find peace.

I find no peace.

Sideshows are where people come to see public displays of their private fears: of deformity, of a disruption in the perceived gender binary, of mutation, of disfigurement, of a crossover with the animal world, of being out of proportion. And that is a sideshow's intention—to frame whoever or whatever is on display as being outside the realm of what's "normal." For the snake act, it should appear that I have such chemistry with the creature that we are almost one. That's what's interesting to see—the snake/human duo who have overcome the predator/prey divide.

I look at the snake. She is moving her head side to side, trying, I'm sure, to find someone to kill. I'm sweating. A few of the other performers come through the stage curtains and into the truck, rushing right to the snakes with open arms and kissy

15

noises and pet names. They've all worked with snakes before.

"Who's a snake? Oh, you're just a snake, that's right, girl," Cassie says as she reaches out both hands and takes the snake. She notices me trying to plaster myself to the wall and breathing hard. "The snakes think you're just a big tree," she says encouragingly. I nod my head, glance out the door to the darkening escape route where a polka band rehearses "America the Beautiful."

"I haven't actually, uh, spent much time around snakes before," I say, ready to be chastised, ready, at twenty-nine, to be treated like a fibbing child, but the admission doesn't seem to faze anyone. Tommy shrugs and Cassie steps toward me.

"Here's the little angel," she says, moving quickly as she drapes the snake around my shoulders.

The snake is cold and so heavy she forces my neck to bend so I'm looking down at the floor, and I taste blood as I bite the inside of my cheek, knowing, like a sword in my heart, that I cannot do this.

⚡

I ended up with a snake around my neck because of a conversation with a giant.

February 2013.

Four months before this snake moment.

Two and a half years after my mom had her stroke.

A town in Florida where sideshow performers retire.

I snuck around back behind the circus tent to an old, off-white trailer, peeling, rusted, with all its curtains drawn. I knocked. Something inside bumped the trailer's wall and the whole thing shook. It was still again.

I could feel my heartbeat under my tongue, pulsing that soft skin like the belly of a panicked frog. Trespasser. That's what the man would say, if he ever opened the door.

I knocked again. Something jostled in the trailer, followed by some clanging. The door opened the width of a human head.

"Yes?" the man asked. He was huge, his neck bending and back stooping to fit his face into the door's opening. In the dim trailer light I could just make out that he was wearing droopy underwear and a yellowed T-shirt.

"Hi," I said, unsure of what to say next, realizing I hadn't planned anything beyond this moment. "I was wondering if I could ask you a few questions about the sideshow. About your life?"

He stared at me.

"I'm a big fan," I said, and smiled, and didn't step away from the door despite his silence.

"I don't do daylight," he finally said. His voice was low, and gruff, and gravelly, like a man who'd been shouting into a microphone for a lifetime. Which is exactly what he was.

"I can come back when it's dark," I said. "I'm a student." I was trying to throw any pieces of my identity toward him that I thought might make him sympathetic. Willing to talk.

He sighed. "All right, then. Come back when it's dark."

I walked around to the front of the tent, paid three dollars, and went inside.

Steel blades flew from a man's fingertips and landed inches from a woman turned sideways, her spine arched. *Thwack*. Knife after knife sliced the wooden board. Stood straight out. A constellation of metal like a saint's glow. Like she was made of prayers. *Thwack*. She did not flinch. Stared at her assailant. I had spent a lot of the past few years feeling tired, half-asleep, in the lulls between emergencies. But in this tent, watching the blades make a new shape around the woman's body, I felt very, very awake.

The knife-throwing pair was performing on a stage inside the World of Wonders, a sideshow at the Florida State Fair. The World of Wonders, the talker outside had said, was the very last traveling sideshow of its kind. I'd never seen anything

17

like it—the Bay Area, where I grew up, was far too PC for a sideshow. But recently I'd learned that there was a town called Gibsonton that was famous for its sideshow performers, and that there was a sideshow performing at the fair just down the road from Gibsonton. I headed for Florida.

I watched the acts twice through. I smiled and rolled my eyes with the rest of the crowd as a human-headed spider told us she's just *hanging out,* covered my eyes as a man hammered nails up into his nostrils. Other performers manipulated their bodies, harming them—or seeming to, or avoiding the harm at just the last moment, when it still felt like things might go very wrong.

But nothing went wrong. They survived.

And I witnessed these miracles they were performing. I was not sitting in hospital rooms, or helping with a physical therapy transfer. I was not talking through options for surgeries.

Instead, I was keeping my eye on the blade as the knife thrower landed the final piercing tip just beside his assistant's head. He turned to the audience, gently nodded, and walked toward the board to gather his instruments. The knife, somehow, always missed the flesh.

The trailer was dark and musty. There was a three-foot- long shaggy spider leg on the floor beside a torn canvas banner. Painted there, a man swung heavy chains from his eyelids.

"The work is very hard. Dangerous," Chris Christ said right away. He co-owned the World of Wonders with his partner, both in business and in life, Ward Hall. They've been together since 1967.

"Putting up and taking down the tent every few days, moving towns. For twelve, fourteen, sixteen hours a day, every day, without stopping. You're always working," Chris said. Each word comes out of his mouth wet and heavy, loud enough to be onstage. Which is where he usually is. He'd been a sideshow talker for years, and chimp trainer, knife performer, inventor of new acts. He seemed twice as big as a regular man, like he stayed in the womb for double the allotted time. His ears stood out wide from his head and dark tobacco snuff trails ran down from the corners of his mouth.

"How'd you get in the business?" I asked him. I pretended to look over his shoulder at the wall as he thought but concentrated all my peripheral vision on his face. This was the face of the sideshow. Creases. Grease. This was a body that chose to take in fire and swords.

"Where are you from?" I asked him.

"Did you always want to be a performer?"

"What does it feel like to eat fire?"

"Does anyone ever get really hurt?"

"Have you always felt like the sideshow was a place you fit in?"

I asked and asked, question after question, until an hour turned into three or four and then he was finally silent. He stared at me across the table where we'd moved once evening light gave way to the pitch-black of late night. He had answered each question I threw at him, asked some of them back to me—surprised, he said, by a young person taking interest in this world. Most people believed it was dying.

"I don't know what else to tell you," Chris finally said. "Have you learned everything you wanted?"

"Yes," I said. "Thank you." I looked around the trailer, locked my eyes on the giant spider leg. There was more I wanted to know. I wanted to know how to make sense of my attraction to this world of illusions and danger. Where the work was physically grueling, where the task was to transform into someone else, someone who could transcend a fragile human body. Someone who was and was not herself onstage.

"You really want to know what it's like inside a sideshow?" he asked. There was a tone in his voice of, what—annoyance? Amusement? I started to pack my notes.

19

"Then come play with us," he said. I met his eyes, sure he was joking. He held my gaze. Raised his eyebrows, expecting my response.

"Really?"

"Why not?" he asked.

"Well . . ." I imagined telling my mom that I'd been invited to join a sideshow. That I'd said no.

I nodded at him. "Okay," I said.

⚡

Four months later, I arrive in Tampa with a suitcase full of family-friendly stripper costumes, selected per my future coworker/stage manager Sunshine's instructions, which I heave into the fifteen-person passenger van that picks me up at the airport. The World of Wonders Sideshow winters in Gibsonton, known to locals as Gibtown, ten miles from Tampa. We're meeting there before we load up and head north. We will follow a semi packed with our show all the way to Pennsylvania and the first fair. The 2013 carnival season opens in eight days, and for the next five months, we'll travel all over the country performing in state and county fairs, living in the semi.

Chris Christ will stay in Florida for most of the season, managing the show from afar, while Tommy will be in charge of on-the- road operations. Tommy is also the show's primary talker, not *barker*—a term that will immediately expose you as an outsider, I learn—and has been with the World of Wonders for nine years.

After I left Florida with Chris Christ's invitation to join the show, I began doubting that it was real. Thought maybe I'd misunderstood. I e-mailed him to ask if it was a joke. Nope, he said, come along. There were a few months left before the season started, so as I finished up at school and prepared to graduate, I sent another e-mail to Chris, checking again. Making sure he remembered it was me, not a real performer.

"I think it would be a great adventure for you," Chris wrote back. "Plus, we could use a little help with PR. You're a college girl. Maybe you can write some stuff."

The van picking me up at the Tampa airport holds Tommy, the road boss and talker, and Sunshine, the stage manager/fire eater. Sunshine, I immediately recognize, was the target half of the knife-throwing act I saw at the Florida State Fair. I feel a little starstruck.

"You tired?" Sunshine asks as I climb in, exhaling her vapor cigarette, "or do you wanna go to a party? Pipscy'll be out with us this season. She's having a going-away party tonight. There'll be friends, family, other performers." Her voice is slow and even. She has the round, watery eyes, coiffed hair, and disappointed pursed lips of a silent-film heroine. "Pipscy's a mermaid."

"I love mermaids," I say. Tommy steers us toward the party.

The van is clean and white with plush gray seats. Blue fuzzy dice hang from the rearview mirror. Sunshine and Tommy tell me about the previous season's thirteen-foot albino python. "I wasn't really paying attention one day," Sunshine says, waving her hand dismissively, "and Lemon managed to wrap herself all the way around my arms and neck, and then slid down my body, pinning me completely inside her coils. *Bad Lemon*, I said. Someone had to come unwrap her so I could move again. It was so funny." She and the boss exchange nostalgic smiles. I hope they don't notice my blanched cheeks.

Lining the road are meticulously spaced palm trees, an intrusion of order in a state with so much wild. Soon, the palm trees give way to concrete art: sculpted geese or the outline of a gator, huge against the wild brush in the background. We're flying.

"No Lemon this year, though," Tommy says. "All the interstate reptile regulations just changed. No pythons across state borders without permits. Pythons and a few other snakes are

21

considered too likely to escape and make new snake colonies wherever they get out. And the permits are expensive."

"So no snakes?" I ask, a little too eagerly.

"Oh, there will be snakes," Tommy says. "Boa constrictors. No permits required."

"Boa constrictors," I parrot.

"You like snakes?" Tommy asks, meeting my eyes in the rearview mirror with his steady gaze.

"I'm going to," I manage.

Apart from the e-mail I'd sent Tommy in which I'd bluffed my skills, I didn't know how much Chris Christ had told the crew about who I was—that I'd shown up at his trailer searching for his sideshow story and suddenly found myself inside my own. I didn't know what they believed I could perform, if the list I'd sent Tommy had been passed around, and I was nervous to ask, to get caught in my lie. I was even more nervous to be thrown onstage with the expectation that I could do something I couldn't—like the actor's classic nightmare of being in a play where you don't know your lines or even what play is being performed.

"What other acts, exactly, will I be doing?" I ask. My voice shakes a little.

"You're our bally girl, which means you'll stand out on the front stage with the talker, Tommy, and help him get people to buy tickets to come into the show. Bally girls handle the snakes, eat fire, escape from handcuffs, and perform magic," Sunshine says.

"Great," I say, gulping, racking my brain for magic tricks I knew as a kid, for some way to apologize and explain I am not an escape artist.

"You eat fire, right?" she asks.

"Yep," I say. Since I've just learned, I look like a fool doing it.

"Then you're all set. I'll teach you some advanced fire-eating tricks, if you want. But we usually just train all the bally girls on everything when they come. You'll learn the other acts sometime soon."

22

My stomach muscles loosen their clenching just enough that I can smile and nod at Sunshine as she turns to look at me. I don't believe her. Even if it's true that they teach many of the performers the acts after they get here, I'm sure they all come with an arsenal of experience I'm lacking.

"Don't worry," she says. "Performing the acts is the easy part of making it out here."

The party for Pipscy is meant to infuse her with love and fun and booze, because, story goes, this will be the first time she's ever left home and she's terrified. She's been performing in the Tampa nightclub circuit a few years, a little burlesque here, *Rocky Horror Picture Show* there, but now, at twenty-two, she's going to try to hit the road. That's all I know about Pipscy when I am introduced to the girl with robin red hair who is jumping up and down just before she takes a shot of Jägermeister with her roommate, a guy at least twice her age who has just had his leg amputated above the knee. It is wrapped in white gauze, which Pipscy helps change two times a day.

"Fuck diabetes," he says, nodding toward his leg. I agree.

"You'll never believe what awesome goodbye presents I'm getting," Pipscy says, pulling me over to a table. She fingers a small pile of neatly stacked bones. "Like this—it's a choker made of armadillo vertebrae—and this," she says, gesturing to a painting of a girl's face hung on the wall, "portrait of me. It's painted in blood." She doesn't say whose.

I'm introduced to Spif, our show's knife thrower and assistant stage manager, who is leaning against the kitchen sink with slicked-back hair and a long beard—the point from which he derives his powers, he says. It splays out like the whole world has a static charge.

I try to mimic his cool lean. "This is gonna be quite an adventure," I say.

"Yeah," he says, "life on the road's fucking crazy."

"I bet," I say. "Wait. Like, bad crazy? Like, scary?" I ask, trying to sound nonchalant.

"Sometimes. But it doesn't matter 'cause I can't die."

I look over at him and expect a smile, but his face is stoic. "How's that?"

"I can't be killed," he says. "I'm a Juggalo."

Juggalos: die-hard fans of Insane Clown Posse, a horrorcore rap group whose listeners drink and spray Faygo soda and, as I just learned, can't die.

"Well," Spif says, "I *can* die, but not until I have a rusty ax, until I know voodoo, until I have a fat bitch named Bridget, and a little sip of Faygo, too," he says, his words gaining rhythm, and then he raps a few lines. It's from one of ICP's hits, Spif explains, "I Want My Shit." What a beautiful idea, that death could come only after the right boxes have been checked. I want to tell him I like the lyrics and why, but I don't want to lay my grief on someone I've just met while standing in the middle of a party. Plus, I'm not sure if I am going to tell anyone here at all. What if I kept the door to that story closed here? I pinch my leg and keep my mouth shut.

Spif fiddles with a horseshoe piercing in his septum, then fingers one of the ten or twelve necklaces he wears on his neck—there are wooden beads, silver chains, an amulet, crystals. "I'm the only half-Mexican I've ever met," he tells me, "who can't speak any Spanish." He's handsome, in his early twenties, with the sort of face you might see carved for the statue of a city's great battalion leader. I like that snippets of his life seem to tumble out of his mouth without hierarchy, those ICP lyrics delivered with the same passion and intensity as a mention of his teenage homelessness.

"Oh god, is he telling you about being a Juggalo?" Sunshine asks, walking over. "You've got to stop him. It will never end." She elbows him in the ribs. "Cigarette?" she asks, looking at him, but before he can respond, Pipscy throws her arms around his neck from behind and pulls him in close.

"Hey, love," he says, burying his nose in her cheek. She purrs. Pipscy's boyfriend, a Renaissance fair reenactor, stands a few feet away, readying to say goodbye to her for the five months we'll be on the road. He doesn't seem to notice.

"So how do these kinds of long-distance relationships work?" I ask Sunshine a little later. She spends twenty minutes telling me about her boyfriend from a warm perch in Tommy's lap.

"I miss my boyfriend a lot, all the time," she says, exhaling. "It's really hard." She gets off the boss's lap and comes closer to me, lowering her voice. "I can't wait to leave this show one day and be back with him all the time. Keep it quiet, but I want this season to be my last. It's my seventh, and I'm tired of this shit."

I ask Spif the same relationship question a little later. "Well," he says, "it's pretty much a don't ask, don't tell situation. What happens on the road stays on the road," he says. "It's hard, though. There's no loyalty anymore."

"So you've been faithful but other people haven't been?" I ask.

He gives a wry smile and looks at me sideways. "I'm not saying nothing," he says. "But what happens on the road stays there."

The party carries on around me, people laughing and talking and doing all the normal party things in their dark-colored lipstick as some kind of punk or hardcore plays in the background and people walk up to one another and know the right things to say, have a whole world together that I don't know how to enter. I feel incredibly far away from everything that's happening.

I excuse myself and walk half a block down the street.

"You make it to Florida?" Devin says when he picks up the phone.

"Oh shit," I say.

"Oh yeah?" he says.

25

"Oh shit."

"Are you okay?"

I tell him about the bone necklaces, the blood paintings, the Juggalo, the law of infidelity. I tell him everyone's in black and a few people are speaking carnie and I am in a collared shirt and cowboy boots and I'm such a square and who do I think I am for believing I can do something like this and who do I think I am for not spending every minute with my mom and I feel out of place, totally, spiritually, physically, Christ, shit, oh shit.

"Well, yeah, isn't that the point?" he says. I stay silent.

Devin's becoming a techie. As I was shopping in Haight-Ashbury's sex shops for fishnets and spiked, studded heels, he was in interviews using words like *productivity* and *interface*. He asked me to proofread his résumé while I asked him what color wig he liked best.

"Kid, you can always leave," he says. This makes something in my soft insides turn to stone. I imagine calling Davy and my mom, telling them that it's too tough out here, that I don't fit in. I think about telling this to the woman who performed tricks on top of a surfer's shoulders, to the woman who worked on an all-male fishing boat in the Pacific a few years later. To the woman patiently O-ing her mouth day after day and hoping a word will come out.

"No, I can't," I say.

⚡

On my seventh day with the World of Wonders crew, all my fellow performers' eyes are on me, the new snake charmer, to see what I do with this beastie around my neck. I will be bold. I touch the snake's body with my hand. My eyes crest with tears. My chest heaves. I can hardly breathe. I'm trying to tell myself not to be scared, that there is no reason to think the snake might hurt me, that people look far greater terror in the face every day, people who are even at this minute standing very

26

close to me. I dig in deep, try to channel that bravery. Exhale slowly.

"Okay, nope, enough," I say, scooting my shoulders out from under the snake. Four sets of arms reach toward me to catch the snake I'm recoiling beneath. They grab the thick body and peel her muscled length from my neck. They move fast. It appears, given the placement of their hands, that they think there is a very good chance I will drop or throw the snake.

"Off, off, off," I say, the tears breaking and dribbling down my cheek. My heart won't slow the pace of its clenching, the thump of its terror.

"Snake lesson number one," Tommy says, creating a quick distance between me and the reptile. "That was a good start," he says, taking in stride my inability to hold the snake, not letting on to any disappointment. "You'll practice again, and it'll feel better, and then you'll be ready to perform with them." He's putting the snake back in the trunk.

"You okay?" he asks. I nod. I am so grateful that Tommy is not the stereotypical boss from the old circus movies who'd throw you from the train in the middle of the night. He doesn't seem surprised by my fear of the snake, by how little I'd known during setup, by my anxious gulp each time I remind him I don't know how to perform the escape artist act I'll be doing tomorrow, or the magic trick.

It seems that showing up here for the bally girl position without any skills is par for the course. My lying was ignored. Or expected. And maybe so is embellishing your own story.

It is 8:00 p.m. the night before we open. By the next morning, I have to be ready to hold the snakes for twelve hours a day and to do it again the next day. And the day after that.

HUMAN HISTORY

One Week After the Stroke

OCTOBER 2010

I would paint her nails midnight. That was my next task. Nail polish. I could focus on nail polish.

Maybe midnight was too dramatic. Maybe coral. Powder blue. A nurse had said—in response to our twenty-fifth question that afternoon about when she might wake up and what a certain toe twitch might mean and what we could be doing to help—"Why don't you paint her nails?"

"Oh yes, she'll be so happy to see some color right when she wakes up," my aunt said. And so we had brought a Ziploc baggie of polishes. Some lotion to soften the cuticles. My mom's nails were chewed to hell. It looked strange, actually, that evidence of living and working and stress on a hand that was now unmoving.

It had been a week since she'd had as big and bad a stroke as you can have and still be alive, as the doctors said. She was put into an induced coma to try to let her brain heal itself a little bit. When she woke up, they'd be able to assess the damage. But don't hold your breath, they said. It doesn't look good.

There were moments when she looked peaceful. Between the ventilator's wheeze and the heart monitor's beep, there was this slice of a second where she was still and her eyes were closed. That's usually when people imagine their loved one is just asleep and will wake right up and be fine. When I started to let my mind wander that way, I cut it off. Blood like an oil spill in her brain. I imagined that instead.

I could touch four walls from where I stood. The door was locked to my right. It even had a deadbolt. The whole great world falling apart down the hall and this small place with a lock and space for just one person. Not like the hospital room itself, filled by nurses in astronaut suits and noisy machines and panic. It was hard to remember I had my own body when I was in the room with my mom and her body. I held the bathroom sink and made myself look straight into the mirror, seeing my swollen nose. My pink patchy skin and mascara smears.

"Human fucking history," I said out loud. "This is the normal cycle of human history," I said, trying to sound like the reasonable person others believed me to be. Mellow, levelheaded. I was trying to conjure that idea of myself, but my chest and guts were filled with a throbbing, acute pain, hot pain, searing. I started pinching the skin between thumb and pointer finger with my nails. People lose their parents and carry on. Human history. We must have some innate biological coping mechanism that enables the numbing of grief. This wound must be mendable over time, because it has to be—because people go on, because a death happens and eventually it's Wednesday, and then Thursday, and somebody has to buy coffee filters.

I brought my face closer to the mirror. I was doing a thing I'd seen people do when they needed to get serious with themselves.

"This is not special," I made myself say, looking into my eyes. My face blurred. Idiot crying baby.

⚡

When I was thirteen, my mom drove me to interview at a fancy private high school. She'd hated high school, had not done

29

well, hadn't gone to college more than a semester here or there. She was unwilling to let my education resemble hers in any way.

We drove farther from our small town's redwoods and oaks, farther from the golden hills hiding vultures and whitening bones. The houses grew bigger and cleaner the closer we came to the school. Fifteen and then twenty minutes of driving, twenty-five, and the houses shone at the tops of long-necked driveways. And we were there. My mom's hands were tight on the steering wheel. There was sweat on her face.

"I guess I've forgotten my pearls," she said as we pulled into the school's arched entryway. The buildings were ivory, the rolling lawns manicured and plush. She brushed the hair back from her ear, smoothed her shirt and slacks with the palm of her hand. We were dressed up fancy. Earlier that morning I had been instructed to remove the boxers beneath the baggy jeans I was wearing and to instead wear some corduroys, a sweater. Wealthy-people clothes. I needed a full scholarship. I wasn't sure whether leaving everyone and everything I knew for this new world was what I wanted or not, but my mom was uninterested in my doubt. She pulled into a visitor parking spot, and we sat in silence for a moment. "I never had a chance like this, you know," she said. She reached into her purse and pulled out her lipstick. "But you," she said, twisting the tube and unfolding her mirror. She stopped what she was doing and looked at me. "You are so goddamned smart." Her voice was sharp, almost angry. She pressed the color to her lips.

My fingernails dug into my skin as I surveyed the students in crisp, clean cardigans and new tennis shoes. I took a deep breath and opened the door to get out, but she grabbed my arm. She spoke very quickly. "You are just as smart as anyone here," she said. "Smarter. Do not let them intimidate you." She did not take her eyes off mine. "I let people tell me I wasn't smart my whole life and I believed them and it almost destroyed me. But you. Go show them. You are very, very special."

⚡

Down the hall, my mother was not dead. The table beside her bed was full of nail polish. Reds. Glitter. Day after day, I sat beside her and painted and then repainted and repainted the nails on her left hand, and her toenails, because they were the only parts of her body we were allowed to touch. The skin on her right hand, the crook of her elbow, and her fingers were covered by tape holding needles in place. There were four different tubes going into her head.

People die.

Of course they do.

And yet, against the lessons of history, against the inevitability of time, against her bleeding brain and how much of her already seemed lost, I felt this small thrumming hope deep in my stomach that she'd recover. It kept me certain that this couldn't be the end. I was terrified to let the hope grow.

"You are not special. You are not special. You are not special," I said to the mirror.

OPEN THE GATES

Day 8 of 150

WORLD OF WONDERS
JUNE 2013

The carnival is waking.

Music blasts from the Alien Abduction ride just to our right, turns up louder, then shuts back off. We're in Butler, Pennsylvania. Carnies I've seen only in grimy T-shirts in the four days we've been setting up at our first fair swagger between rides in bright blue polo shirts, the company uniform, greeting one another with quick nods or, for the older guys, handshakes. This carnival, which includes most of these games and rides, has already played a couple of fairs this season, and the carnies jump from the edge of their rides onto the ground with the ease and comfort of big cats, a strut in each movement, an ownership. We are independent contractors; we travel between carnival companies, working with new folks at each spot.

In twenty minutes, the 2013 World of Wonders season will officially open and the gates will let the marks inside. I will eat fire, charm snakes, perform magic, and escape from chains for the first time in front of a crowd.

The idea gives me tingles.

The rides are all plugged in and lit up and the music is on and the air smells like frying onions and I'm costumed and made up. I meet Tommy inside the tent, ready to go out onto the bally stage with him. I feel like a bird has been loosed inside my body, brushing every organ with its wings until I can hardly keep the big tickled smile off my face, the fear of not actually being good enough to perform any of these acts just behind that.

As the show's bally girl, I'll stand out on the front bally stage with the talker, who alternates every hour between Tommy and Cassie so that they don't blow their voices. I'll be eating fire, or charming snakes, or escaping from handcuffs, or performing a magic trick where I turn a one-dollar bill into a five. I had a fire-eating class. And Spif showed me the handcuffs and dollar-bill acts in five minutes the night before, after I'd stopped shaking from holding the snake. This was nothing like performing in school plays, where the bulk of time was spent rehearsing—here it was trial by fire, as Sunshine called it. You learned by doing. Onstage. In front of an audience. Good reason to get better quickly.

"Ready, Tessy?" Tommy asks, walking toward the bally stage with his bag of swords in one hand, money box in the other. I'm so relieved to see the snake around his neck. "I'll just take her for now," he says, noticing how I'm staring.

"Thank you, Tommy," I say. He flashes me a big, cheesy grin, one that looks suddenly different, used-car-salesman-like, above his sequined jacket, and I laugh. It's perfect.

We climb onto the stage and look out at the midway. Still mostly empty. It's Friday, late morning. We are at the farthest point from the fair's front gates, and no eager patrons have made their way back through the carnival yet, so I have a moment to practice.

"What's your stage name?" Tommy asks.

"I haven't exactly decided yet," I admit.

"All right," he says. "Should I just call you Tess?"

"Sure," I say. But no. I'm not here for that. "Or maybe if you think of a good name, you could just call me it? If you have any ideas?"

33

"Hmm," he says, tapping his fingers along his mouth, beneath the thin black mustache he drew on that morning. "Today, you will see Tex Fontaine eat the fire and escape from these chains right in front of your eyes," he says into the mic. And then, to me, "Yeah, Tex?"

"Sure," I say. "I'll come up with more," he says. "Better names."

A family with two strollers is approaching from down the midway, and beyond them, a few other people are trickling this way, so Tommy starts grinding into the mic, listing the acts we have inside with flourish, a warm-up he calls it, and I practice breaking out of the chains one more time before they're close enough to be able to tell what's going on.

"Ready?" Tommy whispers over to me when a few other people are within earshot. I nod.

"You don't have to wait, but you do have to hurry, they're in there, they're waiting for you," Tommy begins into the mic. I try to stand onstage like I have a purpose for standing onstage aside from wearing skimpy clothes. What pose is right? I put my hands on my hips with one knee bent and feel like I'm posing for a swimsuit ad from the eighties. I cross my arms over my chest and lean back a little bit, but now I'm a teen rebel from the early nineties. Every way I move seems to be a reference to something else. Before I have time to overthink it further, Tommy has gathered a small crowd in front of the stage.

"That's right, we're putting on a free show right here, right now," Tommy says, "you're going to watch Ms. Mimi L'Amour change a one dollar bill into a five, I'm going to swallow this sword for you right here, while Hercules, our massive man-eating boa constrictor, lies hypnotized around my neck," and we're off. The crowd grows from ten people to fifteen. "Inside you're going to see Spidora the Spidergirl, born with the head of a beautiful woman and the body of a terrifying spider." Tommy's eyes sparkle and taunt, like he both believes in all the things he's saying and is letting the crowd in on the game.

34

The crowd grows to twenty. I watch people a little ways down the midway follow the sound of the voice on the microphone like a beacon.

Tommy hands a teenage girl in the audience a dollar bill so she can make sure it's real. "Go ahead and smell it," he says. "Do you smell the mint? That's government. And it stinks." Small chuckle from the crowd. "Hand that bill back to Ms. L'Amour," Tommy says, and I take the dollar from the girl's hand, lay it flat in my palm so it looks like I'm readying to convince them that they aren't being fooled. Tommy keeps ballying, listing the acts, introducing amazing stories that he interrupts with other amazements and promises of astonishment, becoming his own Scheherazade.

With dramatic turns of my wrist I smooth the dollar bill in front of me—the audience's eyes following my fingers as I fold the bill into a flat line. Tommy is pitching our medical mystery. I fold the bill into a long strip and wind it around my finger. Many of the eyes in the audience never leave my hands, sure that if they watch hard enough, pay close enough attention, they'll catch the trick, the moment of the inevitable switcheroo, and beat the game. They watch and watch, and I eat it up, the attention, that belief that enough focus will reveal some secret truth. I'm smiling and just a little unsure I'm doing the act right, but it feels good, very, very good, to be onstage.

Though I have the five ready before it's time, I ramp up the drama, blowing on it in my hand, shaking my closed fist to keep them watching, to make their eyes work extra hard to find the moment of slip and switch. When I finally hold one hand, palm facing me, out to the crowd, Tommy looks over, nods, and says, "Now watch Ms. Mimi L'Amour turn a one-dollar bill into a five," and I flip my hand around, revealing the bill folded into the shape of the number five in the palm of my hand, and a few people smile and shake their heads, a few others groan, a few crane their necks to get a better view as if they are missing the joke, as if there must be more to it.

35

"And now," Tommy says, clanging his sword on the metal pole above his head to get their attention and show that the sword is, indeed, metal, "the sword swallower will swallow a sword." He readjusts the snake, asks for a volunteer from the audience. A teenage girl raises her hand. "Down the hatch without a scratch," he says, and straightens all the way up, puffs his chest out, and slides the sword down his throat. Half the metal blade disappears inside him. I'm as transfixed as the rest of the audience, not having seen sword swallowing up close before. What a beautiful act, the grace, the danger, the seeming impossibility of it even though it's happening an arm's length away. Tommy bends over with the sword down his throat, lets the audience see the metal disappearing into the darkness of his mouth, lets them imagine the tip pressing its point against the sac of his stomach, almost breaking him open, his arms out wide beside him, his eyebrows raised. He leans close to the teenager and, with a gesture, invites her to grasp the sword's handle and she does, nearly brushing his cheeks with her hands. He doesn't gag as it slides out. His lips remain stiff. He watches the girl intently as she cringes while pulling the sword from his mouth. Her father, standing just behind her, has a wide, amused frown, and her mother is snapping photos.

The sword's tip emerges from his body, and Tommy does a quick bow.

"For an opening-day special, adult tickets are only three dollars right now and kids are just two dollars. Snickers is waiting right here with the tickets, so go on in and be amazed by the strangest show on earth," Tommy says. Everyone goes in. A line twenty people long stretches back from the ticket box, and the line draws more into it, everyone assuming something that can't be missed is going on right there. It continues to build as the first people go in, and behind me I can hear the inside show starting. Red is on his stage, welcoming people inside by pounding a nail up his nose, and I'm standing on the far side of the ticket box, waving people in, smiling in my gorgeous glimmering booty shorts, and they keep coming, buying tickets and stepping right inside. I'm dazzled. Dazzling.

"Good turn," Tommy says when the crowd is all in and I walk back onstage. "That almost never happens, where we have a total turn."

"We must have the magic," I say, winking, feeling that this might be the life for me. This might be my most right self. We high-five, and I'm as high as I've ever been.

Our next bally, which we immediately begin, goes just as well, with a one-dollar bill turned into a five and sword swallowing and stories of grandeur, but at the end of the bally, as we stand onstage with ta-da smiles, everybody turns around and walks away.

On the next one, two people come inside.

Next, three more.

We're forty-five minutes into the five-month season, and I feel defeated. Though we're performing the same minishow over and over, now and forever, for every new group that wanders by every seven to ten minutes, each iteration has to look completely new and exciting. And sometimes, they are really unimpressed.

My feet ache. It's been an hour.

My heels are low—two and a half inches, maybe—but I'm not one of the graceful naturals.

Also, the fishnets pinch my waist.

I'm sweating my makeup off.

I'm getting a little short of breath from the cinch of the corset.

When I have a fifteen-minute break a few hours into performing, I closely inspect the corsets the other performers are wearing backstage. Sunshine's corset wraps her body closely, but it seems to fit more like a shirt than a vacuum sealer, zipping up on the side and not bothering with unlacing or relacing at all. Cassie's is the same. And then I think about eating a snack. I'm not sure I could. I don't think the granola bar would have anywhere to go, that it would sit like a mouse in a snake's throat above my corset, a great lump. I reach behind me and loosen the corset further, keeping it still tight, still uncomfortable. I'd performed in a lot of plays when I was younger, and there it doesn't matter if your costume is uncomfortable or you're feeling tired, because the adrenaline is pumping and the performance time is limited. But here, it begins and carries on like a record skipping into eternity. I like this idea—that every day I can try and retry and retry to be better and better at the same thing. That every day I get a chance to redo what I've done before until one time, eventually, I'll get it just right.

⚡

We had a lot of chances to fine-tune our reactions to bad news about my mom. A lot of practice in tightening our face muscles, tensing our jaws, and furrowing our brows while listening to a doctor's update. These were the choruses of our days:

There's a strong chance she will not make it through the night.

There's a moderate chance she will not make it through the afternoon.

Wear the face mask. Wear the disposable robe. Wear the shoe protectors.

There's a 75 percent chance this last complication has been too much for her body to fight.

She will not last the morning.

Use this soap to wash your hands before and after you put on and take off the gloves. Do not remove the protective plastic eye shield from the face mask.

We're going to give you some space.

We'll give you alone time.

This is probably the end.

One day of life-halting emergency.

Do you see the Kleenex?

Don't let her see you cry. She might give up.

Do you see the Kleenex?

Four days of life-halting emergency.

Don't let her see you look like this is hard.

Eat a sandwich.

This is certainly the last degree of complication a person can survive.

A week of it.

Four weeks.

Prepare yourself: we've got to pull the plugs.

How are you holding up? Are your bowels regular?

Four months.

Do not touch her face.

She might live, but what kind of quality of life would she want?

What are her advance directives?

Sir, you can't ignore her advance directives.

On.

Nine months.

A year.

Two.

On.

⚡

It had taken three days to drive from Gibsonton, where the crew had met, to Butler, Pennsylvania, the site of our first fair.

When we arrived, a giant piece of plywood leaning against a fence read big butler fairgrounds. Behind the sign, we parked in a huge, open field, the grass already summer-dry and patchy.

Tommy and Sunshine disappeared into the fairgrounds. I looked at Spif and Pipscy for answers.

"Tommy's going to find the boss canvasman so we know which lot is ours," Spif says. He has opened the van's side doors and lies sprawled across the steps, digging at something under his fingernails with a dagger he's pulled off his belt.

"We don't know already?"

"How would we know?" he asks, shrugging at me. I shrug back. I don't know anything about anything.

Spif relents, explains that the boss canvasman will have created a map of the fairgrounds designating where each ride, game, food truck, vendor, show, and so forth will go. This map is both practical and political, taking into consideration, for example, rides that have a lot of motion with spindly arms— these go in the middle aisle so customers can see through them to more rides they'd like to buy tickets for. A carnival's central walkway where the rides and fast-food joints cluster is called the midway, and you want the biggest attractions, the roller coasters and drop zones, spread on either end of the midway's oval so that fairgoers must walk the full midway and see all the other possibilities as they go. Placement is also dependent on the length and depth of the relationship between the individual joint owner or carnival company and the boss canvasman. Canvasman likes you, you get a money spot. Hates you, you're on the edge of kiddieland.

Near us are a smattering of other vehicles and a trailer surrounded by a small metal fence, inside of which are eight or ten ponies, each bridled and tied to one long metal arm of an octopus, which spins as they tread behind one another in a circular march, bobbing their heads as they step.

"Ponies!" I say, pointing to the little ring of animals and then clapping my hands.

"Greenhorn," Spif snorts.

"Are we allowed to go pet them?" I ask.

"There will be ponies everywhere we go," Spif says. "And cooler animals. Tigers and shit," he says, so I give it up and watch the ponies from afar. Pipscy climbs out of the van and motions for Spif to give her a neck rub.

Inside the fairgrounds, trucks are slowly unfolding. Since

America's highways became numerous and reliable, the circus stopped moving by train; the rides in any traveling carnival have to disassemble and fold up within the space of a truck bed. I'm witnessing a secret ritual here, viewing a carnival's insides. A man is bolting the extended legs of the Octopus out wide.

A pickup truck full of young pink-skinned men honks as it drives by. Every few minutes, another truck passes us as it heads into the carnival entryway, hauling in its bed a load of stuffed animals bundled together in giant plastic bags or a half dozen carnies, and each time all the heads in the truck turn toward us for as long as the truck is in sight.

"Not many women around," Spif says, digging into Pipscy's neck. "They're gonna be real interested in you two," he says. "Watch out."

It sounds like an invitation to trouble and I like it. I crawl over Spif and Pipscy and sprawl on the grass. Let them look. I'm three days in, and though it has been obvious at points that I am not a part of this troop yet, don't get the inside jokes or know the metal band they're playing loud in the van, I am here and part of something spectacular. I'm happy—elated, really, to be here. There was no reason to believe the carnival would be anything less for me than the wonderland it is for most attendees, with the lights and sweets and deep-fried delight. I feel all that—some collective nostalgia—as I watch truck after truck enter the grounds, as the occasional blast of music is tested from a ride's speakers. There is pleasure in the *idea* of the carnival. It has been a long time since I've been overwhelmed with the kind of excitement these first few days have brought, where the future isn't filled with hospital equipment or the terror of loss.

I think about how much she'd love it. How funny she'd think it is. There are goddamned ponies.

An hour after we arrive at the Big Butler Fairgrounds, we unhitch the trailer in our spot. We are at the center of the midway's farthest U-curve. Good to be at a pinnacle point, like the tip of the U, though less good to be at the farthest point from the main entrance.

"Let's get that possum belly unloaded," Tommy says to Sunshine, Pipscy, and me. "Boys, set the stake line," he tells Spif and Big, Big Ben, our show's working man.

I follow Sunshine to the compartments below the trailer's main storage area. We unlock them, then pull the heavy metal covers off these giant versions of the luggage storage beneath a bus. The possum belly is an old circus term for the storage box built beneath a work wagon that doubles as a napping spot.

"The possum belly is a special, special place," Spif says, grabbing a steel tent stake. "It's a place for lots of fun," he says, humping the metal.

"It's where truckers bang hookers at rest stops," Sunshine adds, crouching into the possum belly and looking over the massive stacks of metal tent poles strapped together. "They're called possum belly queens, those truck-stop hookers, so that's what we call whoever is in charge of our possum belly. The possum belly queen. I've been it for years, and it's scary and dangerous and disgusting, so I'm done. Now it's you," she says, turning to look at me. She smiles. "Congratulations."

I feel a little gush of pride. Could they tell what a hard worker I was?

In the possum belly, there are about forty tent poles stacked on top of one another in a precarious pile. Sunshine unlatches the massive straps holding them together, loosening the ratchets slowly. "Come sit here," she says to me, patting the lip of the possum belly. I do. The smell is wet and metallic and mossy, like the inside of a mine, I imagine, or a tunnel through the earth. The stack of steel poles is five feet high and twenty-five feet long.

"I need you to lean all your body weight against this stack," she says. "Plant your feet and really lean. The poles get jostled

42

on the road, and sometimes they all just pour off the stack and bury people."

The steel lip of the possum belly is cracked beneath me, ripped and rotting in jagged metal patterns that look like lacework.

Though she is thin and doesn't appear muscular, Sunshine moves her body in this tight space with the strength and precision of a martial artist, climbing and cinching and grabbing and leaning, intricate movements that make clear this is an orchestrated dance. She pulls poles out one by one as if she were playing a terrible game of pickup sticks that might always end in entombment.

Sunshine slides a pole to one end of the truck. I take it in both hands. It's heavy and dirty, fifteen feet long, and sharp where the metal is corroding and flaking off. I spread my hands wide for more balance and take a few steps. The weight is still unbalanced, and heavier than almost anything I've ever picked up. I drop one end to the ground and then the other. Nobody looks. I pick the pole back up, trying to remember lessons about using your legs, and one side of the pole comes up quickly, much quicker than I expected, and knocks into Spif as he's walking by.

"Oh, sorry," I say.

"Careful," he snaps, jumping back and continuing his hustle toward the truck.

I tighten my grip on the pole, looking ahead of me and over my shoulder before I move it, then spread my hands wide, grit my teeth, and move with the steel. The space around me is not mine anymore but my crew's. In the other crews around our lot, men climb the still-unrecognizable rides to begin wrenching and pinning and joining. Now that I'm here with all this, I feel like a bona fide carnie. Suddenly, my body counts for something. It is working; this is what work is. Look at all these functional limbs whose muscles respond on command.

I move like a tightrope walker. My hands are in the center

of the pole and I concentrate on one step and then the next, a tiny correction, and then the next. There is nobody to call for help if I can't carry it—it is my job to carry it.

Once we finish unloading the possum belly, Tommy opens the container's back end.

We grip the corners of the Feejee Mermaid's coffin. "Never ask what you should do next," he tells me. "Just wait for instructions. But don't wander off or look distracted. That includes the bathroom. Don't go." The Feejee Mermaid's hair is peeling off her face and her plastic tail is chipped. "We'll take breaks sometimes, and you can go then, if you ask first," he says, wiping sweat from his forehead. The Pennsylvania sun is lowering but still strong, and we are moving quickly. Much of the skin I see around me is sunburned.

"Everything has a very specific order. So don't take anything out that you aren't told to. And don't touch anything, or it might fall on you. Last season a giant board fell on Sunshine's head and knocked her out cold," he says. We unload a massive chair with metal plates and wiring.

"What's this?" I ask Tommy.

"The Electric Chair. For Electra, the Electric Woman. She lights light bulbs with her tongue," he says, his voice suddenly changing as if he's onstage.

"Wow. Who gets to be Electra?" I ask.

"Only the bravest among us. Will that be you one day, Tess?" he asks, winking. My stomach flutters.

We drag part of our massive circus tent across the grass in its giant canvas bag. I can't wait to see the bag untied, watch the red and blue vinyl unroll from its log and join the other flattened vinyl to somehow form the structure around the amazement we'll offer onstage. Or, the amazement *they* will offer.

"Don't worry if Sunshine yells at you. Or Red. Red's arriving tomorrow, and he might yell at you. Actually, I'm sure he will.

44

He'll call you a dummy. It's nothing personal. Okay, Tessy?"
Tommy says.

"Okay," I say.

"How you doing?" he asks, noticing my flushed cheeks.

"Sore," I say, patting my arms. "I can already feel some of those circus muscles coming in." He nods, smiles. We've been working for less than an hour. The bulk of setup, which takes sixteen hours on a good day, will come in the next few days, after we scrub the winter off the set and props.

"Well, take it easy," he says, still smiling, maybe hiding a laugh. Greenhorn.

Physical labor is still, as it has always been, a marker of class delineation, and as a middle-class female my life has never required anything more physical than picking up the children I was nannying, delivering burgers to the tables outside. Nothing has ever been asked of my body, not really, not much. But here, straining to keep the pole from knocking into someone's head, there's little I can think about other than the geometry of my movement, the mechanics of my machinery.

"Can I be doing anything more to help?" I ask Tommy.

$$\lightning$$

Can I be doing anything more to help? It's a familiar question. One I had asked nurse after nurse, surgeon, neurologist, physical therapist and then occupational therapist, speech therapist. Nurse this or that would say something or other, new doctor, new thing, and then I'd do that thing,
rotating the arm from the elbow in tight circles
    clockwise
    counterclockwise
    north
    south
    rubbing Vaseline between the toes to encourage blood flow
    the base of the feet

calves, when they aren't in the squeezers
spreading and folding the fingers
and I remembered to do all these things one, two, maybe
four days, and then the new nurse has
the new set of mouth-opening stretches, her jaw between my
thumb and fingers
the lemon-flavored sponge to rub along the gums
inside the lips when I can pry them open
to wet the teeth
see if the synapses connected to taste still work
new knee bends
new holding her hand in my own hand
rotating: thumbs up
thumbs down
thumbs up
thumbs down
thumbs up
thumbs down
singing
humming
staying silent
telling old stories
making up new stories
reading books out loud
except I skipped parts that were sexual or scary or violent
or dangerous or that involved medicine or death, or that were
particularly sad or extra happy, so I read mostly descriptions of
desert plants, the diet of a trumpeter swan, the cycle of power
generation at a nearby windmill.

What else can I be doing to help?

She smelled like plastic and disinfectant, and beneath all
that she smelled like a human mother, my own human mother.

What, exactly, had been lost? There she was, still, in front
of me, alive. The only human being who would ever walk up
behind me, rest her cheek on my shoulder—her surprisingly

tall daughter— and hug my waist from behind, saying softly
as she laughed: *I birthed you.*

⚡

"There's nothing else you can do right now, Tess," Tommy
says.

A clean-shaven man in a visor and polo shirt strides over
to us with a clipboard in hand. He calls to Tommy. "That's a
boss," whispers Sunshine. "Just look at him. You'll know who
they are because they'll have showered, they'll have most of
their teeth, or they'll be riding around in a golf cart with one
leg off the side so they can jump down to solve a crisis while
the cart's still running."

"And kick lazy carnies as they pass," Spif adds.

"Listen up," Tommy says as he walks back over to us. "Boss
just told me there's a new policy. We're getting drug tested at this
fair." All eyes that had been vaguely distracted by something
else are now glued to Tommy's face. "This carnival company is
doing a major push to be family friendly and move away from
their reputation, so everyone's gotta pass a drug test to get their
ID before we open."

"Oh fuck," Spif says.

"You have to pass or you can't be in the show. Boss's orders.
We're heading to Walmart tomorrow night so that everyone
can buy whatever they need to make sure they pass. All of you,"
he says, slower, quieter now, "have to pass. We have no extra
people. The show won't run if you don't."

Spif and Sunshine grasp one another by the arm as Tommy
walks away. "You have four days," Tommy calls over his shoulder.

It is time to make the individual bodies perform feats once
thought impossible.

"Vitamin B3 makes you sweat," Spif says.

"Cranberry juice clears you out," Sunshine adds.

47

"B vitamins," Pipscy says.

Everyone starts moving very quickly.

$$\lightning$$

After five days in the induced coma, the doctors gave her some sort of *wake up!* drug. They wanted to test her level of brain function, to measure what she could respond to, how she could move.

We hovered around her bed.

I thought ICUs would be full of people moving very quickly, but much of the time, there was stillness. Quiet. Like the woman I sat with in the waiting room when I couldn't handle being in my mom's room or when they were doing something to her they thought we might not want to see. The woman was waiting to see if her boyfriend would wake up from a motor-cycle accident. He'd been in a coma two weeks. We waited near each other. She sat cross-legged in the upholstered chair, smiled a lot. Put on lip gloss. Together, we picked up magazines, set them down.

The magic drug went in through my mom's IV. We waited in a semicircle around her bed. Davy, my brother, Sam, my aunt, and my uncle. She would open her eyes, see us there, and smile that smile we all knew so well, the smile of the boss of our lives, the queen, and we'd know that this minor disaster was just another hurdle we'd applaud her for overcoming.

We waited. She would yawn and stretch, say, "What happened?" or "Where am I?" and we'd smile sad, grateful smiles, wipe little warm tears from the corners of our eyes and say, "Never you mind, because everything's going to be just fine."

Two hours, four, twenty-four.

And then, genius, miracle, angels-on-high-or-something, whoever, thank you, her left hand gave a squeeze. Just a little. Just a small squeeze, a *hello someone's here*.

It was the first sign that she wasn't vegetative.

48

She would open her eyes.

She would open her eyes, and then she did.

We crowded around the end of the bed. "Hi! Hi! Hello! Hi, beautiful!" we said. But the bright, bright green of her eyes wasn't there. Instead, there was a slug-gray cover over her iris. Like a cartoon of illness or evil or warning. But this was no cartoon. This was a real fucking sick person whose eyes had changed color and all I could think was *Who is this new person inside her?*, and then hated myself for thinking it. Of course it was her.

It wasn't her.

It was.

The gray eyes weren't looking at us, weren't looking at anyone or anything in particular, it seemed. They stared off blankly.

That's all I could think about that night, those eyes, *whose eyes?*, as Davy, Sam, and I drove back from the hospital to the house. This house that she had spent twenty-two years living inside and fixing up with her bright, bright green eyes, the house that was now filled entirely by boxes. They'd bought it all those years ago for so little, spent year after year digging away chunks of the hillside on which it was precariously perched to make a garden, putting in new windows, saving a year or two at a time for a new appliance. But the rest of the Bay Area housing market boomed and it was too hard to keep up.

The house was filled with boxes of dye and hand-painted fabric from the business my mom had finally had to close a few years before. She'd sold off her painting tables, fabric steamer, washer. Had let go of the small studio/office, already a much smaller space than the previous studio/office, downsizing and downgrading until all that was left were a few mouse-chewed boxes in the dirt basement. Davy hadn't been able to find work after his layoff a few years before. There was no more money to be borrowed, shuffled. Everything was getting sorted and boxed. The house was gone. Sold. There was an empty storage

49

unit waiting for all these boxes and a plan to come up with a good plan.

The move-out date was two weeks after her stroke.

⚡

Our neighbors went to work in the kitchen. They stuffed garbage bags full of open baking soda, warped Tupperware lids, packages of stuffing, chicken marinating in the fridge, ceramic spoon-holders my brother and I had molded as Mother's Day gifts when we were small.

I came into the kitchen where women with large curly hair and turquoise earrings were sorting. The neighbor women volunteered to help, but my mom was the one with the packing plan and so now nobody really knew what to do with anything. Everyone had their own plan. One opened a jar of *berbere*, Ethiopian spices my parents ground by hand with the mortar and pestle they kept under the tea boxes, beside the jars of flour and sugar. The neighbor smelled the spice. "What on earth is this?" she asked the room.

"*Berbere*," I wanted to say. I wanted to say that since my parents could barely afford to pay the electric bill month after month, my mother traveled the world through the kitchen. But I was still trying to synthesize memory into a sentence when the woman with the *berbere* shrugged and tossed it into the garbage bag. Other people's hands squeezed boxes of decorative toothpicks and released them into the bag. Other hands disposed of kimchi.

There was nothing I could do in there, wordless as I was. What arguments were there for keeping a jar with four cloves? Some. I just couldn't find them. I walked quickly down the hallway, heat rising and piling on my face. A few other neighbors were hovering in the doorframe, discussing the best way to tackle the bedroom. Her underwear. Dirty T-shirts. Satin slips. The slips were rolled into tight logs like cakes and lined up next to one another in a drawer, pale pinks and ivory and black, tucked beside a few belts and a Ziploc bag of pantyhose. I didn't want these neighbors to touch the last things that she had touched. The very idea made my lip snarl. I needed the items all to myself.

The details are what drive you mad with grief. Socks that didn't match but that she counted as a pair anyway.

"I'm sure she'll want turtlenecks soon," one of the women in the doorframe said as she reached for a hanging turtleneck.

"I'll do the bedroom," I said, smiling and pushing between them.

"We'll help," the women said, not budging.

"No thanks," I said. "Thank you, though," I remembered to say, smiled, and then shut the door right up against their faces. I hated them there. I knew this was rude. Picking up dirty cups and feeling superior—were they feeling superior? were they overwhelmed by pity?—because these weren't the dirty cups of their own beautiful California homes, which they weren't losing. We needed them. There is no question: they saved the day. Because of their help the house was being packed. Our family would move everything into a storage unit in time and no police would be called to escort us off the land with shotguns, nobody would be bleeding except for our dumb swollen hearts and my mother's head, still spilling, at the hospital.

It wouldn't stop, the bleeding. They tried different drugs, tubes, suctions. It just wanted to give and give and give.

I pulled flattened cardboard into boxes. Taped. Made new containers for the bedroom stuff to live in. Bracelets. Bras. Potpourri sachets. One of my mother's two sisters came in as I started on the sock drawer. I couldn't tell if I was supposed to be crying, if I shouldn't cry. Somebody in the family needed to be the general here to get things done. It was clear this would be me. I'm the heavy lifter. My brother was back at college. Davy was off somewhere, his heart falling apart in huge sloughs. We needed someone around to sign paperwork.

I started filling a box with handfuls of socks. My aunt was doing the underwear drawer beside it. It was okay that she was here. Good, even. A few handfuls in, I touched something hard instead of soft. I pulled it out. In my hand was a huge, multibuttoned vibrator. On its side, it said *The Rabbit*. I blushed quickly and held it by two fingers like it was a dirty diaper. It was heavy, and used by a live body with desire and a whole life far, far apart from me, the life children often forget about their parents having, the life I usually wanted to forget about my parents having. But now it meant something else. It already indicated a former self. My aunt, perceptive and kind, saw the momentary horror on my face, the complicated sadness of what was in my hands, my embarrassment.

"Oh, I was wondering where that was," she said, speaking swiftly. "I'm glad you found it, at least," she said, moving quickly and taking it from me. "And not your brother. My son found mine when he helped me move last. That was embarrassing." In a quick flurry of movement she had the thing wrapped up in another slip and tucked into a sock and buried deep in the box we were packing.

I looked out the bedroom window at the golden hills and remembered a lesson my mom had taught me about keeping yourself safe. If you see a mountain lion, move slowly. Pick up the closest branch and place it vertically on top of your head. Keep one hand on your crown to balance the branch and stretch the other, if you can, out to your side, as wide as it can go, the fingers as splayed as starfish. You are creating a monster. You are becoming a bigger beast than the mountain lion, a beast the mountain lion will fear and acquiesce to as you back away slowly, slowly, horns still on head, wings spread wide, slowly, slowly, eye to eye.

THE DRAGON

One Month After the Stroke

NOVEMBER 2010

It was Thanksgiving. I made lists.

We were crammed into a neighbor's kitchen. They were away for the weekend. My mom was still in the intensive-care unit, infections having crawled into her brain and her blood. She couldn't eat or drink anything because her brain had forgotten how to chew and swallow. We spent most of our time at the hospital. Every day was the last day, the big goodbye, but then there was a new last day. Again and again.

So, Thanksgiving. Some aunts and uncles had driven up, and we all stood shoulder to shoulder in the neighbor's kitchen being good ol' regular Americans. *Cranberries, fresh and canned.* I wrote down recipe temperatures and cooking times. I wrote *celery, butter, russet potatoes, flour.* There was some communal delusion that Thanksgiving would heal us a little. We were big into holidays. The whole extended family loved elaborate meals, decorations, drinking. My mom especially. But we'd forgotten she was the one always in the middle, making all of it come together.

In preparation for Christmas ten years earlier, my mom came home with a thin cardboard box covered in Chinese characters. Without saying a word, she pulled out a red-and-orange flattened shape from inside. "Hold this very gently,"

53

she whispered to my brother on the couch. He was eleven, I was fifteen. She placed one end of the paper in his hands. She took the other and walked slowly backward, letting it unfold between them. One red-orange plane of paper turned into two, then three, then more, strings attaching each section as she walked backward across the living room. When it seemed like all the sections had unfolded, she backed away even farther and the paper kept growing. It kept getting bigger than we imagined it could.

"I've decided on a theme for Christmas this year," she said. The paper kept unspooling, on and on like scarves pulled from a magician's throat. "The theme is: Chinese." She was standing against the far wall, twenty feet away. Stretching across the room was a paper dragon. It had gone from the world of two dimensions into three. It was our year to host Christmas for our extended family.

"The theme is *Chinese*?" we asked. "What does that even mean?"

"You'll see," she said, with a grin like a plotting cartoon character's.

"For Christmas?" we asked, still incredulous.

She sighed. "I'm tired of turkeys and hams, aren't you?" We nodded, but we were not tired of turkeys or hams. In my fifteen years on earth, we'd never had turkeys or hams. We didn't eat traditional holiday foods because they were always boring, according to my mom. We knew about them only as the tropes of other people's worlds from the occasional mainstream movie we were allowed to watch.

She set the dragon down and pulled from other boxes little firecrackers and paper lanterns and big plastic soup spoons.

"Do you kids know what's no fun?" she asked. We shook our heads. "Everything ordinary."

Over the next few weeks, she and Davy were up on ladders every evening. Room by room, they transformed our small house into one of those shops you see in Chinatown so crammed full of goods it was hard to make out one object from the next. There were bright lanterns painted with pictures of bamboo and butterflies and flowers that hung from our lights, and paper umbrellas dangling upside down, and the counter was stacked with fake jade cats and red satin. She filled the fridge with wonton wrappers, tiny mushrooms, and big bundles of greens.

On Christmas, when the eight family members came, they were in equal parts delighted and wary—this fun wild sister, this creative one, this girl always a few steps away from what they understood. The dragon hung by translucent fishing line from hooks in the ceiling above the dinner table, a floating centerpiece. "This year," my mother said as we sat down, beginning a Christmas toast, "we will all be transported somewhere far, far away." Her tone was deeply solemn. There was always somewhere else to be. Some great dream adventure waiting, this time in misty mountains dotted with jade lions.

She was always a little bit elsewhere. Maybe that helped her when one of the doctors stood with his face six inches from hers as if she were deaf and dumb, asking her to stick out her tongue. Maybe she didn't respond to his command because it was stupid, ordinary, and she was distracted by more interesting concerns; maybe she was inside some deep fold of her brain designing a new landscape for her dragons.

We made a turkey. Stove Top stuffing. Pillsbury rolls. It was the first time we had that kind of real American combo. We ate like she was away for the weekend and we were sneaking in as much ordinary life as we could before she returned, maybe teased us, maybe pretended to be grossed out. Every few minutes my brother and I said, too many times, too loud, how good the rolls were. I mean, really, exceptionally good. Unbelievable.

Devin had come to visit me two months before the stroke, late summer, when the biggest challenge we faced was removing twenty years of life from the house. He had not met my family, and I wanted to show him this place before it was gone.

We stood on the deck that looked out over the valley and hills, the dusk giving the high points one final golden glow. Cows dotted the dead grass, redwood trees stretched in wild stripes.

"I could live here," he'd said. "I'd like a place like this."

"Not me," I said. "This place is haunted."

I could hear Davy inside working on an old tiny motor, the clatter of tools, an intensive project he was single-mindedly focused on despite the sea of other, larger, pressing projects closing in. I could hear my mother on the phone, negotiating dates with the Realtor. A little more time, she said, just another week or two. Then: How's your garden?

"But you could have a garden," Devin said. "I could work at Google and make all the money and eat free sushi for lunch every day."

"That's true."

"And you could write steamy romance novels and make millions," he said.

"It's a good point."

"It is a good point."

He told me later that night, after my parents had gone to bed and we were alone, that when I'd gone inside, my mom, empty wineglass in hand, had walked over to him, hooked his arm, and firmly marched him farther down the deck, away from the house.

"Do you know how special she is?" she'd said, turning to look him straight in the face. Her hair was short and silver. People stopped in the grocery store to comment on the greenness of her eyes.

"Yeah, I—"

"Really, exceptionally special."

"I know."

"Do you know?"

"She just loves you so much," he told me when we were brushing our teeth.

✦

"Loosen up, babygirl," my mom said, pushing a shot of tequila at me across the table. "Loosen up, and toughen up." She smiled.

I took the shot and raised it into the air. "What are we cheersing?"

"Adventure," she said, and swallowed the thing down. Small glittery skulls hung from the ceiling like a warning.

"So tell me about why you keep dating people who aren't your equals?"

"Mom."

"Want me to tell you what I think? You're scared. You want to be in charge."

"Let's not talk about this," I said.

"You feel like you need to be the boss," she said.

"That's not it," I said, even though it obviously was.

"Well, what is it then?"

"I don't want to talk about it."

"Sir," she said, meeting the eyes of our waiter. "Two more tequilas, please."

"You can't just get me drunk and make me talk."

She smiled again. "Wanna bet?"

It was March 2007, three and a half years before her stroke. I was twenty-two. We were at a small Mexican restaurant in a strip mall somewhere near the Oregon-California border. The mariachi music was low and the lights were bright, and my mom and I sat across from one another in a small booth against a yellow wall, tequila debris between us. Also, history between us. Some lingering linguistic trail that pointed back to the moment in the kitchen when, at fifteen, in the midst of a fight about a friend's house I was no longer allowed to visit, I told her: "I don't love you."

They weren't just fighting words, though. Since I was

thirteen, I'd known it. I believed it through my early twenties. I didn't love her.

When she looked at me, shocked, the corners of her mouth turned up just slightly as if she were about to laugh, because usually whenever I said something dramatic, she laughed. That's how I knew what to say next. The surprise on her face. "I don't love you now, and I never have. I never will."

She didn't laugh. She looked at me, stoic. We both realized that something in what I'd said was true.

Finally, she turned back to the carrots she was chopping and gave a halfhearted chuckle. "I sure can't wait till you're not a teenager anymore," she said, trying to cover the wound. But I knew what those words had done, and how they were now and forever a part of her world.

Never have. Never will.

"I just want you to find someone who will make you happy," she said, holding up the next shot of tequila.

"I can make myself happy," I said.

"The world is lonely and you are lonely in it," she said. "Get a partner. A good one. It's better that way." Her tequila was still in the air like a vessel of preserved amber that might hold some key to unlocking the future. I raised mine, too.

"That's why I ended up with David," she said. "He's a guy who loves me no matter what. He works hard and loves the family." She paused to suck lime. "He stepped in when it was just me and you, when you were two, and I didn't know what to do next. He built you a little kitchen. Do you remember? A little wooden kitchen. That's when you started calling him Davy. Not David, or Dave, like everyone else, but Davy. He built you that kitchen before he'd even met you."

We drank. It singed our throats.

We were drinking tequila because I was driving from Seattle, where my dad lived, to San Francisco, where my mom and

58

stepdad lived, and she'd decided to join me for the road trip.

When I was two, my mom left. We were living in Seattle, my mom, my dad, and me. And then she left for California. I don't know for how long.

I don't know for how long because how long depends on who is telling the story.

In my mom's story, she was gone just a few days, a few weeks at most, to scope out a new apartment for us to live in. She was leaving my dad, see.

In my dad's story, she took off and there he was, a big burly bachelor man with a two-year-old baby girl, and did he know how to braid hair? No. And would that become a problem when that girl child became insistent, furious, that she have her hair braided the way her mama braided it? Did she throw screaming tantrums so that the bachelor man had to plead with some coworkers later that day to show him how to braid hair and he spent the afternoon practicing on women in his office, getting tips from the flock of expert braiders? Well, yes.

In my mom's story, shortly after she arrived in California, she received a letter from my dad. It said, Bye, I'm taking the baby and we're moving to Canada. He is Canadian, so he can scoot right over and back pretty easily, knows a lot of folks over the border. Not just Canadian, but French-Canadian, and not just that, but Catholic, so he's related to most people. Anyway, there he went. "It's not that he really wanted a kid all to himself," my mom said the first time she told me this story. "It's just that he knew what would hurt me the most." She sighed. She'd decided that my college graduation gift was this truth and told me a few weeks before I finished school. She hadn't told me before, she said, because she wanted to protect the person I believed my dad to be. "Your face could have been on a milk carton. He could have been in prison."

In my dad's story, she left to go have an affair with someone she'd known for a long time, someone she might have been having an affair with forever. She was done with my dad. With me. A few weeks before she left, before he knew anything about the leaving or the divorce or any of that, she'd thrown my dad a surprise party. As they were driving there— he didn't know anything about it—she said she was going to leave him, that she wanted a divorce, wanted out, that she'd be taking off soon. Then they arrived at the party. "Surprise!" everyone shouted as he walked in the door.

I believed his version for a long time. Probably because I didn't see him much. It was easier to be on his side. Each time we talked on the phone, I pleaded for more pieces of the story, wanted to know the ways she'd wronged us. The stories spooled on. Trying to get me legally removed from him. Taking and taking child support, but never using it on me. Not letting me visit when I was scheduled to visit. Leaving me behind, and then deciding to take me back months later, because she'd been guilted into it. Each piece of information was like a wound I couldn't stop filling with salt, an itch already scratched open that I did not want to stop digging into.

And I developed this real allergy to her love. By the time I was ten or eleven, when she touched me, it felt like there was a hot searing poker scalding my skin. I felt like my organs were failing a little bit when she'd hug me, like it was a big fake act she was putting on and somehow my body knew the truth and withered in response to her proximity. I didn't trust her. I didn't think her love was real, because she'd chosen to walk away from my dad and left him all alone, so sad, and angry. Because she'd been able to walk away from me.

If she didn't need me, I didn't need her.

At eight, eleven, fourteen, eighteen, and all the years in between, the more I heard and then embellished in my head, the more deeply I became attached to the story. The more I invested in it being my own story, the clearer it was that the only way to get through life was to be on my own. Me against the world made up of my mom.

When I was a teenager, I spent some time trying to verify

60

truths. Cross-referencing stories, finding outside sources.

What I discovered is that there are even more versions of what happened, who did what, and who was to blame. So I stopped.

In my own story, I decided that there might be truth somewhere in the middle, and that the two stories could both exist as half fictions, as versions of what each of them felt, of how hurt they were by the other.

What matters most isn't actually related to any of their truths. They were trying their best, my mom, my dad, and my stepdad. I love them for that. What matters most is my cruelty.

I don't love you, I'd told her. I never have, and I never will.

It took me so many years, until I was in my early twenties, to figure out that what she wanted from me was love. That she wasn't going anywhere. Maybe she'd made mistakes, but she'd spent years afterward trying to pour that love on me, trying to make me sure I knew that she loved me—always had, always would. It seems so obvious from a distance. But I figured it out so late.

How do we arrive at our realizations? There wasn't any sparkling, trumpet-sounding, aha moment of recognition for me, no tidy turning point. Just a gradual understanding, as I became an adult, met more people, saw some of the world, that the person my mom was did not align with the person I had believed her to be.

The summer before she had her stroke, when I was back with her and Davy for two months to help them with packing and sorting, I decided I'd tell her that I was sorry, and that I loved her. I knew I needed to. I'd choked out the words *love you* just a handful of times in all my memory, but I wanted to tell her that I always had. I was scared, confused, wrong, I was going to say. Maybe it would let the ever-present guilt I carried for being so skeptical and unkind to her finally loosen. Maybe it would mend the hole in her heart she told me I created.

I thought about it when we sorted my old Barbies for a garage sale, drinking wine and dressing them in outfits and posing them on various fruits. We laughed hysterically. Of course I love her, I thought, but didn't say so. I thought about it all the time that visit: when we watched the deer scatter during one morning walk and she squeezed my arm with delight, when she brought me strawberries—my favorite—for no reason, when she was so stressed from trying to figure out where they'd move next and what they could sell in the meantime. I was almost there. I could feel the words taut in my throat, getting so close that they pressed against the back of my teeth like an animal trying to escape. But somehow I couldn't let them out.

I was going to grad school in Alabama, and I drove back in late August. My mom told me on the phone, on that long drive southeast, how much strain losing their house and their community of the last twenty-two years was putting on her and my stepdad. And how much it made her feel she hadn't succeeded. Financially. Professionally. At anything, she said.

It would have been such a perfect moment to tell her that she was wrong, and her life was inspiring, and she was deeply loved.

"Oh god, relax. It'll all work out," I told her instead.

Six weeks later the blood poured into her brain.

WORLD OF WONDERS
JUNE 2013

Red holds a hammer. He has the full moon of a nail's head protruding from his nostril. He taps it in a little deeper. The flat head rests one inch out from the entryway to his cavity, the metal flaring the soft nostril tissue wide. With the hammer's forked prongs, he hooks and slowly pulls out the nail. It glistens. Only the audience members right up front can see the sheen of snot coating the nail, but the rest are practiced in the art of imagination.

There is nobody out front to hear our bally. I'm half-crouched, peeking through the opening in the tent to watch Red perform.

"You want more?" he asks the audience.

"Yeah!" they yell.

"You're sick," he says, pounding the nail into his nostril one more time, bowing a little with the nail inside so they can see that he is filled up, that he is real, that they may now applaud.

When Red first arrives at the Big Butler fairgrounds—the day after our caravan pulls in from Gibsonton—all the other performers run to him with arms open.

We've just started unloading Queen Kong, our taxidermy gorilla in her upright glass coffin, but she needs fourteen hands beneath her heft as she's lowered straight down from the truck, and there are only six of us: Tommy, Sunshine, Pipscy, Spif, Big, Big Ben—the show's working man who we'd picked up in Gibsonton—and me. And then, as if on cue, Red's van pulls up.

"Red!" Sunshine calls, running to him across our lot and throwing her arms around his neck. Everyone says hello, and then Red thumbs at the small man who has just climbed out of the passenger side of his van.

"This is Snickers," he says.

"Snickers T. Clown," Snickers says, tipping his fedora. He's wearing a suit vest with no shirt underneath, and some very worn slacks. He doesn't smile.

"Came recommended through a friend of a friend," Red says. "He'll be our working man and ticket guy."

"And performer," Snickers interjects.

"We just need a working man for now," Tommy says.

"I've got a lot of acts. I've been performing for years," Snickers says. There's a long pause.

"We'll see," Tommy says, turning away. "Anyway, good to see you, Red. We've got your stage unloaded and an extension cord ready for your van."

"Where did you guys come from?" I ask Snickers, who gives me an exaggerated smile that reveals two dimples so deep, they must be scars.

"I met up with Red in Philly. Spent a few days there. Got a kitten from his mom. Then we headed this way."

"A kitten?" I ask, looking around.

"She's in the van, with Red's cat," Snickers says. I look over to the van, but the windows are covered with tan curtains on the inside.

"They don't get too hot in there?"

"There's an air conditioner in the back window," he says. "One of those big ones. My cat's name is Wednesday, like from the Addams Family. I've been performing for years," Snickers says, looking around the tent as he lights up a cigarette. "It's in my blood. They'll put me onstage as soon as they see what I can do."

"What can you do?" I ask. The others have wandered off, back to their various jobs.

He grabs his left pointer finger with his right hand and pulls it all the way back so it touches the top of his hand. He does this for each of his fingers, pulling and pushing them back, then switches and contorts the fingers on the other hand.

Story goes: Snickers was born triple jointed in every joint. He had thirty-six birth defects. Spent his first four years in the L.A. Children's Hospital. "I was their poster child," he says, unbuttoning his vest. "I mean, really. You drive down the 101 and you'd see my cute-ass face on the billboard. They loved me."

He takes off his vest, folds it neatly, and sets it on a stool. Across the right side of his chest and shoulder is a tattoo of a thick, thorny vine, as if one of those popular tribal tattoos had been sharpened at each point. His torso itself is crooked, with a few bones protruding in places I haven't seen bones protrude before, a single point sticking out from just below his ribs, like something inside is trying to escape his skin.

After a deep pull on the cigarette, he tucks it into the corner of his mouth. An exhale, and then he sucks his stomach until it's as thin as a cereal box, with the two wings of his ribs protruding. He contorts his torso, twisting, and something pops with the kind of sound that usually makes people seek medical attention, and he twists further, his ribs moving closer together and his hips going the opposite direction, bones protruding from places I don't understand. He straightens and throws his shoulders back, and there are more pops, and one of my hands covers my eyes except for the slit through which I can't not look and the other hand covers my mouth. He asks if I have a stringless tennis racquet that he can contort his body through. I do not, I apologize.

"My ribs are made of rubber. It's been my dream all my life to be on this show, and I've been performing now for twelve years, so I'm good at what I do. I don't mean to brag, but I'm really good. I'm gonna get a spot as a performer here. I have to," he says.

"Back to work," Tommy calls from the back end. I go.

"Don't be upset," Tommy says, "if Red yells at you."

We're tying canvas straps to the metal stakes, which will bind the circus tent to the earth. "I'm gonna put you on his crew. Just don't take anything personally," he says as Sunshine walks over.

"Are you putting her with Red? Poor thing," she says, stroking my shoulder. "He knows everything and he's amazing, but don't be offended when he insults you."

Cassie overhears and calls from where she's building the stage curtain's frame. "He's gonna call you a dummy. He calls everyone a dummy," she says. "Dummy means he loves you."

"Dummy means he thinks you're a dummy," Sunshine says. "But it's okay. Everyone's a dummy compared to him."

I look across the tent to where Red sits, shirt off, belly round and hard out front. He's bent over an electrical box with a tool in one hand, frowning.

"Red! Tess is on your crew," Tommy calls down to him. He nods and looks away. I walk over, tentative, eager, wanting to show him that I'm the real deal. Tattoos line his arms and chest, an anatomical man bending back with three swords down his throat. Stars surrounding the man. In yellow letters over a red circle on his forearm: *STRANGE*. On the other arm: *FREAK*. A cigarette hangs out his mouth while he fixes a lightbulb with his hands.

"Hi!" I say. "I'm Tess—"

"Bring me a spreader," he says.

"I'm not exactly sure—"

"Go!" he yells, so I start running in the general direction

66

he's pointed, grab Cassie's arm as I hustle to ask what a spreader is, then keep running. Spreaders, it turns out, are long, rectangular metal bars covered with red and blue bulbs that attach to the long banner-line poles to make the frame where everything else hangs. We're testing each section and piece of the banner line's lights, readying to raise it twenty-five feet into the air.

The night before, I'd heard something about Red. An explanation, maybe. Story goes: he married young, had a wife and baby whom he loved ferociously. The kind of love that can only be felt by a person who gets the things he never thought he'd get. Then his baby died. And then his wife died. He was alone again.

"Test the spreaders from the main junction box," he yells. I run toward a huge pile of electronic boxes on a metal cart, hoping for sudden insight about what a junction box looks like, say, but the stack of buzzing transformers and loose cords remains an enigma. I grab at a plug, thinking the prongs might give me a clue, and when they don't, I try to follow the line with my hands to its origin. I glance back at Red, hoping that he might be watching and help, and also hoping he is not watching and has moved on to something else and forgotten about me. He's nowhere in sight. I turn back to my scrambling, untangling cords, and trying to guess how things might power one another, when suddenly he's right behind me.

"No," he says, grabbing a cord out of my hand.

"I don't really know—" I start, but he jumps back in. "Find the flag bag and tighten the slip-ties." I stare blankly. "Fine," he says, looking around for a job simple enough for an idiot. "See all these bulbs in each spreader?" I nod. I do. "Plug the spreader into this junction box," he says, and I realize this is the same job I failed at just moments before. "Check each bulb to make sure it works. If it's a dud, or if one of the bulbs is broken, stick these pliers into the socket, unscrew the base of the bulb, and get a new one in." I look at the pliers he's just handed me. Metal. I know nearly nothing about electricity, but I remember the early childhood lesson about not sticking metal into an electrical outlet.

"Is it okay if I unplug these spreaders before I stick the pliers into the socket?" I ask.

He sighs, turns to walk back to his table. "I guess," he calls over his shoulder. Greenhorn.

I work on my task, moving as quickly as I can to make up for my lack of knowledge. As I hustle back and forth between the junction box and the spreaders, I watch Spif and Ben plug long extension cords into this box and yell at one another to test items in the show and our bunk. All lights and sound and even the little power we get in our bunks are coming from this complicated breaker.

Just as I'm about to finish my task, I hear Red yell, "Unplug the pigtail!" I continue unscrewing the bulb I'm working on and feel a little smug, a little proud for being such a good worker, for finishing this assigned task like a real carnie. "HEY!" he yells. "Unplug the pigtail!" and this time I glance over my shoulder to where he sits to see who is being berated and am surprised to see him looking right at me. "Yes, you!" he shouts. "Are you deaf? Dumb? Unplug the pigtail. Now!"

Again, I have no idea what this means. I jump around to the junction box, study the cords in front of me, hoping one might be—what?— coiled or curly or pink or something. "The pigtail!" he calls again, louder this time. I hold a cord up to him, ask if it's the pigtail. "No! It's real easy. Unplug the fucking pigtail!" he says. "The PIGTAIL! The PIGTAIL!" he shouts, and I'm frantic, pulling cords out one by one and occasionally calling over my shoulder that I do not know what the pigtail is. He stands up from his chair and begins marching over, his shadow approaching like a storm, staring me down, chanting, "Dummy! Grab the fucking pigtail!" and I can feel that heat building in my eyes, the emotional response I've been warned against, take nothing personally, but who can ever be successful at that, come on, who is divorced from emotional response, I want to know, as I keep unplugging and replugging and Red is hollering at me and the rest of the cast has stopped what they're doing to stare at our scene, him screaming, me frantic on the ground, and yep, of course, my eyes brim with tears. When he is three or four steps away from me and I'm still crouched, ready like a stray to be kicked in the ribs and sent away, Tommy suddenly appears beside me, swiftly, kindly, with speed and firmness in his voice, points to one of the four pieces in my hand, tells me to twist until the lines meet, pull the plug apart, and then he disappears. I am saved. Just before he reaches me, Red turns around. He walks back to his chair and flops down heavily, as if I've exhausted him. The plug looks nothing like a pigtail.

In another version I hear of his story, Red's baby died and he went mad with grief and so his wife left him, afraid of the monster he was becoming. In one more version, he left to fight in Vietnam, and when he returned, they were just gone. I hear four or five more versions during the season. Reasons why he lives in his van, why he's been on the road for all these years. How he developed his ability to withstand pain. The number of people he's lost. Whatever the beginning of the story, the ending to each is the same: a man always on the move, always alone.

The next night, when the work is done and fireflies spark, I see Snickers start to walk off between two cars. He catches me watching him and waves me over.

"I wanted to show you a video of an escape act I did," he says, lighting a joint as he talks. "Want some?" he asks.

"Did Tommy tell you that we're getting drug tested soon?" I ask. I don't mean to be a total square, but the threat sounded real.

"Whatever," Snickers says quickly, holding his breath with a mouthful of smoke. He looks toward our semi's trailer, its

69

white still easy to see despite the dark. He exhales. "I've been drug tested plenty of times. Never stopped doing any drugs. Never tested positive. I have my ways."

"Fair enough," I say.

"So?" he asks, offering me the joint again. "A few hits of this won't even show up on a drug test."

"No thanks. Thank you, though. Another time."

"Cool," he says, pressing Play on his phone to show me the four-minute video of his escape act. He narrates on top of the video's narration. His wrists and ankles are tied up in ropes and his ankles are chained to two fifteen-pound dumbbells. He is shirtless and shivers, just a little bit, as he and his two assistants are preparing the act. The videographer giggles quietly a few times. Once he's tied up, an assistant unfurls a black garbage bag over his body and ties the top, and he's rolled into a river. Within ten seconds, he has torn through the bag and is out. Whatever the video lacks in quality is more than made up for by his enthusiasm. I imagine him as a little boy in the hospital, watching videos about Houdini, a man who can transform his body into a miracle. Past what anyone thinks he can survive.

"Well, I'm gonna go find some trouble," Snickers says, winking to me as he wanders away from our truck and down into the deep heart of carnietown, the section of the fairgrounds where all the carnie bunkhouses are pressed together, where the real action goes down. "Unless of course you want to join?" he asks, stopping to look back. I do. Every part of me does. All the warnings I've heard from Sunshine in these first few days only whetted my appetite to get right down into the ugliest, nastiest part. Some piece of my brain thinks a meth habit might be a necessary part of the experience. Would be forgiven. But I see Tommy's shadow walking between Tommy and Sunshine's trailer and the show trailer, and I know enough to try to keep on his—and the rest of the cast's—good side. I shake my head no.

"Your loss," he says, and disappears down into the darkness.

"Tex," Tommy whispers, breaking my stare. Red's blockhead act with the nails up his nose is over, Snickers is sitting in the ticket box beside our front bally stage, and Tommy has spotted approaching marks.

"You ready for the snake?" he asks.

"Yes," I say, meaning no. Meaning, clearly, completely, no. Tommy uses two hands to lift the snake off his shoulders and set her onto mine. She's shimmery and cold, eyes milky blue because she's readying to shed. The meat of her middle rests on my shoulders and throat, sliding across my body as she squeezes my limbs. Approaching kids point and call out, specks of spit flying from their wet mouths. "A snake! A big snake!" one squeals.

A carnie shaped like an apple stops as he's walking by. "Red-tailed boa?" he asks. I nod.

My heart is clomping and kicking with such ferocity beneath the snake's heavy body that I'm afraid she'll mistake it for the quick pitter of a rat's heart, her dinner, and this very thought makes it pump faster and sweat bead on my hairline and upper lip and my wet fishnetted feet slip inside my heels.

The carnie takes a few steps back but keeps his eyes on the snake. "Had me a red-tailed boa for ten years," he says. "Loved her. Had to kill her, though."

"Oh?" I say, curious, but not sure I want to know why.

"I was at the vet buying her some medication, and just as I was leaving, I mentioned how strange it was that the last few weeks I'd been waking up in the night with her stretched out long beside me on the bed. I let her roam free in my house, but she'd never done that before. I was just telling the vet sort of as a joke, 'cause I thought she wanted to snuggle with me. But the vet stopped what he was doing and looked at me so seriously. You need to go home, put her in a cage, and bring her back in right now, he told me. I asked him why. Because, the vet said, she's measuring you to see if you'll fit in her body. She's planning to eat you. I have to kill her. And he did."

Tommy starts laughing his high-pitched cackle that sounds too performer-perfect to be real. I'm about to pee myself.

"Just know that when she stretches out long beside you, it's time to say your goodbyes," the carnie says. "Anyway, boas are sweeties. Aren't you, baby?" he says to the snake. "Better get back. See ya," he says as he walks away, throwing a peace sign over his head as he leaves. I have a lot of questions for Tommy, but before I can get any of them out, he ups the ante.

"You think you can do the dollar-bill trick and still keep hold of that snake?" Tommy asks.

"Sure," I say, gulping, and try to force a smile.

The night before, Tommy had asked for one of my dirty socks when I was getting ready for bed. I'd dug one out of my stash of dirty laundry, a sock I'd worn during a long, sweaty day of setup, and he'd dropped it into the snake cage for the night. So they can get used to my smell, he said. So they'll be comforted by it. But all I can imagine is the sock gripped in one's coils while it is shredded completely by the fangs of the other, the snake's best attempt at a dead animal warning on a doorstep.

Tommy reaches into the ticket box for a dollar and hands it over. Both my hands are on the snake's body, and it takes me a few seconds to rearrange them enough to free a hand to take the bill.

"Know what? How about you just get used to the snake a while," Tommy says. "We'll add the bill later."

It occurs to me that there is no real reason why they should keep me on. And then, as suddenly, that they might not. That they could decide that I don't have much skill or strength or experience or whatever the things are that everyone else seems to possess. They could ask me to leave.

I take a deep breath and resolve to dig deeper. To make myself necessary. To stay.

72

The big beauty lies across my neck.

I feel the snake's tongue flick against my earlobe. I feel it on my cheek. I'm smiling, I'm waving. The kid is pointing at the snake. We are luring them into the tent. I try to focus on that feeling—my job as a conduit of wonder for this kid. I feel the snake's face slide onto the hand I have beside my neck, my fingers pressing against her coil to keep her from strangling me, *calm, calm, peaceful and calm*, I chant to myself. People do this every day. Some people, somewhere. The snake does not want to hurt me because she thinks I'm a tree, I think, and then I feel a sharp pain on my finger. I yank my hand back, hold it up in front of my face. It's bleeding.

The snake bit me.

Now, I die.

I am standing onstage, waiting to die.

Tommy continues ballying. I hold my finger in front of my face for two, three seconds, watching the droplets of blood bloom from the flesh, sure someone will notice and start screaming, but Tommy is getting ready to swallow his sword, and nobody is looking at me. I use the back of my hand and wrist to push the snake's face as far from me as I can get her.

I have been bit. I have been bit by the snake. I repeat these unbelievable sentences in my head.

I do not believe that this snake is not poisonous. Sure, I've been told she's not poisonous because she's a boa, and sure, boas don't bite, they squeeze. But she *bit* me.

I look over to Tommy dramatically, not quite wanting to interrupt his bally but also desperately wanting him to notice. To get ready to catch me as I faint.

"Today you're going to see a girl from California eat fire and drink burning gasoline like you or I would drink iced tea," Tommy tells the growing crowd. "You'll see the Pain-Proof Man, the Icelandic Giant, and Olga Hess, the Headless Woman," he says. This is where I'm supposed to be pointing at the corresponding banners. Neither Tommy nor the crowd seem to notice anything amiss, and so, not knowing what else to do, I point to the banners as he ballys, keeping the bloody side of my finger away from the audience as well as I can.

My finger stings, though after the first thirty seconds, the bleeding only looks impressive when I squeeze the wound, which, when I eye it as I'm waving to a hollering baby in a stroller, does not have two deep fang holes. The snake keeps wrapping her body around me, curving her strong neck toward my face with a kind of coil that looks to me as if she's readying to attack, so I keep strong-arming her head away from mine. My biceps are already quivering with strain.

"You got a hold of that snake?" Tommy whispers when his bally pitch is through. It does not look like I have a hold on this snake. I do not have a hold.

"The snake bit me," I whisper, trying to keep my smile. The words come out a little garbled, like a ventriloquist. I hear the shake in my notes. I hold my finger up to his face and prepare for him to cry out in horror, but as I eye the injury myself, I realize it appears more like a scrape than a bite. A small scrape.

"What? This is a first," he says. We both stare at my finger. It looks, really, like the snake has brushed her teeth against me more than anything else. "Sometimes the snakes scrape against things when they're getting ready to shed to help them peel away some skin. I guess she wanted help from you. She must like you."

"She does not like me," I say, my eyes filling with a heat I know means they are close to tears. Again.

"Do you want to put her down? I can take her," Tommy says, reaching over. I begin to lean toward him, to let the snake get taken from my shoulders. There are bees in my brain, maggots, spiders, a panic of pain and anger. I did not imagine fear would be such a daily hurdle here. I thought the sideshow would be a place to escape it. But here it is. Over and over.

The snake squeezes on, coiling herself around my body. Tommy's arms reach out toward me. I want to take a deep

74

breath, move past the fear, and let myself face the actual creature on my shoulders, so much less terrifying, really, than the idea of her. I want to be bold.

I shake my head meekly toward Tommy and, with as much courage as I can muster, keep the snake half-draped across my shoulders. I smear the tiny bit of blood on my sequined shorts and, not knowing what else to do, smile at the passing marks.

CAKE

Two months after the stroke

DECEMBER 2010

Her eyes were still gray.

She'd been awake for seven weeks. My mom's eyes opened and closed, her hand squeezed ours or a doctor's or anyone's. She had movement in her left leg and left arm and left hand. Nothing on the right side.

Eye color is determined by the distribution and concentration of melanin. Trauma can create heterochromia, a difference in coloration of the iris, due to excess deposits of iron from too much blood in the eye's anterior chamber, among other causes. Nobody knew *exactly* why what was happening, was happening with her eyes. Her brain.

Two months, and we were desperate to understand how far she had or hadn't come. How much she would or would not recover. We asked her to read things. Books. Cards. Writing on photos. She looked at them. Sometimes her brow furrowed. Sometimes she placed a finger on the photograph, on the letters. Then she looked away. We didn't know if she couldn't read them, or if she just couldn't express that she could read them, or if she just didn't want us to talk about any of it because she was so frustrated.

We asked her to write her name. Nope.

To draw a picture of a house. Of a circle. Of a person.

Could she nod? No. Sometimes she moved her lips or eyebrows like she was trying to talk but had forgotten which part of her face made the sound come out.

Could her tongue go to one side or the other to mean different things?

What if she held objects to express different wishes? What if she picked up this cup for no, this stuffed bear for yes?

What if we use an iPad, a laptop, flash cards? What if she does?

For weeks, then months, we try this. We try everything. The professionals try everything. All the tricks.

"Oh, she's had a stroke?" I hear from neighbors, acquaintances. "That's terrible. My uncle had a stroke and had to be in the hospital for almost a month before he was up and walking and talking again. I'm sure she'll recover soon."

It has been two months, and she has not recovered. The doctors keep telling us that she will not recover. Davy spends all his time at the hospital trying to get her to recover.

Will he find a way to get her to communicate? Yes, he says he is certain. He is goddamned positive.

Can she move her hand so that her thumb points down for no, points up for yes?

Davy sits beside her bed. "Cutie," he says. "We want to help you communicate, so we know what you need and want. Okay?" he asks.

She is looking right into his eyes.

"I'm going to help you make a fist," he says. He gently bends the fingers on her left hand in, straightens her thumb so it sticks up. She is making a thumbs-up.

"Great, that's so great," he says, smiling hugely at her and then looking over his shoulder at my brother and me, making sure we are witnessing the beauty. "When your thumb is up like this, it means yes, okay?"

"Na na," she says.

"Great," he says. "Okay, relax your hand." He unfolds her

fingers, kisses them, and sets them down on the bed. "Let's practice. Is your name Teresa?" he says. She raises her hand. I stop breathing.

She flexes her fingers, relaxes them. Holds her hand in the air for three seconds. Every muscle in my body is tensed. My brother is chewing on his thumb.

She clears her throat. Extends her pointer finger. Sets her hand back on the bed. She looks at Davy. Her eyebrows are tensed and furrowed, there are lines across her forehead that signal distress, lines we have come to know too well.

"No problem, honey. Let's try again," he says softly and slowly. "Is your name Teresa?"

She raises her hand quickly.

"Good," he says. "Now see if you can make a fist."

She makes a fist.

"Yes," he says, talking quicker now, "and now stick your thumb up," he says. She moves a few of the fingers on her hand, looks at it, looks at him, looks at it. She thinks about it. Stares and stares. Wiggles a few fingers. And then she sticks up her thumb.

"Yes, yes, yes!" we all three yell, my brother and I jumping up and down, Davy clapping. My mom is beaming, this tender smile that stretches from the midline of her face across the left side, her eyes jumping back and forth among the three of us, watching our joy.

Davy jumps up and grabs the physical therapist as she is passing. "Come see, come see!" he says, pulling her into the room.

"Teresa," Davy says. She has set her hand back on the bed. "Am I your husband?"

She is still smiling at him.

"Am I your husband?" he asks.

"Na na na," she says.

"Can you give me a thumbs-up to answer the question, honey?" he asks.

"Na na," she says. Her hand remains on the bed.

"Remember the thumbs-up you just did? She just did one," he says. "Can you do that again, to show Linda?" he asks. She is looking at him. She knows he wants something. "Right here, with this hand," he says, tapping her hand on the bed.

She picks her hand up, holds her arm out straight from her body. She knows we want something from her. Insurance will only pay for therapy—physical, occupational, speech—if the patient makes continual, measurable progress. We need progress. We are desperate.

She sticks her tongue out in concentration. Licks her lips. All our starving eyes, staring.

"Am I your husband? Thumbs-up or thumbs-down?"

Her arm is still out straight. She bends her wrist and her flat hand folds ninety degrees down. The lines crease her forehead again and she is staring at us as if she knows this isn't what will please us.

"That's okay," the therapist says. "I've gotta run. I'm so glad to hear you made a thumbs-up. Let's try it again tomorrow, okay?" she says, but my mom's mouth stays in a grimace. She is working. She is working so hard.

"See you all tomorrow," Linda says, closing the door behind her.

"What does Linda know?" Davy says. "Anyway, you'll show her tomorrow. Ugh. Linda."

My mom's brow releases a few of its creases. She sighs out a big huff of air.

"You ready to try again?" he asks.

"Na na na na," she says.

He will do anything, everything, again and again, to give her a life.

A few days later, Davy and I were sitting in the hospital's hallway, waiting, while my mom's blood and brain fluid were being sucked out for more tests. In the two months since her stroke,

79

with each step she took toward healing, another crisis occurred—a head wound infection, more internal bleeding, additional small strokes, another required brain surgery—she'd had six brain surgeries already—septic shock, on and on, so it was impossible to keep track of how many or which steps forward or back we were taking. There was just constant crisis, and her pain.

The kindest thing, the doctors said, would be to pull the plugs.

What kind of life will she have now?

Would she want to live it?

Would you?

It is not painful, the hospice workers told us, all of us scrunched in one visiting room, to starve to death. We'll just cut off her feeding tube. It's peaceful.

That seems untrue, I said.

Well, we give them a lot of morphine, one of them said. And then your body just shuts down. It's natural. Not unpleasant.

Not unpleasant?

Well, the hospice worker said, taking my hand. You know, she said, and smiled a frowny smile that made the pockets of her cheeks stand out like overstuffed strudels.

The terrible truth was no. I don't think she'd want to live this life. I wouldn't.

Davy and I left the hospice conversation and sat in the waiting area. His back was to the windows overlooking giant trees that might have been hiding mountain lions, anything was possible. It was early evening, and the light was gold and coming in shafts through the window and holding in its arms the ordinary beauty of floating dust particles, and we were both staring at them. It had been two months, only two months, but there was exhaustion to contend with already. There was the turmoil of sustained emergency, which seems like an oxymoron—that emergency could be long-term— but it was, sustained. We were in it. He leaned his head down away from the light and shaded his eyes with one hand. His voice was higher than usual.

"I don't think I will be able to go on if Teresa dies," he said. I nodded. These are the kinds of words we know to use in times like these. Like *times like these*.

"I mean, I won't go on," he said. His hand still shaded his eyes. He wasn't using abstraction. This was not the story of the American hero who endures and endures. This was, he thought, the end of his love story. Which was the only story that mattered to him.

I thought about my brother. I tried to imagine what his life would feel like, at twenty-one, to lose both parents at once. My stomach dropped six floors to the street and my heart was pounding and I felt desperate to run the three hundred miles that moment to my brother's college and knock the kegs away and gather him up in my arms and grip swords to slice open the guts of anyone who approached.

I nodded at Davy with total calm, accepting the terms.

$$\lightning$$

It's her birthday. Seven months after the stroke.

Davy orders a cake. It must be covered in brown icing, he says. To look like leather. There needs to be a handle on one side of the cake, and little patches of brightly colored frosting made to look like postage stamps. One must say *Paris*. Another *Venice*. *Germany*. In the center, as if written on a luggage tag, ice the words *Visualize Travel*.

A sweet idea, we all agreed. My brother, my grandmother, my two aunts, and I heard the cake plan in separate phone conversations in the week or so before her birthday. Sweet to daydream about something like that, like a unicorn.

My mom was living at an acute rehabilitation hospital. Neighbors, nurses, and other family members came to the party Davy threw for her. They sang. They ate the *Visualize Travel* cake. I didn't.

I stayed in Alabama, trying to keep my head above water in

school, trying to protest the idea that this birthday might be her last. People told her how good she looked for sixty-five, and in the video I watched of the party, which kept panning back to her in a wheelchair out on a wooden deck, her head is moving around all the time, like there are bugs flitting toward her face that she must escape. Guests lean in low and close to her to express their love, talk twice as loud as normal. She looks at them. Looks away. It is hard to know if she wants to respond but can't, and feels too frustrated to hold eye contact, or if responding is just one of an infinite set of possible movements, and looking away, to an evergreen's low branch, is the one she chooses right now. There is no such thing as too much love. But somehow, it is clear that this is too much.

I watched the video and watched the video. I watched myself not being there, watched her overwhelmed with well wishes. For a while I was going home every few weeks, and then after a while, after the first three months, I went back every couple of months, but it was never enough. Every time I went I thought about dropping out of school to stay with her, because that is what a loving daughter would do, but then I kept not doing it.

A month after her birthday party with the *Visualize Travel* cake, I came home for a visit and Davy stopped at a travel store on our way home from the rehab facility. "Be right back," he said to me in the car. He returned clutching maps and travel books on Italy.

"We're going to eat pasta and drink wine and look at the fountains," he said, using the knuckles on his hands to jab at the tears beside his eyes. I think about my mom's tracheotomy. The sound of the nurses suctioning the phlegm from the quarter-size hole in her throat because she cannot swallow, because she was choking too often on her own saliva.

"We always wanted to go when we retired," he said. "If we ever had the money."

"Do you have the money?" I asked.

"We'll find a way."

"What way?"

"We're working it out."

He didn't give me any more information and I thought it would be rude to keep asking, thought maybe there wasn't actually a way, and the plan would fail, and we would all remain home, safe. They'd just had to sell the house. How would there be money for the trip? How would a doctor okay her to travel? How could they decide to leave us behind? None of it seemed possible. But even the far-off, distant, impossible idea of it made me feel like I didn't fit inside the car anymore, that I couldn't sit beside him without exploding.

"Do you really think she'll be able to travel?" I asked. I tried to keep my voice soft and tender, but there was a knife in it.

"She wants to."

"How do you know?"

"She's always wanted to."

"And now?"

"I asked her. Very clearly. And she very clearly responded *yes*."

"She did *not* respond yes! She cannot talk! This is so selfish," I wanted to scream at him. "So dangerous! So dumb! So terrible to take her somewhere far away to die!" I wanted to list all the threads of idiocy and self-obsession that would have concocted this plan, but I stayed quiet. I was afraid of him cutting me out. And I was afraid that it wasn't just about her. Maybe he needed something, a wish, a dream, to keep him going, too.

We drove in silence for a few minutes, him wiping his face and neither of us looking at the other. Living in our own private continents across the chasm of the gearshift. Both our hands moved to our wet eyes at the same time and then there was only one of us and a mirror image. Wiping away the evidence. As in the human brain, connection across hemispheres is nearly impossible.

83

HAIR INGREDIENTS

Day 9 of 150

WORLD OF WONDERS
JUNE 2013

Story goes: a woman became a carnie because she fell in love with a Ferris wheel. She called him Bruce. For seven years they traveled together. Then, in their eighth season, a hurricane hit their carnival and Bruce was destroyed, sent to a junk lot in New Jersey. She followed him there and, after finding his remains, asked him to marry her. They were wed. She's working at a sandwich shop to save enough money to have Bruce shipped home to her in Florida.

I am not yet in love with any of the machines but also in love with all the machines. Seeing the half-assembled rides during setup was almost embarrassing, like I was glimpsing them in their underpants, not yet all dazzled up with long stiff arms and flashing lights, blaring the summer's pop hits. But I like seeing them at night. Powered down. Sleeping.

We've just returned back from our first Walmart trip.

You want to meet a bunch of carnies? Head to Wally World after midnight when the carnival is in town. Hope they're a little high, jovial. Hope they're not squaring off in their rivalries, that food jocks stay in cereal while the ride jocks are in canned soups.

Walmart is an American carnie mecca. It's cheap, familiar, and the only thing open after the fair closes late at night when we have the opportunity to restock food. Tommy tells us to meet back at the van in an hour, setting us free inside the bright halogen city. "I recommend that everyone take advantage of the, uh, facilities," Tommy says as we're walking inside, glancing my way. "As you know by now, the fairgrounds don't always have the cleanest bathrooms," he says.

"Or bathrooms at all," Sunshine pipes in.

"Right," Tommy says. "And here you've got air-conditioning while you shit and unlimited toilet paper. It's a shitter's dream."

Our nine days on the road haven't included any climate-controlled, toilet-papered, locking bathroom stalls, nor has there been any time to be alone, so even a few minutes by myself in a cool stall is exciting. As are the thousands of possible items to buy stacked in neat rows.

After the bathroom, I wander. When I was packing for the sideshow, I didn't know what to bring. I still don't totally know what I need from this shopping trip to see me through until the next, not really, though one thing comes right to mind. I've been sleeping on a plastic-wrapped mattress with a leftover sheet from last season, my sweat gathering and pooling around me like I'm a package of hot dogs left out in the sun. Separating sets of bunks in the semi's back end are wooden boards that create the suggestion of tiny double rooms, though there are no doors. My personal space for the season is the two-foot-by-six-foot bed where I sleep—which also acts as my bunkmate's step stool for getting onto her bunk—and the small plastic drawers beside it. At least I can try to make my bed my own.

I head over to bedding and am not surprised to see a few others from the crew.

"Why are these so expensive?" Spif asks, walking slowly down the aisle as he eyes the price tags beneath each plastic bundle of sheets. Fifteen, twenty, thirty bucks. "It's just a piece of cloth," he says, not picking up any package. "Fucking capitalism. This is some bullshit."

"Over here," Pipscy calls, her face free of the bandana she had veiling it all day to keep the sun off. She's at the end of the aisle, fingering stacks of brightly colored sheets that are priced well below the others. We walk over. The sheets are stiff, the kind of material that will stand up of its own accord. They feel more like the papery sheet draped over your lap at the gynecologist, but they are less than twenty dollars.

"Still expensive," Pipscy says.

"I gotta go take a draw," Spif says.

"Me, too," Pipscy says.

"Already got one," Sunshine says, walking up behind us.

"You need one?" Spif asks me as he starts to walk away. "Or you got money?

I start to answer that I need one, that I don't have money, that I've been in grad school for years and living on nearly nothing, but I stop. The truth is, I have a little bit of money in my bank account. A very little bit, but it's there, enough to buy sheets and some groceries at least. This, it seems, is not the case with the other folks on my crew. This job certainly doesn't pay much. And it's seasonal. As a greenhorn, I make $275 a week, minus taxes, though the others who've been out longer likely don't make much more than that. Still.

"I'm good," I say. I could probably get the jersey sheets, six dollars more, softer, more absorbent, but I don't. I'm embarrassed to have money for jersey sheets. I pick up the cheapest, scratchiest, most miserable sheets I can find, because that's the team I want to be on.

I'm instructed to get myself food for the next few days—up to a week, Tommy says—plus whatever else I think I need to survive in the bunkhouse. I buy a pillow, the cheapest one I can find. I buy tiny cotton shorts for sleeping, as the bunkhouse is absurdly hot inside the metal truck's container; a small clip-on reading light for my bed; and food: peanut butter, bananas, apples, pretzels, tuna, granola, hummus, and water.

In the semi's hallway, we have one tiny fridge, college-dorm-room-size, for all of us to share. But things here are not like things in a college dorm room. Not because this world isn't full of dreams for the future or folks who like to get rowdy and fucked-up on a Friday night, but because here is "like" nowhere. This is its own universe, enclosed by chain-link fences and kept just outside cities off long dirt roads—close enough to visit but far enough to forget. I'd always assumed the fairgrounds were outside town for reasons of space, but I'm also realizing that there might be suggestions of quarantine.

Back from our store run, I'm walking the darkened dirt road to the bathrooms when suddenly, from nowhere, another body is walking directly beside me, as if it always had been.

"I seen you," the body says. "At Walmart."

Crevices shine from the curtained windows of trailers parked along the road. The sliver of moon does not cast much light but beneath the picnic tables causes shadows to appear as decomposing bones in a shallow grave.

"Oh. Yeah. We just did a food run," I say. He comes closer, and his face enters a slant of light. His cigarette smoke snakes up past a sweat-stained baseball cap. Smooth, tight skin across his cheeks makes him look like someone is holding his head closed, too tight, from behind. He pulls the cigarette out to exhale, and as he does, he smiles and worms his tongue out the side of his mouth. As we round a corner, two small lights above the bathrooms illuminate his whole face, sweaty and sunburned. I'd been warned about carnies a few times already. This one doesn't seem especially harmful, and I have a sense that he, or any carnie, really, might be a piece in some puzzle I need to solve here.

"How many seasons you been out?" he asks, and I want to lie to sound like a pro, but don't.

"This is my first," I say. "First fair."

87

"Holy shit, a greenhorn. You won't ever be the same after this," he says. He has a thick southern drawl, so I ask him where he's from. If we are friendly, maybe he'll tell me more. Maybe he won't do any of those vague, bad things I've been warned about.

"I'm from Atlantic City, New Jersey," he says. "But I put on this accent in order to catch these northern girls at the fair. They love the accent." He laughs. "You know who is the most beautiful girl?" he says. "That one you were with at Walmart. Red hair. Black pants. Ass like there's no tomorrow." He means Pipscy. She is, indeed, beautiful, and has a Jessica Rabbit–meets–animé punk look she lives inside wholly and with confidence. She wears layers of long sleeves and jackets and wool hats in the daylight, tank tops at night. She's desperate to keep her skin white as a geisha so she will be cast as Snow White in the dead princess version of *The Rocky Horror Picture Show* when she gets home.

"I know how to spot a true lady," he says. "My IQ is five points less than Einstein." We're right beside the bathrooms, and part of me is relieved to be talking to a real live carnie, a man on the inside, a roustabout, and to find that he's no different from other strange men I've encountered, but another part of me is exhausted, desperate to take the three further steps that will put me in the bathroom next to running water, to wash the layers of dirt off my face and walk back down the darkened road and climb into the truck and go to sleep and try this all again tomorrow. Do better, be stronger.

"Well, I better get going," I say.

"Wait," he says, stepping closer to my face, licking the edges of his mouth with his pointy tongue. "I'm gonna tell you something." His hand grasps my forearm. "Do you know the secret to making hair grow longer?" he asks, taking off his cap and running his fingers through the short mess of brown hair beneath. I shake my head no. "Take calcium pills. Calcium is one of the key ingredients in hair," he says, coming closer until his mouth is pressed up close to my face. "Every chick wants longer hair," he whispers. He fingers the tips of my hair. I can feel the thump of blood in my neck, and the hairs rise on my arms.

"Well, I'll be seeing you, then," he says, and turns to walk away. I smile, unsure whether I've made my first carnie friend or invited trouble. Wondering whether there's a difference. "I'm quite sure I'll be seeing you," he says, his back to me, and he begins to whistle, the notes all wet in his mouth. I'm standing still as the rain begins again, and somewhere down the road, there are children warm and asleep in their beds who will come to this carnival, and all of us, even the greenhorns, even the ones who rub a stranger's hair, will be in charge of their joy.

I duck into the bathroom. Cassie and Sunshine are inside brushing their teeth and turn to face me immediately. "Never, never, never talk to carnies," Sunshine says. "If you do, it's like a free-for-all invitation for them to come to you anytime, wherever you are. They'll try to pull some moves that I'm sure you won't like. They will never leave you alone."

"I'm sure it'll be fine," I say. "He didn't seem that bad."

"You just wait," she says, a string of foamy toothpaste stuck to her chin. "You'll see."

The other carnies I've interacted with so far—the group I waited with for drug testing two days before the fair opened—didn't seem so bad either.

There are six carnies in front of me, all of us crowded inside the back end of a big RV, waiting our turn to enter the small bedroom/office space up front for drug testing. We'll pee into a cup in the attached bathroom.

It's impossible to know anyone's age because of what hard sun does to a face year after year, plus everything in the carnival seems to be taking place outside linear time, where each day feels as though it were stuffed with a dozen days: the day of clanging metal while the Ferris wheel, which had arrived late, was being scrambled together; the day of learning to clean clothes and dishes in the bathroom sink; the day of thinking and thinking and still not knowing who from home would be there to answer a call.

This day inside a day is a drug test, and the man right in front of me is leaning back against the wall, giving his armpits a rest from the crutches he holds in his hands. Up ahead, a carnie comes out of the bedroom, nods to the rest of the men in line, and leaves.

The man right beside me has his foot all wrapped up in a big white bandage. On his other foot he has a regular sneaker. I keep glancing down at the big bandaged foot as he is telling me about the gator one-off where he works. One-offs, he tells me, and single-o's are sideshow offshoots, and as opposed to the ten-in-one, where one price gives you admission to ten or more acts, single-o's cost fifty cents or a dollar and let you see one thing: the world's largest rat, smallest horse, fattest pig, or, in the case of the carnie with the bandaged foot, hugest gator. He likes the work, he says, because he can sit in the shade all day.

These men in line don't seem nervous, unlike my fellow performers, who have spent the last seventy-two hours taking midday jogs in all their clothes to try to sweat everything out. A few family-owned carnival companies had recently started drug testing all their employees, the bandage-footed man explains, in an attempt to make customers feel safer about the carnies operating the rides and to decrease the employee drama. Plus, it might help to break the stereotype that all carnies are meth heads.

"Are they?" I asked.

"Depends which shows you're talking about," he explains. "Depends which carnies."

The previous year at this fair, local drug dealers had lost all business for the two weeks the carnival was in town because of how hard and cheap the carnies had been pushing their own goods. In an act of retaliation, the townie dealers had called the cops on carnietown with some specific information to share. In the middle of the night, searchlights and sirens broke into each trailer as helicopters and SWAT teams rolled in from all sides. The carnie bunkhouses are inside long trailers—sixty feet or longer—filled with tiny rooms, two or three beds in each, and from the outside many of them look like portable bathrooms. In the bunkhouses, the SWAT team found a meth lab and an enormous drug supply.

So here we are, one year later on the same fairgrounds, and more than half of the folks I've talked to have a Ziploc baggie of someone else's pee tucked into their pants.

"You get caught in a ride?" one of the carnies in line asks the man in front of me, nodding toward his bandaged foot.

"Or your gator do that?" another asks.

A few people snicker.

"No, no, none of that," the bandaged man says. "Happened before the season."

They all nod.

"That girlfriend of yours?" another asks, and he laughs again.

"Shit," the man says. "Nah, she's trouble, but not that much trouble."

They are all quiet for a moment. I think the conversation is over.

"Y'all know I got diabetes real bad," he continues. They nod. "Diabetes makes it so you can't feel your hands or feet too well anymore," he says. "One night my girlfriend was working a night shift and I was at home with the dogs. We got this big husky and this little Chihuahua of hers. Anyway, I went to sleep and the little dog had all this energy and was kinda just running in circles like he did a lot. But I fell asleep.

"Next thing I know I wake up to screaming. My girlfriend is standing at the end of the bed and looking down, and I sit up and look down, too, and I see all this blood. 'What the hell's going on?' I ask her, but she's still just screaming and she starts to lean down to pick up that little Chihuahua, but then she stops and backs away. He's covered in blood, too."

91

The boss coughs in the next room and a child screams just outside the trailer door, but we're all leaning toward the man, silent.

"Anyway, I kind of sit up straighter and look down at what my girlfriend's looking at and I start to realize. All the blood that's everywhere is also all over my foot, and the little dog is there just gnawing and gnawing, and I look again at my foot and realize it looks real weird and I look at the dog again and that's when I see it. In his mouth, the dog has my big toe. He's chewed it off my foot."

We are all silent, staring at the man's face to see if this can be true, staring at his bandaged foot to imagine what's underneath, what's not, if there are little leaks of blood on the gauze for proof if we look carefully enough.

"Holy shit," one of the guys says.

"Couldn't feel a thing, 'cause the diabetes has gotten so bad," he says.

"Did you shoot that dog in the face?" another asks.

"Oh no," the man says. "He didn't mean it. I love that guy. Still let him sleep with me at night."

⚡

The morning after Walmart, I wake up sore all over, achy, and scoot out of my bunk. I'm getting used to the soreness now, ten days into being on the road with the show. It is 8:00 a.m., work call not for another hour, and the morning air is cool. The silence at this time of day isn't anything I can hear in the carnival at any other time. I've found, already, that getting up just a little bit early, if I can muster it, gives me time to walk the grounds or sit outside with a book, a slice of calm and solitude before the day's work begins.

I step into the trailer's main area, our dirty, wooden backstage home, but immediately stop, a few inches short of kicking a foot. A body lies face down on the floor. My breath catches for a second, imagining a body lying in ambush ready to turn and attack, or a murder scene. Quietly, quickly, I step over the body's legs, my back pressing against the semi's wall, and tiptoe around toward the face. A hat covers most of it, but just below the brim I see those dimples: Snickers.

My panic drains and I stare down dumbly, wondering how comfortable those dirty, splintery boards are. I hear footsteps come up beside me. "Is that Snickers?" Spif asks.

"Yep," I say.

"Why is he here?" he asks. I look at Spif's face. His eyebrows are raised, hard wrinkles on his forehead like he's just had to ask the most ridiculous question he could imagine.

"No idea," I say. I bend down to shake him, but Spif grabs my shoulder and shakes his head no.

"This is one for the boss," he whispers, and carefully steps over Snickers's sleeping body as he climbs down the steps to Tommy's trailer.

Tommy emerges a few moments later, disarmingly uncool with messy hair plastered to one side and basketball shorts, very unlike the punk rock hero I'd come to expect, and stands beside Snickers. He says his name a few times, then reaches down and shakes his leg. Snickers stirs, blinks open one eye so slowly it looks glued shut, painful.

"What're you doing, man?" Tommy asks, no humor in his voice.

"Hey, Tommy," Snickers says, a genuine smile beginning on the side of his mouth. His face hovers an inch off the ground.

"Why are you sleeping here?" Tommy asks.

Snickers makes no move to peel himself off the floor, but keeps blinking up at Tommy with that smile. I notice, then, two bottles against the wall not far from his head. One bottle of beer, the other, water.

"I didn't want to be late for work call again," Snickers says, still smiling, a little defiantly this time, like a child who believes

93

he's outsmarted his parents. "So I thought I'd sleep right where I needed to be when I woke up."

"Strike two," Tommy says, turning to walk back into his trailer.

I follow Spif back to his room.

"Is this a baseball kind of situation? With three strikes?" I ask.

"If you're lucky."

"I didn't know." "

You'll be fine, Goody Two-Shoes."

"Tommy said strike two—when was strike one?"

"Oh, it was nonyo."

"Nonyo?"

"Nonyo business."

"Oh."

"Don't be late for banners," he says, crawling back into his bunk.

⚡

I wander outside, feeling the morning sun on my face, smelling the dirt. There's a peace I feel from the sun and the earth smell, something that harkens back to camping trips and hikes, a one-with-nature kind of solitude. Even though it seems like the carnival is a place where there is no nature, in some ways, it's really nature presented at its most extreme. Beside our show, for example, is the world's smallest pony. A sign hanging over the pen says so. The fair has a few of these. World's largest rat. Heaviest horse. Littlest pig. The biggest and smallest always attract.

Instead of paying for a bally talker like Tommy or Cassie to stand out front and work people in, a grind tape plays over loudspeakers while the carnival is open: "The only living horse smaller than a cat, inside, alive, today." As freak shows became less popular in the second half of the twentieth century and show budgets decreased, the grind tape became a necessity.

94

Each of the grind tapes for the single-o's here sounds old, both the voice and the tape, like an invitation to an earlier world, before those enthusiastic inflections were used as jokes, back when stranger things were on display.

There was a famous grind-tape recorder named Peter Hennen, one of the best in the business. Story goes: Hennen called a friend in the middle of the night and said, "I've got a good one! Listen: 'See the little girl born to live her entire life underwater. She can't come out or she will die. She's in there now. She goes to school in there. You can come in and see her. You can ask her questions. She may not answer you.' " Was it a real mermaid? his friend wondered. Could it be?

Hennen was giddy, and explained that when you walked into the single-o, there would be a giant fishbowl with a few goldfish swimming in it and a sign with this disclaimer:

GOLDFISH DO SPEND THEIR ENTIRE LIFE UNDERWATER.
THESE ARE GIRL GOLDFISH AND THEY GO TO SCHOOL.
THEY LIVE IN SCHOOLS.
ASK THEM ANYTHING YOU WANT.

It's amazing that the single-o's work. But they're always cheap, and what's inside is never an explicit lie according to what has been advertised. The world's fattest pig is pretty big. And the Giant Battalion horse is a Clydesdale, which *is* large. Why don't people warn each other? Maybe they feel foolish after wanting to believe they were going to see something truly exceptional for fifty cents, or maybe they want others to fall for it, too.

The world's smallest horse bally tape runs in a loop while Leo, the joint's operator, leans back in his camp chair with a newspaper. He reads each page meticulously. Our PA system blares the same acts we're talking every seven to ten minutes. I can't imagine how dreadful it is for Leo. And yet, every time I walk on or off stage, passing close to the mysterious trailer allegedly holding the smallest horse, he waves and smiles.

After work one day, as we're rolling banners—an activity we do each night to preserve the thirty-foot-high hand-painted canvas that advertises all the acts we have inside—he catches my eye and points at his horse's trailer. Did I want to see it? I trot over when we're finished, climb the few steps, and there, in the recessed center of the platform, see a very small pony. It's about the size of a golden retriever. I make some clicking sounds and hold out my hand, but the pony does not look up.

"I grow orchids," Leo says. "That's really what I love." He takes out his phone and fumbles his thick fingers across the small buttons, breathing heavily and cursing quietly when the buttons aren't taking him where he wants to go. I look down at the pony, steadily munching hay, taking no notice of my presence at all. "Here," Leo says, coming up right beside me. On his screen is a photograph of a tiny violet orchid. "And here," he says, showing me a snow-white large-petaled flower next. "They love it on my boat. It's parked in Florida. You can come stay with me anytime," he says. "You're always welcome. Remind me of your name again?"

"Tess. Thank you," I tell him. "They're beautiful." I'm amazed by his level of kindness toward a stranger. I imagine, in another context, that this kind of offer might come across as creepy, but he seems wholly focused on his flowers, and I have no reason to distrust him.

"How many seasons have you been out?" he asks.

"This is my first," I say.

"Oh, you seem like a real pro," he says, and I think about my Band-Aid finger and sore muscles and snake tears and nearly laugh out loud. "Well, the truth is that you'll never be the same after doing this," Leo says. "This kind of life changes you."

"You're not the first person who's said that," I say.

"Folks who spend life on the road are just different."

"Do you mean that in a good way or a bad way?" I ask.

"That all depends," he says, smiling. "Gotta wait to find out." He pulls up more pictures of his orchids.

It seems so obvious—that whatever life you're living will change you. But it's not something I was aware of as a kid, not something kids are aware of in general—that their world is particular. I didn't know my version of America was different from anyone else's.

My America was full of women with armpit hair. A lot of musical events happened at my K–8 school, which doubled as a community center and day care with a rainbow painted above the door. There were drum circles and concerts on the scratchy grass, and my family would trek down to these events like everybody else. The women would stand up and sway their bodies along with the music, slowly at first, speeding up as they raised their arms to the sky for a fuller expression of the music entering them, and that's when their soft, sweet armpit hair would emerge, and their skirts would twirl around them like trumpet flowers, and wafts of pot and sage would rise—it took me years to understand those scents as separate from one another. Sometimes men rose up, too, and swayed with half-closed eyelids like gentle ogres, and it was all sort of nice. It was what I understood America to be.

My mother shaved her pits. She shaved her legs. Sometimes. Once a week, she taught me. Well, from the ankle to the knee. Never shave above the knee, she told me, because there aren't really hairs up there anyway, but the ones that are there will grow back black and thick like thorny vines.

She stood up when the loud music moved her like the other moved women, but she didn't raise her arms to the sky. She snapped, or moved side to side, foot to foot. She swayed her hips, smiled, took sips of wine.

Once, when I was twelve or thirteen, I couldn't believe the

97

number of times she asked me to dance with her in one after-noon. Come on and dance, she called to me. Stop being so shy, she said sweetly, and smiled, both her hands out to me, snapping with the rhythm and then beckoning me over, and I wished above all else to be invisible. Or dead.

I surveyed the scene around me. The town, mostly these women, carried out ongoing campaigns for the blue-bellied salamanders and campaigns to preserve the open ridges and campaigns for the spawning salmon and campaigns to create meditation retreats for the children. We were the children, and we ate miner's lettuce from the side of the road, and there was love—local, free-range, organic love. I wouldn't have said, as I looked at the pom-poms of their pit hair beaded with drops of sweat like beautiful cobwebs, that I didn't envy them. That kind of looseness, that total I-don't-give-a-damn-ness. I think my mom felt the same. I could see her there, bouncing side to side, talking to a friend but eyeing the wild mothers, wondering if letting go completely was a trick she would ever be able to perform.

It would be easiest to say *she was this* and *she was that*—a free-spirited smiling hippie in this free-spirited smiling hippie town—but she wasn't. She was, partially. She was complicated. Like everyone. A part of her wanted to be loose in the world, an ecstatic celebrator, and another part of her desperately wanted to be accepted by the wealthy pearl-wearing women who hired her to paint fabric for their draperies.

My mom and Davy had moved to this drum-circle town because he'd found a job close by, and they were part-time hippies and she was full-bellied pregnant with my brother. I asked my mom, years later, how she could have left my dad and married someone else so quickly. I didn't ask it kindly.

Sometimes, you just have to make the best choice for you, even if it's not the pretty one.

As soon as he'd heard that my mom was splitting up with her husband, Davy had left his job as chief audio engineer at

NPR without another job, packed all his things into his car, and driven across the country from D.C. to San Francisco. For her. For the possibility of her.

Fate's the word Davy used. Finding each other again, getting married, him finding a job. A year after my brother was born, we went to a portrait studio in the mall. There were bears and plastic roses and wagons and piles of empty Christmas packages along the walls to use as props. We chose the wagon, set my small brother inside. I kneeled next to the wagon like an obedient little pioneer with my hands clasped tight in my good girl's lap. I already knew, at five and a half, that I was the add-on. That I was not a core member of this nice, new, fated family. I stayed quiet a lot, afraid to remind anyone else of what they must know, too.

"Hello, love of my life," Davy said to my mom. She was on the couch, had just woken up from a nap. After ten months in the hospital and rehabilitation facilities, she was released to his care. He rented a small apartment for a few months, had soft blankets and shower stools and raised toilet seats and all the accompanying products that are supposed to make recovery easier. She was alert, alive. Still paralyzed on the right side of her body. Still without language.

Her head wound was fresh again, as it usually was, because of the number of times they tried to stop the bleeding, to implant drains and tubes and magnets and replace the bone flap and take it back off and replace it again, off, on, off. There were a lot of infections. Constant infections.

She was home with Davy for a few weeks, then back to the hospital. Then back home for two months, then the hospital. She started having seizures. She had soaring temperatures. She fell. Hit her head. She would go back into the hospital, and the doctors would help how they could and Davy would be there every day and my brother and I would visit when we could, and then she would come back out and into his care, and he would do the best he could to care for her, an amazing job. But something would happen, another infection, weakness, wound trouble, whatever, and off they'd go to the hospital again.

"Italy," he whispered to her. "Just keep thinking about Italy."

⚡

After we close, I find I've been marked. By the snake, again, though differently this time. I held her today, still afraid, but she hadn't drawn blood, and I'd tried to commune with her, sending her a sense of peace. I peel the sweat-sticky corset from my torso; my ribs finally expand with a full breath and ache with the relief, like the pain of a hand finally warming up after hours in the cold. Papery snake scales are stuck all over my skin. They cling everywhere, binding to me from the heat of the day, my fingernails filling with the rough flakes of snake as I run my fingers over the indentations from the corset's ribs.

I lie down in my bunk, legs and feet aching, ribs hot, and close my eyes. Try to breathe. But quickly, I feel a heavy weight grow around my neck, a cold smooth body pressing into my throat and moving down my sternum. I know that there is no snake on my body, that I am lying safely in bed, exhausted, dirty, alone, but still I feel it, not only her weight and chill but also the expansion and contraction of her muscles as they move, her face pushing hard against the side of my face as she slithers up and over my head. People who've lost limbs sometimes feel phantom pains—could the same happen here? Maybe this will be the way life is from here on out, the weighty presence of that giant boa constrictor around my throat whether she's there or not.

Still, the presence of the snake isn't what keeps me awake. I am afraid of a recurring dream. It was always set somewhere different— a car I was driving, a room I was walking into— somewhere innocuous. When I'd enter, just out of my sight, from the back seat or behind a corner in the room, I'd hear

100

my mother's voice. She'd say something very quiet, almost imperceptible, and I'd look around until I found her. She'd be right there with all the other dream people doing banal things, suggesting a right turn ahead or wondering if the sandwich bread was whole wheat. I filled with joy. There was her voice, that familiar song I hadn't heard in so long, and even as a dreamer, I knew these words were a gift. That her voice was, somehow, a miracle. And every time, that sweet happiness I felt would slowly start to fade as I looked around at all the other dream people, who acted as though it was normal for her, for any person, to speak. That was the moment I'd realize that her voice wasn't real. That her words were ghosts of words she had spoken years before. Realizing that made time start happening faster, so I'd ask her to speak again, turning from the road my car was hurtling down, craning my body all the way around since our car could not crash in this dream, so I could get right up against the words she couldn't possibly have said—*What? Can you say it again?*—but she never did, of course, my recognition of its impossibility killed the fantasy. *But I'm inventing this dream!* I wanted to shout, *Please speak again*, and sometimes she would take her palm and bring it softly, softly up to my cheek, her eyes meeting mine with their mirror of green, and I knew there was a lesson I was supposed to understand about acceptance. I refused it. *Please speak again*, I pleaded with her, *Tell me what to do, please? I didn't hear you? Please*, again and again and again.

LET'S US HAVE FUN

Two months after the stroke

DECEMBER 2010

Story goes: Sidonia the Hungarian Baroness began sprouting a beard just after giving birth to a little person. He weighed one and a half pounds. The baby's father was Baron Anton de Barscy, a burly four-hundred- pound man who lost his fortune and was forced to flee Hungary just as their new child arrived. Taking their new life in stride, the family decided to begin touring as performers. 1885. They traveled with the circus together for many years, seeing the world, amazing audiences with their family story that was almost too good to be true.

Davy told us the incredible story of the de Barscys before we went to sleep, or around a fire at our camping spot, five miles into the redwoods from where we lived. The son, Davy would say, Baron Nicu de Barscy, was my first friend.

The de Barscys came to the United States in 1903 and continued performing together until the baron died in 1912, after which Sidonia the Hungarian Baroness married the Long-Haired Cherokee Buck Man, another performer on the circuit. The reorganized family continued playing circuses and sideshows until Sidonia's declining health in 1923 caused the Long-Haired Cherokee Buck Man to leave her for a performing dwarf named Doletta Boykin. Sidonia died in 1925, and, after performing another decade, Nicu retired to a small town called

Drummond, Oklahoma, that they'd passed through on their way elsewhere. Davy's grandparents lived next door.

In the kitchen, there were a table and chairs made for a two-and-a-half-foot-tall man. When Davy, at seven, was invited in, it was the first time his legs didn't dangle down from a chair, the first time he could rest his elbows comfortably on a table. He fit there. He was ecstatic. There was not only the magic of this Hungarian aristocrat living close by and performing in circuses and sideshows and traveling the globe, there was also the fact of finding, as a child, a world that seemed made just for him.

As a kid, I loved these stories. The idea that out there, somewhere, a weird, wild world awaited. A world that fit people of all sizes, where everyone was normal because nobody was. I kept the stories tucked away like tiny prizes I'd occasionally allow myself to admire.

⚡

Two months after my mom got sick, two months into the hospital and rehab facilities and emergency goodbyes and brain surgeries and therapies and grim consultations and leaking blood and brain fluid and crises and recoveries and humming, I met a carnie in Tuscaloosa, Alabama.

I was walking with Devin back to our respective apartments from a bar.

The carnie was slumped against a bank on the town's main drag in the middle of the night.

This was two years before I heard of the World of Wonders, two years before I knew anything about the town in Florida where sideshow performers went to retire.

I'd been in California most of the time since my mom had her stroke, saying goodbye and goodbye and goodbye, but she seemed not to be dying just yet, so I was back in Alabama. Trying to be totally, completely, absolutely normal.

We saw the man and asked if he needed help. He didn't respond. We shook the man by the shoulder and his eyelids retracted slowly like a toy losing its batteries and he said, "I work with the carnival and I lost it."

The streets were filled with souped-up Ford trucks accelerating under the feet of hammered frat boys. We were nervous about what might happen to this man if we let him be, and charmed by the idea of the carnival, and so we said, "Come with us." We bent down, one on either side, and held his elbows as he swayed to his feet.

"We'll get you a taxi," Devin said, "to take you back to the carnival."

"Where is the carnival?" I asked.

"You know where," he said. I wanted to know where. I wanted to have a sixth sense for that sort of thing, but I didn't.

We stepped to the edge of the sidewalk, looking for a miracle cab in this cab-less college town, hoping a driver might know where the fairgrounds were. We stood for twenty minutes and no cabs passed. We couldn't get any on the phone either, or find any information about any fairgrounds.

"What do you do in the carnival?" I asked, standing close to the nodding-off man while Devin waved and thumbed at passing cars. We were now hoping for a generous stranger.

"Rides," he said. "The Gravitron. And more. A lot. Let's us have some fun. Let's go have fun."

I looked at Devin, still frantically trying to wave down a car. Good-hearted, loyal Devin. He saw my look, walked back, and pulled me down the street by the elbow.

"We are not taking him back to my place. No," he said.

"No," I agreed. "That would be a bad idea." We looked at the man, now wide awake and singing something to himself as he looked up and down the street. "But maybe not that bad of an idea. A real carnie. Let's take him back to your place. You've got beers. I've got so many questions."

"He's not a lost puppy," Devin said. "We're taking him to

104

the Downtown Pub. They'll know what to do to help him." I had no good arguments against this.

The night was warm and swarms of blond girls filled the air with their floral perfumes, and sometimes I could howl with how much I wanted that easy life, but tonight we had captured a true American vagabond carnie. And maybe he'd be able to tell me about life on the road. About waking up beside a Ferris wheel. About a world where people who couldn't fit anywhere, did. It was the most excited I'd felt in two months.

The man slid into the booth beside Devin. I poured us beers as the man nodded off and then woke back up with a shock and looked me in the eyes. His were a clear light blue, bright and almost white, somewhere between a glacier and a blue Slurpee.

"Let's have fun, us three," he said. Devin huffed and left for the bathroom.

The man's eyelids did not spasm or close. He was looking at me, right at me. "I really think we could be something, me and you," he said. I swallowed hard.

"What really happens at the carnival?" I asked.

"Everything," the man said, then paused. "You could live with me in my trailer," he said. "I have a TV in there."

I laughed, laughing at myself for feeling drunk and serious, sipping my beer and looking around the bar. We were both quiet until Devin started walking back toward us. The man reached across the table and grabbed my hand in his.

"Run away with me," he said quietly, urgently, those blue, blue eyes wide and staring me down. "Run away with me to the carnival." I couldn't swallow. Tears started pouring down the sides of my cheeks.

Devin hurried toward us and, from a few feet away, yelled, "Hey! What the fuck did he just say to you? What's wrong?" I tried to wipe my eyes and paw toward him an "all's okay," but nothing was coming across to anybody. "What'd you just say, buddy?" he said, standing tall over the man.

"No, no, it was nothing," I said. "He said nothing bad."

"Doesn't look that way," Devin said.

"I gotta get back," the man said.

"What?" Devin asked, not looking away from me. "What was it?"

"Let's have a drink," the man said, sipping his beer.

"He just—" I said, trying to decide how much truth to tell, deciding to tell all of it. "He asked me to run away to the carnival. I've been waiting my whole life for someone to say that."

"Jesus Christ, kid," Devin said. "Jesus Christ."

THE MOON IS APPLE PIE

Day 14 of 150

It's the Fourth of July, a Thursday, and our seventh day performing. Sunday will be our last day at this first fair, and we'll tear down through the night and immediately move on to a fair in Ohio.

But not yet. It's 9:00 p.m., and the sky has just darkened. We have three more hours of performing ahead of us. Suddenly, a boom causes everyone to flinch as fireworks begin behind our tent, shot, it seems, from a big parking lot on the other side of carnietown. We can mostly see them from the stage, pausing our ballys because we can't talk over the boom of the explosions, and people are holding each other around the waist, back to front, like they are getting their portraits taken and pointing and sipping beers in big plastic cups, the whites of their eyes like little moon mirrors for the colors in the sky.

Tommy watches the fireworks, too, but looks out over the crowd every few seconds, a little fidgety. We haven't made nearly as much money at this fair as we should have to keep everything afloat, and there are only a few more days until we close here and move on to the next fair. We have a big audience primed to go inside if only these damn distractions would stop. The show's financial calculations were worked out before the season began, and include minimums for how much the show needs to make in each spot in order to go on to the next spot. This information isn't discussed with the cast, but I can glean it from the stress each day as the midway's thin crowds walk past our tent.

"Inside, you're going to see an Icelandic Giant—" Tommy begins, but a firework explodes and drowns out the rest of his sentence. "Free show, free show," Tommy calls, and a few heads turn toward him for a moment but snap away when a series of booms take over the sky. Even I can't look away.

Tommy nudges my arm.

"Light up your torches," he whispers into my ear.

"Now? Isn't it, like, un-American to take attention away from fireworks?"

"What's more American than trying to make a buck?" he says.

I light them up.

I remember that in my fire-eating class our teacher had warned of gasoline burps, teeth cracks from heat, tongue blisters, and scolded me, sternly, not to get pregnant while sucking in gasoline fumes. None of this matters when I ignite the torches onstage. All I can see is the gas canister beside me, into which I dip the torches, shake off the excess liquid, and pick up the lighter. I am aware of the audience watching me ready the flame. I am not thinking about how many brain cells I lose each time I swallow some of the gas, which happens, just a little bit, each time. I light one torch, then touch my fingers to the other gas-soaked head and squeeze. I bring my hand to the lit torch and pick up the flame. It stretches, like a piece of chewed gum, between my thumb and pointer finger. I carry the flame to the unlit torch and light the head with my fingertips.

Fire eating, long used in Hindu, Sadhu, and Fakir performances to signify spiritual attainment, became popular with sideshow and circus performances around 1880, a mainstay of touring acts. It's not hard to see why. The eyes that are within

108

fifty feet of our bally stage flicker over to me, then back to the fireworks, then back to me. What's happening in the sky is spectacular, but the brightness of those lights is farther away, and one by one people start a slow zombie walk toward my fire, the same sort of draw I often see when the torches are lit, like there is never any choice but to seek the flame. We gather a small crowd as I run my fingers through the fire, wipe the torch across my arm, blow one out, and then light it again using my fingertips to carry the fire. The crowd grows, the fireworks still behind us, and I feel a little thrill to have stolen the attention. Tommy begins his bally, working it extra slow and long to give more time for a larger crowd to draw, the thunder of the fireworks lessening, the glint of his sword bright, reflecting the fire as he licks it and lets an audience member feel its heft, the burn of the fire in my mouth, the weight of our responsibility here to keep ourselves afloat just like real, good, hardworking Americans.

We turn a huge crowd. The show will go on.

The next morning when I wake up, Tommy's massive shadow is blocking all the light from the doorway as he stares at the bunk beside mine. On it, Snickers is stuffing clothes into a duffel bag. Tommy's arms are crossed, a more serious posture than I've seen him make, a throwback perhaps to his days as a professional wrestler in New Jersey. I sneak over to Spif, who is connecting cables on the far side of the trailer.

"What's going on here?"

"Snickers got the boot," he says.

"Third strike?"

"Guess so," Spif says, attention still on the cords in front of him, as if this event didn't merit even the smallest glance.

"What'd he do?"

"All I know's he went down into carnietown last night and got involved in more trouble. Don't want to know the details. Don't care. Guy's a prick."

Snickers begins singing to himself, laughing as he grabs

109

something from the main trailer area, close to where we sit. I try to give him a pity smile, but he just keeps laughing, shaking his head.

"What I care about is being shorthanded for teardown tomorrow night. And out a ticket guy. He fucked us over on that," Spif says.

"Don't worry. You saw my guns during setup. I got you," I say, elbowing him. He snorts.

"You wanna know how you can really help me out? Give me a blow job," he says.

"In your dreams," I say, and wander off to the bathroom, pleased that he thinks I can handle some coarse teasing.

I feel bad for Snickers, for how heavily he wore this dream on his sleeve when he arrived, and how quickly he failed it. A man who had a hard life and finally thought he'd made it to his destiny. I'm sad for him but also nervous at how quickly a person can get thrown off the show—he's been here ten days. The carnival takes all kinds; it is often a place for people to find work who can't find work elsewhere—people from other countries, people with drug problems, people with criminal records, people with mental instabilities—but there are still rules, still a code to follow that can be broken, which will mean immediate removal. I don't understand the codes yet. I'm not even sure I know them. When I ask Tommy about it later, he brushes me off. "Just keep showing up to work call on time," he says. "And don't believe that this will ever be easy."

⚡

Sunshine and Spif spend half the year splitting the electricity bill and the other half traveling around the country as performers in the show. Both from Camarillo, California, they have been friends since they were very young. They lived close to one another, had classes together, spent time together after school. But things got hard.

Story goes: Spif was homeless. As he's telling me, he's twisting the silver rings on his fingers, revising and looping to make sure the details come out right. We're sitting backstage after day eight of performing, trying to wind down. "My friends were letting me crash on their couches for a while, but then they got sick of it. I didn't have anywhere to go. I ran out of couches, and then ran into Sunshine." He laughs at his joke. Sunshine has walked down to the bathrooms to take a shower, but her presence as the boss backstage is never far off. "When I told Sunshine I didn't have a place to stay, she immediately told me to come over with all my stuff."

Later, I ask Sunshine about her and Spif's story.

"I needed help," Sunshine says. After a long bout in the hospital, her mom was just about to return home at the same time the landlord required everything out of their house for renovations. "I was in a panic, and completely alone," she says. But then there was Spif. He moved into her living room and they lent each other a hand. And he never left. That was three years ago.

Spif talks about his early days in juvenile hall, his involvement with gangs. He's twenty-three now and has been out of trouble for years. As he's talking, he plays with a paper flower he bought earlier to give to Pipscy because she's been feeling down. It's hard to imagine him as a kid interested in trouble. Especially around Sunshine. They often lock arms and skip to wherever they're headed.

This is Sunshine's seventh season with the sideshow. As the stage manager, she's in charge of behind-the-scenes operations—music cues, show order, break rotation—and also controls the loading and unloading of our semi. But the thing she's known for, the thing the little girls outside the tent whisper about as they're walking away, is her fire-eating act. She does tricks I'm far too scared to try—like the human candle, where she traps and then lights gas fumes in her

111

mouth, blowing a flame out her O'ed mouth as casually as if she were blowing a bubble.

She stands onstage in five-inch heels, her stick-skinny legs in sheer black tights below a black skirt and corset, her fingers removing two long torches from a canister of gas. The torches are ignited. She carries the flame with her fingertips, blows fire, swallows torch after torch and then lights the flame from the tip of her tongue. Moments later, she returns to the stage with Spif and stands on the knife board as he throws the bouquet of metal around her body.

There isn't a day they aren't together. But it hasn't always been that way. This is Spif's second season, so for years he'd stay at home half the year while Sunshine was touring the country. Then last year, when she was preparing to come out for her sixth season, Sunshine began thinking about asking Spif to come along. She'd never invited anyone out to work at the sideshow before.

"You don't bring just anyone," Sunshine says. "You don't actually bring anyone." She'd watched as other performers brought friends or family out to work the season and then seen them sneak off in the night never to return just as many times. The hours are long; the work is hard. There aren't many who can hack it, and vouching for a person who then leaves the show in a bind can be a big problem. In all her years, there was nobody in Sunshine's life she thought could make it. Until Spif.

Spif took the leap. He joined Sunshine for the season and stayed the entire time as the ticket man. A dedicated worker who proved himself quickly, he soon earned important crew jobs for setup and teardown. The bosses also saw his potential as a performer. For this, his second season, the bosses have taught him a few acts. To lie on a bed of nails. To throw knives around a live human target—Sunshine.

Later that night, a 3:00 a.m. storm sounds like a train breaking through a mountain of bricks. Spif leaps from his bunk, bounds down the hallway, and is outside, wrapping the electrical equipment in plastic in less than a minute, dropping the banners to protect them from high winds.

"You gotta keep proving yourself here," he says to me the next morning, when I asked him how he knew he was the one who should get up and fix what needed fixing. "It's my job. My responsibility."

Between acts, Sunshine listens and asks questions as Spif describes the storm's lightning, the proximity of thunder, then rolls her eyes when he moves on to describing a cute girl in the crowd. Mid-conversation, without speaking, they both stand and disappear through the curtain onto the stage. She will rely on him. He will rely on her. Loud, moody rock music plays onstage, but the sound of metal sinking into wood, with each thwack, is louder than the sounds coming from the intricate speaker system. So is the applause at the end.

Sunshine and Spif's story was not unfamiliar. I'd been hearing similar themes in my mom and Davy's story my whole life.

Davy's father, DS, played trumpet at the University of Oklahoma in the late 1930s. He was set up on a Coke date with a freshman sorority pledge in Kappa Kappa Gamma. She'll be short, someone told him, slender and real pretty. Her name's Mary Francis. He's always carrying that trumpet, someone told her about DS. They met for a Coke. That's the part I know. I like to imagine they shared the same straw, and he wanted to know about the mountains she grew up around, or about her older sister, the firecracker everyone talked about. It was her first date ever. She had just arrived at college. Mary Francis is my mom's mother.

They had a good time but decided to be just friends. He continued to play his trumpet around town, she danced with the Kappas. One night, at a party, she noticed another horn player in a different band who wouldn't take his eyes off her while she was dancing with friends. At the set break, he lowered his

113

instrument, approached, introduced himself as Everett and asked her for a date. Three years later, they married: my mom's parents, Mary and Ev.

DS had met his own sweetheart by then, Lenore, and the two couples, Ev and Mary, DS and Lenore, breezed around Oklahoma in fast cars and danced late into the night, until World War II was declared. Ev was shipped off to Germany. DS was asked to stay as the town's dentist.

This should be a made-for-TV movie.

Ev was the commander of one of the ships that landed on the Normandy beach on D-day. World War II marched forward, every telegram and knock on Mary's door a heart-stopper. Seven months after Ev headed out, she had a baby, Judith, my mom's older sister. Ev lived in a hole on the beach in Anzo for six weeks, writing a letter each morning with the paper pressed up against the dirt wall beside him. And then, shock.

Deep shock.

Shock to have survived. The only person, of all the men he knew over there in his three-year stay, who returned without a scratch. Not a goddamned scratch, he still repeated sixty years later.

Ev returned to Oklahoma. Lenore and Mary became pregnant at the same time. In February, Davy was born; nine weeks later, to the minute, Teresa was born. My stepdad, my mom. Dave and Teresa spent three years being babies together. They rolled around in the grass, drooled on each other. And then Ev and Mary left with their girls for California.

Seven years later, when Dave and Teresa were ten, Dave's family was lured by their friends out west, rented a house right down the street. 1956. In the long, hot summer drive across half of the country, Lenore told story after story about their long-lost friends from Oklahoma with two beautiful daughters who loved to hula dance and ride bikes. The stories printed deep on that romantic ten-year-old boy's heart, and he felt some sort of binding love even though he hadn't seen this Teresa since he was a toddler. When they finally pulled up to Ev and Mary's house, Dave jumped out of the car. Out the front door walked a tan little girl in a romper with bright green eyes and a swagger. She asked if he wanted to be in her gang. He tried to kiss her. She said she wasn't that kind of girl. He touched her arm. She had the softest skin he'd ever felt.

$\lightning$

It's closing night. Day ten of performing. We've been instructed to have our bags packed and thrown on top of our bunks in order to make space for stage pieces that have to slide under the beds. Our drawers need to be closed, hanging items—like the sweaty fishnets I hang from a protruding nail in the wall to dry each night—put away, back end swept, minifridge emptied, work clothes out and ready to change into as fast as possible once the wheel goes off at 10:00 p.m. exactly. We completed the tasks the night before, because work call that morning was 9:00 a.m. And now, at 9:30 p.m., while most of the carnival still appears to be operating normally, I see twice as many carnies moving twice as quickly between rides, cords wound in the shadows, translucent trash bags full of unsold popcorn and soft pretzels laid beside food joints like little tombs.

At 10:00 p.m. exactly, the big wheel goes off. All across the lot, screams of "Wheel's off!" echo down the midway.

"You have ten minutes to go to the bathroom, get out of your costumes, pack them up, get into your work clothes, and meet back here," Tommy tells us.

"Then what happens?" I ask.

I get a hard look from Sunshine. "You'll find out. Go!"

And I do.

We pack the show up through the night, a task I thought would be easy since we'd set up less than two weeks before, but I can't remember how this dance began. I have no idea how to put anything away. Each task I'm assigned—dismantling the head-less chair, folding the tent walls—require precision to ensure the objects stay in good enough shape to set up again, and physically fit in their exact space in the truck. No room for screwups. The next few spots we'll play have shorter runs—just five days performing. I'm glad that the time between setup and teardown will be shorter; less time to forget how it all works.

I want to get my hands back on the electric chair, to feel its magic as I dismantle it, but I keep getting directed elsewhere.

Radios blare from every joint and we work straight through until 5:15 a.m.

"Get a few hours of sleep, if you can fit on your bunk," Tommy says. "We pull out of here at nine a.m."

Sunshine has a vapor cigarette clenched between her taut, bony fingers as she grips the steering wheel. The jump to Ohio is four hours, four luxurious hours where we can lay our heads against the plush headrests of the van and take in the rumble of the plastic clasps on the windows as they pound out the beat of Sublime turned to max volume.

We stop for pizza. Everyone orders cheese, I assume because it's cheapest, but it comes out that nearly everyone is a vegetar-ian. All my carnies are vegetarians, I think, delighted with this little phrase I've just invented. I say it, quietly, to Cassie on the seat beside me once we're back in the van.

Not *all*, she corrects. And not *mine*. And not *carnies*.

"We are not carnies," Cassie says. "Well, I used to be one. But not anymore."

"That's right," Sunshine says from the front seat, very matter-of-factly. "We're showpeople. There's a huge differ-ence. We're above the carnies."

Showpeople. Has a nice ring. But so does carnie.

"There's a very clear pecking order, and you should know it. Top line is bosses, of course. Then showpeople. Then carnies. And the big carnie rivalry is between game and ride jocks. Ride

116

jocks have more power, because they can let pretty girls go to the front of the line and they gather bigger crowds, but game jocks make more money. Easier to swindle the marks. Foodies are at the bottom, obviously, though some of them make a killing. Don't call a performer a carnie, okay?" Sunshine says. "Like, ever."

"Right," I say. "Sorry."

I want to change the focus from my blunder.

"How long have you been a vegetarian?" I ask Spif, who is sitting behind me in the van and twisting his septum piercing with both sets of pointer fingers and thumbs.

"A while," he says. "I can't eat animals because I know they don't want to be eaten."

I nod, start to turn back around in my seat, but he continues.

"The first time I ate mushrooms, I was tripping and walking around outside and I found a bee. He was in a pool of water, kicking his legs and flailing around. I bent down to get a closer look and the bee started talking to me."

"What did the bee say?"

"I can't tell you. Don't remember. But we had a whole conversation, back and forth, talking about all kinds of shit. I pulled him out of the water. I knew as soon as I finished talking to him that I could never eat another animal."

"I only eat fish," Sunshine adds. "And alligator. Did you hear what the pope just did, though? He proclaimed that rats were also fish so that people in South America could eat capybaras on Fridays."

Our van was following the sun, west along highway 80 and then 90, skirting the base of Lake Erie as we passed the kind of strip mall that was indistinguishable from every other strip mall all over America. The TGI Friday's, the China Buffets, the Starbucks popping up when we whizzed through an affluent area—never near the fairground. I'd know we were nearing the grounds when I started to see pawnshops, Quik Marts, or old

117

factories. The carnival was not a place for the wealthy, though the cost of an evening there could quickly add up.

"You know what a group of ferrets is called?" Pipscy asks from the back seat. We shake our heads. "A business. When I get out of here, I'm going to have a business of ferrets business."

We laugh, and keep on to Ohio. I'm trying to play it cool, but I think I might be falling for my carnies.

THE SOFTEST SKIN OF ANYONE IN THE ENTIRE WORLD

Two years and eight months after the stroke

JUNE 2013

Davy gets up each morning in the dark to pay bills and schedule appointments. He researches how to visit a Venetian glass museum in a wheelchair. Tours of the David for the handicapped. The opera. Bathrooms in the cruise ship's dining area. Size of shower in the room. He clicks and scrolls between websites, writes notes, scrolls, reads, writes notes.

When light comes in the window, he goes back into the bedroom and sits on his wife's side of the bed. She stirs, her good leg bending and straightening. "Morning, cutie," he says, leaning low to wrap his arms around her torso before he pulls her upright into a seated position and shifts her hips so her legs reach down off the bed.

"Na na na," she says quietly, hoarsely. After four months with the tracheotomy, it was removed and she could make sounds again. She'd grown strong enough to swallow and cough on her own, lived with Davy except for when she had to go back to the hospital for an emergency.

She presses and releases her lips with little smacks just after she wakes every morning, like each new day has a taste she wants inside.

119

With one arm slipped beneath her good arm and one arm reaching over her bad one, his body stands in for her right side and they pivot to the wheelchair. There were disasters and then emergencies and then crises, and now this day after day. It is quiet.

"She has the softest skin of any person I've ever known," he told me when I was young, when I was a teenager, recently at the hospital. "It's surreal. Touch it. Here. No, touch it."

As an act of kindness, or apology for tragedy, a lot of people give my mom lotion. It comes in the mail, in birthday packages, appears on their doorstep. Maybe they know about the skin. Want to help preserve that miracle. But I find myself, when I help clean out drawers, with an armload of lotions, lilac, eucalyptus, rose, fresh linen, in glass bottles and blue jars, in plastic tubs, oblong or circular, organic, elixirs, Chinese, tubes for the eyes, for daytime, for scars, for nighttime, and the metaphor of trying to carry so much is too obvious and also fundamentally right, that leaning stack piled against my chest, against Davy's, even though we know, we know, it will tumble.

The house they rent, close to the house they sold, is entirely covered in wood slats like the hull of a ship. It seems that they might always be about to embark. My mom is in her wheelchair. Not Bubbles, the off-roader, but the regular insider called "the chair." She spends all her time there, except for when he lifts her onto or off of the toilet or into or out of bed or the car. Occasionally I lift her onto or out of something, but I often feel like an intruder. There's so much tenderness required for transporting a paralyzed body. Sometimes I hide in the other room when it is time, because I am a small, scared person.

There had been a trip to the emergency room two months earlier for the wound on my mom's head, which wouldn't heal right. It was where they'd permanently cut away the bone plate to allow enough space for the swollen, bleeding brain. The incision would not heal. The skin around it was dead. Months and months. Infections came. And then she started having seizures. A month before I leave for the sideshow, she's in the hospital for seizures. They are scheduled to leave for Italy three months after that.

A week before I leave for the sideshow, she is back home. The days become regular again. Bills. Laundry.

My mom's back is to me, wheelchair scooted right up against the couch. She stoops slightly forward and then straightens up, her left arm disappearing in front of her and then arcing out wide as she straightens again, a gray T-shirt between her fingers. In addition to relearning how to do many tasks as she slowly heals, she must learn to do them with her left hand.

A pile of clean laundry lies on the couch in front of her, T-shirts and socks and bras and sweatpants that I had been planning on folding very soon. Any day now, in fact. But here she is, the mother I spend hours convincing myself isn't the same person living inside her body anymore. Because what would that be like? How would it be possible to carry on?

Here she is with a rumpled gray T-shirt between her fingers, shaking the wrinkles out.

I hold my breath. She shakes a lot, little spasms. Sometimes big ones. Seizures. I haven't seen anything like this in almost three years—my mother, right there, completing a chore.

She sets the T-shirt down on the couch, away from the pile of laundry, and smooths it flat with the palm of her hand. She cannot see me behind her. Here is her bony hand, the one that was always covered in different shades of dye from her textile business, and more recently, the hand that was hooked up to so many IVs that it took on its own face and attitude, a medical Medusa.

That hand was the only thing that moved in the first months when it didn't appear she'd ever really wake back up. I watched it like watching would conjure a prayer. Watched it twitch against the starched white hospital sheets, move slowly up from her side, trembling, toward her head to touch the skin covering

121

her brain on the half of her head where her skull had been removed. Watched it touch her eye—here, now here—dried blood, dried rivulets of brain fluid against her temples. I'd watch that hand make its way back home to her side, tremble, and begin it all again, that journey up to try to understand what it was missing, here and here and here. I'd grab it to kiss it still and whisper terrible apologies and the hand would rest calm and motionless for a moment before it pulled away, readied to move on. She moved on and then they made her come back.

She spent a full month in the ICU after the stroke. Each day was the last day. Then the new last day.

Six weeks after the stroke, when the doctor got her to sit up in a chair, propped up by pillows on all sides, for thirty minutes straight, we clapped like mad.

Two and a half months after the stroke, on New Year's Eve, she waved a noisemaker we'd brought in to celebrate. Yes, yes, let's celebrate! Davy, my brother, and I said. She started physical therapy. Sitting up without pillows. Standing up with the help of a few therapists and slings.

A brain infection sent her back to the ICU.

Then she had to start all over again.

My mom's palm flattens each crease with careful rhythm and precision against the couch. I don't help. I want to see what she can do. If she completes the task, then my assumptions about what she is capable of are wrong. Then I am underestimating her.

It took me a few days after she had her stroke to say the words *I love you*. They were fire in my lungs. I knew they needed to come out. *I love you*, I said, very quietly, the words slurred. I tried to say it more. *I love you*, when I left the hospital for the day. *I love you*. I was just never sure if she could understand it.

She folds in one worn sleeve and then the other. Smooths the creases. Smooths the collar, evens out the sides. Her other hand remains tucked unmoving in her lap but this hand is grabbing the bottom of the T-shirt and folding it up against the shirt's shoulders, creating a rectangle perfect for stacking in drawers, this little miracle of normalcy on a couch in a wooden house on a cool spring evening. She cannot talk or walk, but this. Here it is, a chore. Ordinary life.

We talk a lot about packing. Though I leave for the sideshow two months before my parents leave for their trip, I spend a lot of time navigating the half-packed suitcases strewn across my parents' house. Day by day Davy prepares carefully for The Trip—his term for the long, dangerous journey he is planning—but that doesn't assuage my unease.

One afternoon, my mom is in the bedroom napping.

"I just want to see her face," Davy says, "seeing the bridges in Florence." He is arranging pill bottles in the outside pockets of one of the suitcases. To fit a four-month supply of anticonvulsants, antihypertensive agents, osmotic diuretics, antibiotics, pain management medications, fiber pills, and vitamins, there are giant Ziploc bags filled with the translucent orange tubes, and white tubes, brown plastic tubes, bottles in all shapes and sizes filled with tiny morsels of health. Another suitcase is entirely filled with adult diapers. The right size is hard to find, and instead of risking it, he is bringing the entire three-month supply. There's a bag with orthotic braces. There's a bag that is used exclusively to hold the second wheelchair, Bubbles. There's just one bag with their clothes: seven outfits each, Davy has determined, stuffing into one of their toiletries bags a large bottle of Dr. Bronner's in order to do laundry most nights. Redundant thumb drives with copies of their medical records, advance directives—of which my brother and I both have copies—tucked into various pockets. Audio-recording equipment for one of the bags so he can capture the sounds of the streets around them.

Eleven bags total.

Over 250 pounds.

Plus the sweet beauty who will be sitting in the chair.

"It will make all this worth it," he says. "Seeing her face see the water in Venice."

He is counting out the week's pills into the seven-day strip of containers. "There's a secret spot in Rome I found when I was nineteen. It's off the main road in one of the squares. I wandered off there when I was alone, when I was just a teenager. I bought some dope off a guy in a back alley, and, almost by accident, ended up smoking in this hidden garden with broken sculptures. It was the most beautiful place I've ever been. That's what I want most on this trip. I want to find that place that I used to think was magic. I want to show Teresa that magic."

DAUGHTERS
Day 20 of 150

WORLD OF WONDERS
JULY 2013

Our caravan—one semitruck pulling the show, the fifteen-person passenger van pulling Tommy and Sunshine's trailer/the office, and Red's van—pulls into a small fairground surrounded by houses that have metal bars over their windows. We're in Maumee, Ohio. A few joints are here already, unfolding their giant wings, pinning and joining and stretching out for the imminent arrival of little feet, but much of the fairground is still empty and waiting. It's much smaller than the last spot. We sit in the van while Tommy talks to the boss canvasman. We aren't supposed to interrupt the boss when he is talking to other bosses, or get out of the van when we aren't told to, or walk near other joints during setup, because it is a dangerous affair that requires hard hats, which the people setting them up only sometimes wear. Those metal pieces—which I want to think of as spring petals unfolding from their metal stamens—actually swing and clang and break and people get hurt, badly hurt, during setup. The general rule is to stay out of the way.

The afternoon light is waning into a pale gold, and unlike the paved, smooth Butler fairgrounds we left just that morning, 230 miles back, here dirt roads carved into grass act as the midway lying between huge floppy trees with bright green leaves, willows maybe, and little yellow dandelions. As we wait, flecks of firefly light burst around us. On these new fairgrounds, I will be better at eating fire. Less afraid of snakes. I'll lure more people into the tent. I'll get better at what I need to do, focus more acutely, so my brain has less space to catastrophize elsewhere.

We've been on the road together two and a half weeks. Because our first fair was so long, we've put up the show only once, though beginning setup this time feels a little easier, a little less intimidating, even though we are all tired.

A dirt bike pulls up to our lot bearing a huge guy who wipes his face with his forearm, spits, and lumbers over to the van on thighs the diameter of a steering wheel. The boss had posted a Craigslist ad for a new ticket guy, since he'd had to fire Snickers. The new guy is stopping by for an interview, which is basically a way for Tommy to see if he'll be:

    a. strong enough to potentially move heavy things, and
    b. tough enough to actually stick around and do it.

The guy approaching us is even bigger than Big, Big Ben, our working man, and the prospect of adding a big guy to our team is alluring, another bull to take some weight and get that tent up fast.

Tommy sweeps the new guy out back to talk, and walks him around and through the tent like the boss at a construction site, gesturing with his hands and pointing out items they pass, items that require work. He's sussing the new guy out, watching the way his body moves. I wonder if the working man job is one that has to be done by a *man*. The women on our crew, after all, do a lot of hard labor.

The gendered divisions of this work were explained to me my first full day with the World of Wonders, when we went to pick up our show from where it had wintered in Gibtown. Our van pulled into a junk storage lot, several acres of wild Florida vines and trees where carnies park big rigs and half-broken Ferris wheels in the off-season. The rust of a once-yellow bus peeked out from years of moss and low-hanging kudzu and I

126

heard there was a man who lived somewhere in the middle of it all, watching over the big machines that were brought here to rest. There was no way to see the edges of the place.

Though the yard was full of rides and a few old circus cars, no other sideshows winter there because there are no other traveling sideshows. Traveling sideshows are a cultural fragment stomped out by science and social progress. Public perception began shifting at the end of the nineteenth century, as more information about the medical conditions freak shows displayed became known, then even further with disability-rights legislation in the 1950s and '60s, as restrictions were established on who and what and how a person could be displayed onstage. Nowadays a few nightclub shows include sideshow performers and travel an adult circuit. There are still two stationary sideshows—one at Coney Island and one at Venice Beach, though the Venice show was just booted from their home on the boardwalk.

But the World of Wonders is the last traditional traveling sideshow. It only survives because the people who are part of it will not let it die.

Through palm fronds and the folded masts of a pirate ship in the Gibtown lot, I saw the carcass of our show for the first time. Giant red-paint lettering with a gold shadow covered the side of the truck; gold curlicue embellishments decorated the corners. The entire side of the semitruck read:

WORLD OF WONDERS
THE AMAZEMENT SHOW

About a third of the way down the semi's container stood a door with a large red star and the printed words *Show Personnel Only*. A big dumb grin spread across my face that I tried to hide—to the rest of these performers, this was nothing to get excited about—but I couldn't conceal my merriment. Just a few months ago, I had stood in the audience and gawked at dangerous beauties living a life worthy of this truck. At one moment in that first show, during the bed of nails act, the backstage curtain had blown open and I'd caught a glimpse of a performer backstage. She was sitting on a folding chair, hunched over a cup of instant soup. Noodles dangled from her mouth. There were empty chairs on either side of her and some trash on the ground and everything looked dingy but was flooded with natural afternoon light. The extraordinary ordinariness of it was mesmerizing.

And now here was the history and the great vagabond life contained in this painted semitruck in a junky storage lot, and all we had to do was clear away the kudzu and we'd be off.

It wasn't quick.

There were critters inside. Rusted fastenings. Sunshine chain-smoked while Spif and Tommy did the heavy grunting, and I was told to sit on the side and watch. Pipscy practiced a burlesque act.

"Used to be the girls sat in the shade while the boys did all the physical work on the show," Sunshine said after I offered to help Tommy and he refused.

"But it took forever. We sat there for hours watching the guys struggle, wasting time, because the bosses—Chris and Ward—didn't want us getting hurt. Precious flowers, that kind of thing. But one season five years or so ago we had a really tight jump and it didn't look like we were going to make it to the next fair in time, so we girls just got up and just started helping. And Chris and Ward realized there was some stuff we could do. Some. So we got jobs. There will be plenty of time where we'll be doing those jobs. They're not easy. They're just not these jobs."

"It seems like there's at least something we could do here to help," I said.

"No."

"Okay," I said, not really believing her.

"Chris and Ward still want us in showgirl costumes with feathers in our hair. They're traditionalists. So we've just gotta take what we can and not push it sometimes," she said.

An hour or so later, the boys had the trailer and cab hitched and we were set to go—less than twenty-four hours after I'd landed in Florida, it seemed we were ready to hit the road.

"We've got to go pick up our indentured servant," Sunshine said with a straight face.

We pulled up to a mobile home with a huge canvas duffel bag sitting outside.

"Big, Big Ben, our working man," Tommy said. "He's our muscle."

"He's the sweetest guy in the world," Sunshine said, "but when he tries to kiss you, yell loudly in his face and smack him. He'll learn."

The cicadas' heavy chirps pressed into the van as we swung the door open for Big, Big Ben, who lumbered out of the mobile home without looking at the van ahead or calling back to anybody inside. He popped his bag onto his back as if it were empty and loaded it into the trunk. He said nothing. He was in his late twenties, had pink cheeks and a mouth full of crisscrossed teeth.

"Benny!" Sunshine yelled, and he stifled a smile as he shifted in his seat. He sighed.

"You ready, Benny?" Tommy asked.

"I guess," Ben answered. "I told myself I wasn't gonna do this again, but here I am," he said to nobody in particular. He had the thick arms of a gladiator.

Story goes: he had been working for another carnival company for a few years and had a contract that would have kept him there for a few more, but our bosses bought the contract off the other owner, releasing Ben from his obligation to one company and beginning it with another. As the story was told, Ben smirked, looking out the window. I couldn't tell how much of the story was real—I didn't think people used those kinds of contracts for manual labor anymore.

"Is that story true?" I asked him quietly. He smiled again and shrugged.

He's retarded, one of the performers told me later, when Ben wasn't around. He's just slow, another corrected. He's had some head injuries, Tommy said. An accident. And an aneurysm. He's the sweetest guy in the world, they all agreed.

"Wait till you see him with a sledgehammer," Spif said.

After the burly guy on the motorcycle leaves our new spot in Ohio, I ask Tommy about whether he's going to hire him. "Probably," Tommy says. "We need someone who can hack it. I knew the last one wasn't gonna work out."

"Snickers?" I ask, surprised. He nods like he's answering the most obvious question in the world.

This alarms me—that Tommy can know something like this ahead of time with such certainty. I ask him about it again a few days later, trying to sound as casual as possible.

"There's a test I know," Tommy tells me. We're out on the bally stage one midweek afternoon. "The test predicts whether a person will stick around through the season or bail."

This fair is slow and hot. July in Ohio. People are fanning themselves with 4-H programs and their faces are pink, coated in sweat and seeping grease from funnel cake. They glisten like appetizers.

"I knew Snickers wasn't going to make it. Knew it right away."

"What's the test?"

"I can't tell you," he says.

I sigh, readjust the snake.

"Fine, but you have to keep it a secret. I don't want this getting out and giving people insider knowledge," Tommy says.

130

"There are two things. First, during setup, if someone covers their ears while we're pounding in stakes, they're not gonna be able to hack it."

I think of the piercing ring of the metal sledgehammers pounding the long, steel tent stakes into the ground, how it first hits your ears as a *ting*, but before you can even register the whole *ting* it has shot inside your brain and covered it in metal and each of the individual notes carries its own heavy symphony and even when the sound is over and the men are moving on to the next stake after pounding the first fifteen or twenty times, the *ting* still dominates the inside of your skull and you have to hope nobody tries talking to you.

"So if someone covers their ears, they're too sensitive to hack it?" I ask.

He nods.

I turn my face quickly, so he can't see the blush that's formed on my cheeks. Did I cover my ears? Was I too sensitive to be out there? I remember on the very first day of setup that I wanted to cover my ears. I wanted to because Pipscy was, and she seemed to fit in so well with the crew—knew some of them already—so I thought I should mimic her much of the time. But I also remember how deeply I had wanted to seem tough, able to withstand whatever was going on. Had I covered my ears?

"What's the second?" I ask.

"The big talkers. If someone comes in talking about how much experience they already have, how tough they are, how working here has always been their dream, whatever. The ones who make it sound like they already know what they're doing? They'll never make it."

I think back to Snickers on that first day, rattling off shows he'd done and how much he deserved to be here.

"The work we do isn't easy. It takes a lot of guts and resilience. Humility. Flexibility. I'm just saying I've seen this to be true many times in my nine years here," he says.

131

"Did I cover my ears that first setup?" I ask, trying to make it sound like a joke.

"I dunno, Tess," Tommy says with a smirk. "Did you?"

The new working man's pale, wet biceps are bigger around than the giant poles he's hauling across the grass. He shows up each day on that motorcycle. His name is Steve. He responds to people calling his name by jutting out his chin at them. But he's sweating and working hard and only occasionally wincing and reaching down to grip his side, and I want him to stick around. More hands on deck.

"You from Ohio?" I ask.

"Yep." "Seems nice."

"It's shit. Only reason I stay is because of my daughters."

"Oh—how many daughters?"

"Two. They're a pain in the ass. Child support and all. But I like to get to see them. Saw them just a couple weeks ago."

"What did you do before this?" I ask him a little later, when we're on break. He wipes a mustache of red Gatorade from his lips.

"I've been on disability for a while," he says. "I got into a real bad accident last Fourth of July."

"Fireworks?" I ask.

"Worse," he says, lifting his shirt up. The skin across the side of his waist is puckered and crisscrossed, knotted almost. "Cannon fire."

"No shit."

"Yeah. My friends bought a small cannon. Civil War kind, I think. And we loaded it up with gunpowder, but for some reason it wouldn't shoot. I leaned over to fix it, and, yeah...," he says, trailing off.

"So you shot yourself with a cannon?"

"We all loaded it," he says.

"Did it make a big hole?"

"More like a lot of small holes. My daughters thought it

132

was really cool. It was, in a way. My ex-wife helped take care of me for a while. But she was a bitch. I'm so glad she's gone," he says, unable to contain the grin across his face. "We got divorced after she walked in on me with two other girls," he says.

"I'm surprised she stuck around after the first girl," Sunshine says. "I wouldn't have."

"She didn't have a chance. They were at the same time," he says, the smile erupting through his face like a pimple bursting.

The sideshow men love to show photos of their daughters. They each have a few choice snaps on their phones, which they pull out and swipe through with obvious pride. The first time Spif did this, after setup one night at our first fair, he flashed a photo of a tiny girl in a bathing suit, another photo of her in little running clothes, always smiling up toward the camera.

"She's hella smart," he said. "She looks at a picture of a dog and says *woof woof*, and she looks at a picture of a shark and says *dunna, dunna*, you know, like from *Jaws*." He looked off into the distance with half-closed eyes and tilted his head, as if he were looking right at his little object of love.

On our last day of setup in Ohio, I ask him about his daughter again. About the kinds of things she likes. I want to see him light up that way again. "Well, she likes animals," he says, excited again.

"Whenever she sees a shark on TV, she says *dunna, dunna, dunna dunna*."

I can't tell whether this is the only story he wants us to know, or the only story he knows. Maybe whatever else he has, he wants all for himself.

The little girl, two years old, is at home with his ex-girlfriend and her new boyfriend. The daughter doesn't know Spif is her father. That's the agreement they have. He can see her every few weeks or months, and she can know him as an uncle.

"*Shark Week* is the fucking best," Cassie says a few days

later, backstage during a slow afternoon. The conversation is about the best TV shows to watch stoned.

"Listen to this. If you ask Becca what a shark says, she'll say *dunna, dunna*," Spif says. "It's so fucking cute."

It is hard being on the road and staying connected to the other people in your life.

After our show closes on our second day performing at the Maumee County Fair in Ohio, I call my mom and Davy. I'm tired and grumpy, but before I can start to whine, Davy details the new off-roading tires he's attached to Bubbles. The tires are huge, he tells me, monster-truck- size.

"The streets of Italy are all cobblestone, and we're gonna have to move quickly to find the best cafés and go to all the museums we wanna go to."

I ask him how the planning's going, and he sends me a six-teen-page document with lists of all the port cities their boat will stop at, key attractions in other cities they are determined to see: the David in Florence, the opera in Venice.

"It's great," he says. "Some water taxis in Venice have ramps that can fit a wheelchair on them. It's probably for loading goods, maybe wheelbarrows of pastas," he says, chuckling. "A full wheelbarrow of tortellini." He sighs. "I wonder if they ever use a crane?"

"Are you making lists of hospitals in the area?" I ask. I start to sweat. Thinking about them over there, about them remaining over there, makes me feel like I'm sliding out of my body.

"Yeah, yeah," he says dismissively. "We'll have all that stuff."

"Great," I say. Pause. "It will be so great." I spend a lot of time imagining all the things that might go wrong on this stunt. If she has another stroke. If she falls. If she seizes and falls out of her chair and hits her head on the David's goddamned foot. If Davy has a heart attack and she is alone in the room and she cannot help him and he cannot help her. There are so many ways they might suffer.

My brother and I have a plan. We have been putting aside money and have credit cards with high limits. We have agreed. Should it be necessary—and it will probably be necessary—we will drop what we are doing and get on a plane to wherever they are. We will rescue them. It's all we can think to do.

Nevertheless, I pitch my voice high and enthusiastic on the phone to match their spirits. I don't want them to know my terror. I want to be as brave as they are, and so, taking a breath and channeling my stage persona, I tell them I'm proud of what they're doing. The stage performer can be delighted for the adventures they may find. She can be brave and strong. She loves her family and has always told them so. She is not the daughter researching the repatriation of remains.

They have to get off the phone. Too much to do. I stand alone, offstage, outside the tent in the hot, wet night air, and the tears fall and keep falling.

⚡

Sometimes, a sideshow can save a daughter.

A two-pound baby, deemed a "weakling" by the hospital, is expected to die. It's 1920, and hospitals do not have neonatal facilities. Story goes: the baby's father wraps the baby—Lucille Horn is her name—in a blanket, hails a taxi outside the hospital, and heads to the sideshow at Coney Island. The baby's twin had just died in birth, and he was not willing to lose both children. Up until the second half of the twentieth century, hospitals did not have the equipment to keep premature babies alive.

When Lucille's father arrived at the sideshow, a sign charging admission—twenty-five cents—was up over the door. Inside, all along the walls, teensy preemie babies of every race and class were on display in steel-and-glass incubators. Some cried, others slept in a swaddle. The exhibit was run by Dr. Martin Couney, a pioneer in neonatal incubator research. The medical community was more than skeptical.

135

Dr. Couney funded his research by charging admission to see the tiny babies in their translucent worlds. Over his long career displaying the babies—from 1896 to 1940—they were also shown at World's Fairs, amusement parks, and anywhere else he could find an audience. The money enabled Dr. Couney to keep the babies alive without cost to their parents. It's unclear whether he studied with some of the other pioneering doctors of the time whom he claimed to have studied with, and even more dubious whether he was actually a medical doctor at all. Regardless, he kept thousands of babies alive—6,500 of the 8,000 who came into his care. They would have otherwise died. Dr. Couney passed away in 1950, not long after his incubators were finally accepted by hospitals for regular medical practice.

After six months in the incubator, Lucille went home with her parents. She lived for ninety-six more years.

⚡

Sometimes, a daughter has to step to the side.

I called my dad when my mom first had her stroke. She was his only marriage—brief, and wondrous, and terrible. They've been divorced since I was two.

She had a massive stroke, I told him.

"Oh god, oh god, oh god," he said.

"We don't know what will happen," I said, my voice trembling. "It doesn't look good."

There was silence on the other line, the sound of muffled choked breathing. "I just can't believe it," he said. "I was always so sure that we'd end up together as old people in rocking chairs."

"Dad—"

"We'd be chain-smoking on a porch somewhere in a cabin in the middle of the woods."

I was shocked. All I knew of what they thought of one

another was from their twenty-four divorced years of fighting, threats, legal action, and assertions of the other's cruelty.

"I never stopped knowing that would be my future," he said.

"You hated each other."

"Yes," he said. "And we loved each other. Just two rocking chairs, and the sounds of birds. That was the plan."

I was stunned. Silenced. I was standing in a parking lot. I had walked out there thinking this generic, anonymous space would be a perfect location for my grateful tears when I had a conversation in which my dad finally started showing up like a dad. I had thought maybe I could talk to someone who used to know my mom so well about how scary this time was, how much already felt lost.

"Two rocking chairs on a porch sound pretty nice," I finally said. My voice was not trembling. It had happened so fast— this reminder that he was the person he was. That he would not just start acting like a different person, like some version of a dad I wanted him to be. He had his own pain, his own wishes.

"She couldn't wait to start smoking again, once she was old and it didn't matter anymore," he said.

I hadn't realized between all the times that he told me how much he hated her, how terrible she had been to him and to me, that he also loved her. That most of all, he loved her.

I felt suddenly extraneous in the conversation, in my father's idyllic future with his ex-wife.

This was a new layer of pain I hadn't anticipated. I had this deep sadness over my mom—losing her, in whatever form that losing was going to take. But then there was a next level, where the people I turned to for help and love, Davy, my dad, were so immersed in their own pain that they had no space for anybody else. There wasn't anyone left to be the grown-up and help me through but me.

I thought about what my dad was like when I was young, about what story he would have told if someone had asked about his little daughter. What he would have known. There was one story I could remember he'd told about how when I was three to six months old, every day at 4:00 p.m. I'd get fussy and cry and nothing could stop it. Until one day he set me on his forearm, my head in his giant palm, my butt tucked into the crease of his elbow, walked around our apartment, and sang.

Old Dan Tucker was a good old man, he sang, my pinched, hysterical face screaming up at his, *he washed his face in a frying pan, combed his hair with a wagon wheel, and he had a toothache in his heel*. He sang this over and over, the same little song, and eventually my wailing lessened, and I watched him, and listened.

Maybe this was his shark tale. Maybe when someone mentioned a baby who wouldn't stop crying, he'd tell his story about fitting his daughter's tiny head into his palm and walking back and forth across the living room until she was soothed by a nonsense song sung from a father's mouth.

MUD

Day 20 of 150

The bathrooms closest to our tent are also nearest the livestock barn, so by our second day in Maumee, Ohio, the showers are filled with giant clumps of mud and grass, and the lights have acrobatic bugs circling them and dive-bombing human intruders. The 4-H kids clean up here after their time in the pigpens, and then we clean up here to try to look like starlets. As I come out of the shower, avoiding as many of the mud pits as I can, bent over beside a sink with her pants down around her ankles is Cassie, rubbing white cream for heat rash onto her butt cheeks.

"Oh hey, babe," she says, looking at me upside down from between her legs. "Need any rash cream?"

I chuckle and glance over at Pipscy, who is bent over the sink behind Cassie, dousing her hair in red hair dye. So far, she's changed her hair color twice since we've been on the road. Pipscy is wearing a crop top and low-slung cotton pants, and, it appears, has a long string of crusty black pubic hair lining the top of her waistband.

"Pips, you ...," I start to say, but don't know how to finish the sentence. I start laughing again, and she glances down to her waistline.

"My tattoos!" she yells, starting to laugh as well, and up closer I can see them, peeling and smudged temporary tattoos of swords and skulls, rubbing away to black flakes.

"I can't get real tattoos because of my acting career, so I put on these temporary ones sometimes," she says.

Cassie, butt in the air, calls over, "It looks like an STD is growing from your snatch up your body."

Pipscy, in perfect cartoon form, widens her eyes, O's her mouth, and then leans over to inspect her disease. She starts laughing, and Cassie and I start again, too, Cassie still bent over and rubbing rash cream for babies into her butt cheeks and upper thighs, and the ridiculousness of all this, it all feels perfectly strange, and the easy laughter feeds and builds and becomes louder and harder, laughter that takes over all three of us and works its way toward hysterical, the work and sweat and tears of the last weeks all rushing out of us in a torrent. It is good. In eight hours, we will wake up and hoist the banners and set the props and get into costume and perform each of our acts and then perform them each again and again and again and again and again, until the fair closes its gates at ten or eleven or midnight, with no breaks, no days off, for 130 more days. But that's tomorrow. Tonight, right now, we're just three people laughing hard in a muddy bathroom.

Eventually, Pipscy and Cassie walk back to the tent. I stay behind, brushing my teeth, washing my face, rinsing out underwear and my cereal bowl in the sink, trying to learn better laundry and dish-washing techniques as I go. A few people come in and out of the bathroom in the ten or so minutes I'm there, but I must not be paying close enough attention because a woman startles me as she bursts from one of the stalls. She's wearing her game joint shirt. I know that a lot of folks use the privacy of bathroom stalls to smoke, snort, and shoot things, and in my few weeks on the road I have already seen a few pairs of feet peeking out the bottom of the stalls, toes facing the back wall, the body leaning hard against the stall's door.

140

I assume some variation of such activity has just taken place, so I keep my eyes on what I am doing in the sink, tempted as I am to look.

The woman pauses just outside the bathroom stall. She is still as a statue, so I venture a glance. Her dark hair is pulled back into a ponytail so tight it tugs at her skin and makes it hard to identify emotions on her face. I follow her attention to something in her hand, ready to see a pipe or syringe. Carnie stuff.

It's a pregnancy test. She keeps her eyes on the small white plastic device for another three or four seconds. She doesn't move. I don't breathe. Then all at once, like the video of this moment is finally allowed to play, she steps from the stall and walks quickly over to the large garbage can in the corner of the room. She throws the test inside and walks out the door into the night's bright lights.

Either answer on that stick might have been wanted, anticipated. Either might have been devastating. This is a hard place to think about taking care of anyone else, or losing the opportunity to do so. I slow down as I walk past the garbage can on my way out. Maybe I could find her game, befriend her. Offer her—what? I press both palms against the door, push my way out of the bathroom, and send a vague wish up into the starry sky for all daughters.

The next morning, Thursday, the Maumee fair opens with a whimper. A few young mothers with strollers wander the midway, and a couple of old folks smile at us and keep shuffling along.

"Where's the section with all the rides?" I ask Tommy.

He spreads his arms wide to the section we're in. There's a Gravitron, a janky Zipper, a boat ride, and that's it. A small, small country fair. Physically, we're the largest thing on the midway by a long shot, and the most outrageous, too. On the other side of the pond in front of us, a safe distance from our depravities, are a number of barns full of horses, cows, sheep, ducks—the usual assortment of 4-H kids and their mothers'

141

apple-pie-baking competitions. The barns stretch across much of the fairground.

This fair has a cause. I'm not sure if all the fairs have a cause, but this one announces it on the loudspeakers with increasing frequency. "Attention fairgoers," a nasaly voice calls through the speakers. "Please come to Horse Barn Three at two p.m. for a presentation on pollination awareness." There are informational sessions. Evening meetings. Another meeting is called the night before we open to discuss what to do with lost fair children. The loudspeaker also announces when we can pick up ice each hour. It announces when Buffo the Clown's show is about to begin. Someone behind the microphone must have been denied high school announcements, because there is a continual stream coming from the speakers, and between that and the band playing just across from us, covering the 1950s' greatest hits, it's hard to get in a full sentence of our bally on the mic before something cuts us off. We will start to build a tip, a few interested folks stopping to look at the snake, and we'll reel them in a little closer, but then Buffo the Clown will cruise by on his Segway and the pygmy goat parade will be announced, and the folks who had stopped beside our tent develop wandering eyes and move on.

We have to pause the inside show six or seven times throughout the day, because despite our best efforts we can't get anybody to come into the tent. Tommy drops the entry price from three dollars to two dollars. Consults with Red backstage. As the day ends, Tommy's eyes reach farther and farther down the midway as he searches for an audience to invite over for a bally. If there were a way to throw his voice across the pond to those 4-H barns, for example. If only they could see what wonders we have inside, what fun. Few people come. His upper lip keeps sweating long after the sun has gone down.

⚡

142

"What are your days like?" Davy asks on the phone. It's hard to know how to answer, how much detail to give.

"We get up, and perform all day, and then go to bed," I tell him. "It's fun," I add, to make sure they aren't worried for me.

"Sounds fun," he says.

What I don't say is:

8:00 a.m.: Wake up.

8:10 a.m.: Walk through the fair to the bathrooms, hope they are open. Squeeze in a shower, if you can, or just brush teeth/wash your face/wash out tights or underwear to wear the next day if you didn't manage to do it the night before.

8:20 a.m.: Eat breakfast. If you are the first one up, you have first dibs on the mini-coffeepot. Fill the filter with a few scoops from the Folger's can in your room, pour bottled water into the trough. If you aren't the first one up, wait until the coffee is poured into someone's mug or soda cup, or barter: one cup of theirs for one of yours, later.

8:30 a.m.: Hoist the show's banners, set the props on inside stages, open the mummy cases and turn all the spotlights on, set up the electrical system on the bally stage, test the sound, test the lights, count out change for the ticket man.

8:50 a.m.: Get into costume. Fix your hair like a showgirl. Full makeup. Do this all in the dirty back end of a truck.

9:30 a.m.: Set props on bally stage, make last-minute run to bathroom, count out change if you talk a ding, one of the extra moneymakers inside the show. Ready your individual props.

10:00 a.m.: Open the show.

10:02 a.m.: On the bally stage, hold the snake.

10:09 a.m.: Turn one dollar into a five.

10:18 a.m.: Turn one dollar into a five.

10:33 a.m.: Turn one dollar into a five.

10:37 a.m.: Escape from handcuffs.

10:44 a.m.: Escape from handcuffs.

10:50 a.m.: Escape from handcuffs.

10:59 a.m.: Escape from handcuffs.

11:02 a.m.: Tommy leaves bally stage, Cassie comes onto bally stage, begins talking.

11:03 a.m.: Escape from handcuffs.

11:12 a.m.: Escape from handcuffs.

11:23 a.m.: Escape from handcuffs.

11:34 a.m.: Hold the snake. Try to hypnotize passersby.

11:49 a.m.: Escape from handcuffs.

11:58 a.m.: Escape from handcuffs.

12:00 p.m.: Cassie leaves bally stage, Tommy comes onto bally stage, begins talking.

12:04 p.m.: Escape from handcuffs.

Etc.

1:30 p.m.: Break. Walk around the tent, up the steps, and into the trailer. Lie on your bunk in the dark room and massage your feet. Eat a granola bar.

1:45 p.m.: Escape from handcuffs on the bally stage.

Details: Do this all while standing in high heels on a wooden stage set atop the asphalt midway. The sun will not be so bad in the morning, but as you stand there for an hour, two, four, eight, twelve, the sun will burn your skin despite the sunblock—there's never enough to last as long as you'll be out there— and you will sweat and sweat into your corset, down your dress. You are standing onstage, and so you are always displaying yourself as if someone should look at you.

1:52 p.m.: Escape from handcuffs.

1:59 p.m.: Escape from handcuffs.

Details: Listen to the bally, don't listen to the bally. Know not whether you are listening to the bally or whether the sound track of the bally is just looping in your unconscious. Watch people walk by. Pay attention to their outfits. Count the number of jumbo stuffed prizes. Be surprised by the number of jumbo stuffed prizes. Play games with strangers. They won't know you're playing. Look at one as he passes and try to telepathically convince him to buy a ticket. Fail. Fail better.

144

Etc.

Etc.

Etc.

4:30 p.m.: Break. Walk off the stage, down the midway to the bathrooms. Back to the trailer. Eat a sandwich.

5:00 p.m.: Escape from handcuffs.

Etc.

8:15 p.m.: Light up your torches and eat fire.

8:28 p.m.: Light up your torches and eat fire.

8:33 p.m.: Flirt with man in front row who won't look away.

8:48 p.m.: Light up your torches and eat fire.

8:49 p.m.: Massage cheeks for ten seconds because they ache from smiling.

8:52 p.m.: Light up your torches and eat fire.

9:00 p.m.: Light up your torches and eat fire.

9:14 p.m.: Light up your torches and eat fire.

9:15 p.m.: Vow to eat fire better than you ever have before, because the turns are too small tonight and you know you need more bodies in the tent.

9:16 p.m.: Wink to a group of teenagers out front who aren't sure whether they want to come in.

9:21 p.m.: Light up your torches and eat fire.

9:24 p.m.: Wave to the same group of teenagers who didn't come in.

9:29 p.m.: Light up your torches and eat fire.

9:41 p.m.: Light up your torches and eat fire.

9:48 p.m.: Light up your torches and eat fire.

9:57 p.m.: Light up your torches and eat fire.

9:59 p.m.: Beckon the leader of the group of teenagers over and light your fingers on fire just for him. Watch him buy a ticket. Watch the others follow.

10:00 p.m.: Watch talkers switch places.

10:07 p.m.: Light up your torches and eat fire.

10:15 p.m.: Light up your torches and eat fire.

10:20 p.m.: Remember that you have forgotten to drink

water for a few hours and wonder whether your headache is from dehydration or gas fumes. Chug water.

10:22 p.m.: Light up your torches and eat fire.

10:36 p.m.: Light up your torches and eat fire.

10:44 p.m.: Light up your torches and eat fire.

10:45 p.m.: Tell the drunk man that you will not give him your number right now but that you will consider it if he goes into the show.

10:51 p.m.: Light up your torches and eat fire.

10:59 p.m.: Gather with the rest of the crew around the bally stage. Watch the Ferris wheel.

Note: At 10:00 p.m. on the luckiest nights, but usually 11:00 p.m. or midnight, and sometimes 2:00 a.m., Tommy will make the call that you are about to perform your last show, and you'll speed through the acts, cutting the least impressive parts, making sure the last stragglers in the audience feel they got what they came for, and once they go, your crew will come sit out on the bally stage for the last few minutes as the fairgoers leave, smoking cigarettes and comparing notes on the day. Sometimes, when the day has been too long, they sit quietly, all faces turned toward the big wheel. That's the sign. Nobody on the fairground may shut down under penalty of a big fine until the fairground bosses give the A-OK to the Ferris wheel.

11:02 p.m.: Wheel's off. And then the echo down the midway, Wheel's off! Wheel's off! Wheel's off!

11:04 p.m.: Untie the banners, drop or roll them, unplug the sound system, take the props off the front stage, put the snake away and turn her heated blanket on, close the mummy cases if there is any chance of bad weather. Clear the stages.

11:22 p.m.: Decision.

(11:28 p.m.–12:13 a.m.): Will you grab your shower bag and shower shoes and a few pieces of dirty laundry and run for the showers, hoping the line isn't too long, hoping the water is warm, hoping someone hasn't taken a crap in the stall?

(11:28 p.m.–1:13 a.m.): Will you grab your wallet and hop in the van with Tommy or Sunshine if they are doing a Walmart run, to try to stock up on peanut butter or granola bars or tampons or sunscreen or drinking water because who knows when the next store run will be?

(11:28 p.m.–12:25 a.m.): Will you think of a friend or lover waiting to hear from you and call them, sprawled on your bunk or on the grass in the tent?

(11:28 p.m.–2:19 a.m.): Will you relax and chat and have a drink with your fellow performers, shooting the shit, having your tarot cards read, decompressing from the day?

Whatever you choose, do it fast, because before long if you're not in bed, the wake-up time will be swiftly approaching and you won't even be able to believe the idea that you'll have to do it all again. And you will wake up and swear that tonight, this night, you will go to bed right when the show is over, get a long sleep, "catch up," as they say, but when the last act is over and the banners are wrapped that night, your body will be buzzing with the adrenaline of performing, with the exhaustion mixed in, but more than that, your brain will be awash in relief for having finished the day and you will forget how tired you are, will feel this overwhelming need to have a little downtime, just a little while to unwind and talk to people other than the audience, and so you will, and will stay up too late, and will go to bed a little more relaxed, and will wake up once more in near disbelief that you have to do it all again.

$\frac{\ }{\ }$

The next morning I wake up and do it all again.

"America the Beautiful" wakes me. The recording is old, crackly, broken up behind a woman's overly vibrato voice. It is 8:00 a.m. I know it is 8:00 a.m. because the rodeo stadium blasts "America the Beautiful" across the fairgrounds at this same time each morning, a carnie alarm, an ironic paean to

147

America's opportunities that many of the sleeping men within earshot haven't ever been able to access.

American carnivals are made up of many non-U. S. citizens: Mexican, Central and South American, South African laborers who are willing to do intensely grueling physical work. I've heard a lot of folks in the business praise the melting pot of the American carnival. Whereas the stereotype of the rough-and-tumble carnie usually brings to mind a toothless, tattooed white man, in reality the carnivals are largely run by non-Americans. Away2xplore is a South African company that hires South Africans to work a carnival season in America. *We pay for your airfare***, the website advertises. The asterisks let you know that in exchange for your paid airfare and a weekly check—dependent, mostly, on commission from what you sell—you work a full season, which ranges, per the website, from six to ten months. There are no exceptions.

"Positions open now for Ride attendants/Ride operators, starting from next month! Operating your ride whilst playing the latest music and meeting lots of girls. If you like hands-on work while getting your hands dirty and want to be the most popular boy in every town, this job is for you, for sure!"

Many of the carnies I meet have had trouble with the law. The carnival companies don't ask lots of questions, so carnivals are full of people with histories—ex-cons—that preclude their working other kinds of jobs. Some years ago, when the law would come to the carnival looking for so-and-so, whomever they asked would plead total ignorance and word would bolt down the midway like rigged bowling pins to the ear it needed to find, to the ear that needed to hear *Get lost*, and that person would, usually to rejoin somewhere down the road. This place has all sorts of secret songs being sung in frequencies I can't hear.

"America the Beautiful" ends and I stretch out in my bed, sore, but my feet hit the wooden wall at the end of my bunk and my hands hit the wooden wall at the head and up above;

opening my eyes toward the morning sun, I see a dick and balls and clown face and *fuck you cunt* written on the slats of the bunk above. If I reach my arm to the right, it will press against the truck's metal wall. My left arm does not quite reach the other wall, but it's close, almost touches, and if I stretch out my foot across the two feet of space beside our bunks, it will touch. Then I can be touching all four walls at once. Two small plastic bins with three drawers each sit at either end of the room, one for each of the bunks. One drawer I fill with food, one with costume accessories, one initially with underwear and socks until I hear that panties go missing all the time if they are visible from the doorway, clean or not, and so I bury them in my suitcase and stick T-shirts in that drawer instead.

I walk into the main backstage area. Red is sitting back there, which is unusual. He's sipping from his Big Gulp coffee mug and brushing his long orange hair.

"Morning," I say. He grunts. I try to move slowly and not keep my eyes directly on him, like I would around an eagle or fox, something rare to get close to in the wild. I don't want him to flee.

"I'm gonna make coffee. Want some?"

"Won't say no," he says. We move near one another in our separate worlds, though I'm aware of every sound and movement he makes. This sideshow hero. This madman. This meanie.

Each creak of his chair makes me nervous he might swat at me or, worse, leave. I have some idea that Red knows a secret about this place—about performing or illusion or magic, I don't know exactly what—something that he has come to understand through all these years on the road. Like Yoda. Like he might be able to tell me what it is I'm actually doing here.

"Where you from, Red?" I ask him casually.

"Philly," he says, the *p* a little stronger than the *ph* sound as his tongue shapes syllables against his toothless gums. Last season, he had one tooth. It was aching. He bought a bottle of

149

vanilla Smirnoff and wiped most of the rust off his pliers. He drank the entire bottle backstage, fell off his stool, and passed out before he could pull the tooth. In the morning, hungover and about to climb up the steps to perform his first act of the day, he reached into his mouth with the metal and yanked the tooth. Blood trickled down his chin onstage.

"619 North Highland Street," he says, and I nod, pour the coffee. He continues: "41A Main, 3055 14th Avenue, St. Clarence Home for Boys, West Philadelphia Orphanage, Presbyterian Children's Village, St. Vincent Home for Boys. Let's see," he says, gathering the hairs from his brush and balling them up in the palm of his hand. His hands are not inked, but the rest of his body, from neck to ankles, is covered in tattoos. Tigers, anatomical men swallowing swords, shields, crests, dragons, planets, and between each tattoo, small dark stars making constellations.

"One time all the orphanages were full when another foster family sent me back, so they put a bunch of us in an institute for retarded children," he says. "All the other kids eventually got sent somewhere else. But I stayed." I follow his glance out the doorway to his van, where one of the kittens is coiled on the dash, her white fur nestled between a wooden statue of the Buddha and an empty McDonald's milkshake cup.

He opens his fist and lets the Ohio breeze take the orange nest of hair. "1401 Kensington Avenue," he says. "A home on Cahill Road, can't remember the number," he says after a while. "I forget a lot of the details now." But every address seems a stopover on some Homeric odyssey almost too perfect for the story of a grand-champion sword swallower.

"The Millers, the Thorps, the O'Callahans," he says. He hasn't talked to me at all in the three and a half weeks I've been here, has barely even made eye contact with me. I'm amazed this ordinary question pulls out a string of answers like scarves tied to one another that a magician pulls from his mouth. I'm amazed that the addresses are tied to names, names to memories, and before I know it, he tells me that at sixteen, he opened the door of his foster house one morning and peered out at the snow piled high on the street. It was February. Very cold. He stepped outside. And then took another step. Another. Then he didn't stop. Walking is, in its most basic form, the act of falling and catching yourself. Fall, catch. Fall, catch. It is an act of *travail*. Can it be a pilgrimage without a known destination? He walked for thirty-one days.

AND THE LOW SKY OPENS

Day 23 of 150

WORLD OF WONDERS
JULY 2013

Behind the Gravitron 3000's crown of American flags, the sky's looking more and more like a bruise. Even the performers from California—half of us, earthquake people— know that a sky going green and purple means tornado, and one by one Pipscy the mermaid and Spif the knife thrower and Sunshine the fire eater peek around the edge of the tent between acts to look directly onto the emptying carnival midway. The low sky opens with rain and bursts of wind that knock over a tank of Rastafarian-painted hermit crabs beside our show. Sunshine widens her eyes at Tommy. She hisses, "Thomas. Close the show." They've been slamming their trailer door for days. He shakes his head no and everyone ducks back. But not Red.

Red stands in front of the big striped circus tent in his kilt, arms crossed over his bare belly. Inside, he has just swallowed a tire iron. Here, he appraises the ceiling of clouds as a dribble of spit weaves through his red beard stubble.

"Well," he says, voice barely audible over the wind, "I know I'm gonna die on these stages. Today's as good a day as any for that." He claps his hands with false finality and turns back into the tent. I nod in agreement. I know this doesn't make much sense, but the corsets I wore and chains I escaped and the

152

taxidermied Icelandic Giant I glued back together all precluded danger from feeling much like danger. Or maybe it's the bright lights. Or that it feels a little good to be reminded that there is always more that could be lost.

Tommy and I stand in the drizzle on our bally stage. "You don't have to wait, but you do have to hurry," Tommy bellows, but he's cut off by the loudspeaker announcing the pygmy goat parade again.

My wrists throb. I've escaped these handcuffs thirteen times today, but that's the job here, a little pain, a little delight, always a calculation—what will it take to woo the two teenage girls yawning as they watch our bally. *Look at my danger*, I urge through a squint in my eyes. *Imagine yourself locked up.* One of the girls starts texting.

Red pounds the flat steel face of a gearhead tent stake farther into the dirt with a sledgehammer, the *ting ting ting* and occasional spark just over my right shoulder as I wink to the teenagers. I'm learning the art of distraction. Thunder cracks. Red prepares for the deluge.

"Now watch Ms. Mimi L'Amour escape from these chains. Her world record is five seconds. Can she break it?" Tommy says, and begins the countdown. I plant my feet hip distance apart and take a deep breath. "Five!" he shouts, and I spin fast to face the tent behind me, my back to the audience, "Four!" throwing my arms down hard in front of me to loosen the chains, Red pounding the steel, "Three!" one and then the other wrist is out and lightning flashes and I have the chains in one hand, start my spin back to face the audience, "T—" but the loudspeaker interrupts: "Attention fairgoers. This is a tornado warning. All attendees of the Lucas County Fair must evacuate the fairgrounds immediately," and the thunder cracks again right on cue and everyone across the fairgrounds is suddenly moving very quickly.

"Banners!" Tommy screams back into our massive tent. I clamber down the bally stage, already drenched, as the seven other performers meet me at the front banner line. The banner bearing the two-headed Egyptian princess billows and snaps like a ship's sail, cracking and giving in to the storm.

I imagine the tornado splitting all the banners down the line, the boom of toppling poles like cannon fire, and the ship below suddenly tipping and sloshing as the waves crash farther onto the deck, the ship four days out to sea and unrescuable while deckhands are tossed into the waves, and then it's not deckhands flailing as they sink below the churning sea, it's my mom, her paralyzed body sinking like stone.

"Banners! Go! Go! Go!" Spif screams. Hands are flying, sequins throwing off the rain. We yank the slip-tie off the metal pole, unwind the rope holding the top of the banners taut, its tail splashing to the mud below. Breathing hard, we wrap and wrench the ropes around each of the canvas rolls, muscles shaking, looping slipknots and cinching, squeezing each banner tight, squinting against the onslaught. "Tighter!" Tommy is screaming, each of these banners a few hundred bucks we can't afford to replace.

Ropes slap the mud puddles and spray. Mascara and eye shadow smear our faces. My fishnets are splattered and as I'm running to the next banner my heel sinks into a puddle and I stagger, my shin hitting a rusted tent stake, which grabs and rips my fishnets, cuts my leg open. Blood. "Go! Go! Go!" Tommy screams, pointing to the next banner, and I go.

The rain falls harder and harder, sheets and buckets and daggers of it hitting me from every direction as the wind makes it impossible to hear nearly anything but the high-pitched cry of emergency coming from somewhere I can't see. Carnies run toward the cinder-block bathrooms. On the other side of the fence, one or two fairgoers linger, a few cars speed away, but mostly they're gone. Just as they do each night, carnival bosses shut the gates around the fairgrounds, locking our performers and hundreds of carnies inside.

"Seek immediate shelter!" a policeman calls through a

154

megaphone. But Big, Big Ben has the nine-foot boa constrictor across his arms and is slowly coiling her back into her box. He is in no hurry. There's work to be done. He purses his full pink lips at the snake, kissing her on the mouth as hard rain devours him and the thunder cracks.

The sirens bounce off the cow barn. Rain pounds. Red screams for us to untie the tent's sidewalls, thick vinyl seventy feet across by forty feet deep. A huge gust of wind could find any opening and pick the tent up from the inside, ripping it open or carrying it into the sky. This will not happen today. We will not be afraid.

"Are you crazy? Get to the bathrooms!" a carnie with a snarl of blond curls hollers as he runs. It's time to go. The wind plasters our hair to our faces and then all of a sudden stops dead. A second. Two. And then it picks up again, the tree branches whipping one another as they're stripped of their leaves, the flags on top of our tent snapping and cracking. Gold glitter smears across Pipscy's face beside me. I catch her eye for a moment, and it's wide and spooked but goes right back to the ropes she's tying. It's time to go. We live in the back of a semitruck and we won't leave. We make less than forty bucks a day and we won't leave. Inside the tent, we dart and dodge one another, locking the mummy cases, tying up curtains, gathering knives. We tie and twist. The wind sounds like a train. We lock and pin. The Feejee Mermaid is safe in her coffin. The headless woman's mirrored chair is well wrapped in wet pillows. Though Queen Kong isn't the last taxidermied gorilla in the world, her presence here, alongside her freak family, makes the extraordinary individuals a collective of ordinary love, and that, *that*, is reason to tie her blankets tighter despite the opening sky.

In the end, Tommy finally yells for us to get the hell out of there, though it's almost impossible to hear. The rest of the fairground is emptied of people and the wind is throwing hair across our faces like whips and the sky is mauve. Sunshine, Spif,

Pipscy, and I all run, no longer able to dodge puddles, past small tree branches that have come down, past food tents leaning sharply away from the wind, and finally make it to the cinder-block bathroom already stuffed with carnies. We're breathing hard, can barely see for the makeup smeared across our faces, the membrane of storm water covering our bodies. We take paper towels to wipe our eyes and laugh with the hysteria of danger, unsure what else to do. Sunshine inspects my cuts. I inspect hers.

"Where's Red?" she finally asks.

We look around, but he has not made it into the bathrooms. Someone with a weather radio says the tornado has touched down a mile from our carnival. We push past the other carnies standing in the doorway and peek our heads out the bathroom's mouth, craning our necks toward our big tent down the midway. It's almost impossible to make out what's what, but I'm pretty sure I see Red just outside our tent, two of the center ropes wrapped around his hands as he throws his body back against the wind, fighting that tornado himself, a battle—anyone would say—that there is no way he could actually win.

I can see him there, openmouthed, laughing up at the sky.

⚡

Half an hour later, the wind has slowed and rain lightened. A few breaks in the clouds let some dim sun through, and one by one the rest of the bathroom huddlers decide the danger has passed and leave the building. One of the women has been on her cell phone much of the time. "Oh lord, oh Jesus," she'd said to the line, "I just wanted to talk to you, honey, one last time." Another was chewing gum with a rhythmic grind and stood at the edge of the bathroom door with her phone out in front of her as if it were a mirror, though instead she had it recording the rest of the world outside. A man stood beside her, chewing and spitting sunflower seeds onto the tiled floor.

"I'm going to check on Thomas and Benny," Sunshine says,

shouldering her way out of the bathroom. We follow her, stepping over torn branches and wet leaves and a smattering of game prizes—soggy stuffed cats and inflatable baseball bats strewn about like forgotten toys. Though it was unlikely there was carnage back at the tent, I pictured our comrades' bodies tossed onto an upturned tent stake, impaled in a stack of floppy flesh like speared fish. Or knocked over the head by the fallen giant. Decapitated by a plane of glass.

When we reach our lot, Red is sitting in the front seat of his van reading Facebook. Tommy is inside the tent, whistling and sweeping water off the stage. Big, Big Ben is in the truck.

Time stills. We are standing on a precipice between realities—the fear and drama of the last hour, which is keeping my throat tight, the top of my chest hot, and the regular, much-rehearsed motion of what we're about to do again.

We open the mummy cases, shaking off the leaves and rain. Spif checks the electrical. Within fifteen minutes, Tommy yells that we're opening back up in five minutes, so for those of us with smeared makeup and blood- and mud-covered legs, we should do our best to fix it, quickly, and get back onstage. "The show must go on" trope can't ever have felt more true.

Once I climb the bally stage, I see the rest of the carnival squeezing itself out as well. Crazy Craig the Clown gets back on his unicycle, tries to juggle, and falls off. It's hard to tell if his struggle is sincere or performed. A honk comes from down the midway and some of the thin crowd parts and Buffo, the World's Strongest Clown, emerges, smooth and straight on his Segway, honking horns and ringing bells, his face clown white with a large kidney-shaped red mouth. Where had he been hidden to preserve his makeup? And who had been working out in the rain to make sure his show didn't blow away? He leaves a small white smear against his overripe biceps after he kisses them, those little pythons sticking out of his American-flag-printed denim vest. The engine in his Segway purrs its high-pitched whine.

"Did you know the inventor of the Segway just died by accidentally riding his Segway off a cliff?" Cassie whispers over to me.

I snortle.

"Well, kids, this is just a reminder that Buffo's next show is at six this evening," Buffo says to the crowd. Crazy Craig still hasn't managed to climb back onto his unicycle. He's looking at Buffo with half-lidded eyes, three juggling clubs in his hands.

"Everybody gather round and listen to the weirdos!" Buffo says into his megaphone, pointing at our stage. His style of mockery is predictable in the boring way a jock mocks an outcast in the high school cafeteria.

And the rest of the day continues on as usual.

Later, I call Devin to report on the tornado and because I am scared, though not from the tornado. I mention the tornado, assure him all's okay, and move on quickly. I am trying to remember things about my mom from before she got sick, and I keep finding long gaps in my memory.

"I don't remember her at all," I tell him.

"Sure you do," he says. "You have to."

"I keep trying, but she's always just in the corner of the room as my memory sweeps through the house. I can see her for a moment, but most of the time she's gone."

"You don't just lose a person like that," he says. "Twenty-five years of memories don't just get deleted."

"I think maybe you do."

We are both quiet a few moments.

"She was authoritative," he says. "Commanding."

"She was commanding," I parrot, catching, for just a moment, some memory of a stern arch in her eyebrow.

"She laughed a lot," he says.

"That sounds right."

"Remember the bricks? She was going to make special bricks."

158

"No."

"She had just seen bricks somewhere with animals or patterns printed into them, and she decided she was going to make some. She was sure she could do it. How to make the mold, pour the mix. She was just going to do it."

"God."

"Right? Remember?"

I try to conjure up an image of her chiseling molds, measuring concrete and stone. I can't see the bricks Devin is talking about, but I can see her hands doing a thing like that. Bony, raised green veins, chewed away around the nails. Her hands were often splotched with the stains of dye she'd use for painting. She was a textile designer, had her own business for years in our garage and then in a little studio she rented a few towns over. Hand-painted fabric for high-end customers to turn into drapes or upholstery. The business always just broke even. Custom-designed orders for spas and rich people's homes.

"The music comes on when you enter the room, automatically," she explained at dinner ten or so years before her stroke, after visiting one of her clients at home. "The woman had an obvious facelift. She looked surprised the whole time I was there. It's so silly, a facelift," she said, "and so expensive." She pulled the skin taut across her throat and chin with a hand. Our dinners cooled as we watched her. She did the same to her cheeks. "But there are places you can go where it's not so much," she said. "Mexico. You fly down there and have the procedure and a whole vacation, all for cheaper than doing it here."

"Mom. Why would you even talk about doing something like that?" I asked, not kindly.

"You don't get it," she snapped at me suddenly. "You don't know what it feels like to get old. Just wait. Wait until you don't recognize yourself in the mirror anymore."

My brother and Davy, as usual, stayed out of it. They knew about stray bullets.

"In the morning there would be fresh fruit, and then beers in the afternoon, and all the while...," she trailed off, pulling the skin taut against her hairline. "Take it easy, missy," she said, looking at me. I hadn't taken my eyes off her. "I'm not actually going to do it. I'm really just thinking about the ceviche." She licked her fingers as if they were covered in lime. "Anyway, you've got your brain to rely on. So you'll never be bothered with this stuff," she said, smiling at me before she stood up from the table and left. She stayed in the bathroom a long time. We ate our dinner.

"Did she ever make those bricks?" Devin asks.

"I don't remember," I say.

"They had dogs or pheasants or something on them. I wonder if she made them."

"I bet she did," I say.

"I bet so, too."

THE DEPARTURE

Two years and eight months after the stroke

JUNE 2013

On April 7, 2013, she is back in the hospital after a series of seizures. She has high blood pressure. She is indicating head-aches. Her body won't stop its shaking. She is in the hospital, then out.

 Their trip is three months away.

 I leave for the sideshow.

 Two months.

 One.

 Bags packed.

 A friend drives them to the train station, helps them board.

The last time I saw them, a few days before I left for the side-show and two months before they left for their trip, my pile of new costumes was on my parents' kitchen table.

 The table was in the new house my mom and stepdad rented. Well. First there was the single room Davy rented—I figured out how to cook rice without a stove, in the toaster oven! Davy gloated—then the tiny apartment under tall bay trees, and now this little yellow house. Inside the house it is dark and out the window is a creek and an expanse of grass. Deer graze and neighbors' dogs poop and run and outside it's always the yel-low or gold or brown of wild California grass.

We were all preparing to leave. Them to Italy via a boat across the Atlantic for three months. Probably they won't come back—I can't imagine my stepdad returning without my mom, if it came to that. He said as much in the hospital. He wouldn't go on without her. And now his life's central task is caring for her. What would there be for him to come back to?

I'm leaving for the sideshow for five months. Maybe I will come back. We are all already performing.

How will she be able to tell him if she's sick? neighbors asked, family asked. Will he know if she is tired? Will she know what to do if he gets hurt over there? Could she go get help?

Don't know. Maybe. No. No.

The rest of the kitchen table is covered with bottles of pills and piles of diapers and small plastic salt and pepper shakers and maps of Italy. Their own costumes in neat piles. Checklists. Mine: Eyeliner and tampons crossed out. Theirs: Packs of AAA batteries and hats crossed out.

My pile of costumes has sequined shorts and glittery headbands. I imagine Davy covered in glitter and my mother in a sequined pantsuit, and there's a laugh track in my head as he explains the kind of weight he'll carry across Italy.

Also in my pile of costumes are two pairs of industrial-strength fishnets. My mom scooches toward the table in her wheelchair and picks up the black ones. She stretches the foot between her pointer and middle finger on her left hand. Lace. Shadows. Honeycomb. She stares at the fabric, running her finger over it. Where do these take her? There's that scene in *Good Will Hunting* where Minnie Driver says she'd give her fortune back for just one more day with her dad, and I used to think, Bullshit. No way that's true. Now I have a desperate, wild need to know what the feel of these fishnets means to her, what they remind her of, and now that's not something I can know. My hands are twitchy by my side. Prepared for the moment when we'll rehash the scene where she brings the thing she's just picked up to her mouth and sticks it inside, and my

162

never-gentle- enough voice reminds her the thing in her hand is fabric, not a glass of water, is lotion, not a slice of apple, is tweezers, is a stone, and my hand will quickly but firmly move to her hand and guide the object away from her parted lips, and I will feel sorry for having done so.

But maybe she knows all that. Maybe she's looking at the footed fishnets and remembering herself at sixteen on a stage in San Francisco, drawing spontaneous illustrations for the judges of the Miss Junior California pageant. The stage would have been lit brightly, would have been hot, and the air all around would have smelled like vanilla and sweat and Tahitian Sunsets and the other smells of girls ripening into women. All those high heels. They're competing for the title. My mother, the young woman, the artist, has bright green eyes with flecks of orange, and the judges call her up for the talent portion of the event. She hasn't told her family, anyone, she's tried out, or won the smaller competitions to get there. She just saunters out, pen in hand, and, eyes closed, doodles all over the giant paper pad facing the audience. A mess of lines and jags and dots are on the page. She opens her eyes, winks at the judges, and sets a timer for three minutes. Frantically, what were two disparate flecks on the page become the eyebrows of a whale. Two lines meet beneath her wrist and grow into coral, algae, sunken ships. A universe grows between her fingers, a seascape, a story, and the pen and the paper and the judges are not inside it but they are close and hungry for it, and isn't that most alluring of all, being right next to something special?

The dogs outside the window have picked up the scent of a doe. They circle the ground, their snouts down. Nature carrying on.

She sets the fishnets back onto the costume pile and starts to pick up the tutu, stops. Holds still. Imagine there's a spotlight on her.

An epiphany approaches.

We hold still.

We're looking at her looking past the table.

The judges can't take their eyes off her.

She pushes the tulle aside, finally, and the show continues.

Or it doesn't.

I don't know, because the planet of her head is unreachable. Maybe the show has just begun. Maybe she's in a musical.

She hums.

My mom's travel clothes are folded into suitcases. Thin material, easy to rinse and wash in a sink, clothes made for American tourists traveling to hot countries. This after the sequins onstage and the high heels and the wink to the judges with the pen in her hand. Is this in her character still? Is she still her same character?

I'm telling her the story of where I found each of the costume pieces as she paws through them, because they are the places she taught me when I was young.

The thrift shop down the street from the Ethiopian place on Haight, the San Rafael ballet store, the costume shop in the Mission, and she nods sometimes, and I keep talking, saying whatever I'm saying because there's safety in noise.

Davy places a bowl filled with yogurt and cereal in front of my mom. Her wheelchair is scooted right up against the lip of the table, a spoon by the bowl's side. A metal stick with a concave dome. A silver object, shiny, beautiful even. It is familiar. It is a part of the world of ordinary objects, although what is ordinary anymore?

Silver oval, silver line, sheen.

She grasps the spoon's handle and picks it up. Holds it six inches from the tabletop. The spoon as meteor, as mirror, as muddled lifeline to another world. Brings the spoon up to her face, hesitates, then rubs it softly along her cheekbone.

"No, honey," Davy says. "Spoon."

She pulls it away from her cheek, sets it back down on the table.

Spoon.

What good is a word without its meaning? Is there a meaning? Is the meaning there, deep, like a song she recognizes with the lyrics on the tip of her tongue?

Spoon.

She picks up the spoon. Sets it down.

She reaches into the bowl with her thumb and pointer finger, pinches a flake of cereal, and brings it up to her mouth. Chews. Her fingers return to the bowl, three fingertips in this time, a scoop of purple yogurt on her pointer and middle fingertips, a journey up to the mouth.

Silver lollipop. Moon.

She takes the spoon in her hand, sets it back down.

Fingers in yogurt, licking each off, sucking the little pools of sweet from beneath her long nails after each scoop, this yogurt now honored and loved and savored like the last smear of birthday cake frosting.

She picks up the spoon, dips it into the yogurt, takes a scoop. Brings it to her mouth. Opens her mouth. Puts the spoon inside. Closes her lips around the metal moon, the silver half egg. Pulls the spoon from her mouth and chews the food still inside. All these familiar actions. All the steps in on ordinary life. She eats on her own, drinks by herself, in her own time. Relearning how to be in the altered world.

There's a photograph from the train station my brother sends me the morning after my parents leave. My brother, standing on one side of my mom's wheelchair, is in his dressy work clothes and smiles his huge bright smile, the one that makes people adore him immediately. His obvious happiness and casual hand on my mom's shoulder is an uncomfortable contrast to my grandmother, my mom's mom. She stands on the other side of the wheelchair. She wears a bright yellow coat and white gloves and holds a disposable camera the exact color of her jacket and has the smallest, saddest smile. Her eyes don't meet the camera, but slide instead to some distant corner on the floor, or maybe they weren't focused on anything at all. She is ninety-eight years old.

Their train will take them from Emeryville, California, to New York City, where they will spend a few days recovering before boarding the ship to Europe.

Here they go. Say goodbye.

"I am sure I'll never see them again," my grandmother tells me on the phone. "There is my beautiful daughter, and I'm sure I've just said goodbye."

Do you see a hankie waving from the window? Are their hands outstretched toward those they are leaving behind?

No. Their eyes are focused straight ahead. We can only make out the shadows of the backs of their heads.

⚡

I slip out the backstage door when everyone is off taking showers or calling people at home. I want to feel the anonymity of walking through a big city, anonymity I thought I could have as I walked the fairgrounds, until I realized I was in sparkles and a bustier. In this darkness, maybe I have a chance. I don't want anyone to see my face while I swallow the fact that my parents are gone. They've been on a train taking them across the country for about twelve hours, not entirely too late to convince them to change plans and go home. But I don't call them.

Lights remain on in a few of the joints being scrubbed down, but most of the fairground is covered in shadow. Where is the moon? There were nights the moon shone on all the sleepy people of the darkened world but curled up her light over the fairground like a woman stepping over a puddle, keeping what should be dark, dark.

I walk past a bounce house and a table covered by tubes of incense. Through the glow of a single streetlamp on the next midway I can make out the top of a small barn. I love all the animals here. Their small noises all night, their dirt smell.

There is a group of young sheep in a pen outside the barn. I can hear some activity on the other side, farmers or 4-H kids hosing out a pen maybe. For a minute, before they are corralled back inside, I can stand beside the sheep, alone, peaceful, and if I crouch low to where one is eating, I can just hear its sweet jaw grinding that hay. But then I hear the low whir of a motor.

I turn around, and barely visible is a golf cart with two men inside. The golf cart is a common fairground device for getting through small aisles quickly, usually reserved for bosses, so I expect this is just two bosses doing late-night checks on their joints.

"Come here," a voice says, and I can make out an arm beckoning me over. It occurs to me that if there is someone here who owns the sheep, maybe I am doing something bad to them, disturbing their peace in a moment when prizewinning sheep need peace.

I am not remembering that when you are approached by a mountain lion, the first thing to do is stop moving, face the cat, and make yourself as big as possible. You make the lion believe you are not such an easy target.

I walk over to the golf cart. As I get closer, I can make out something reflective on their chests.

"Nice night," one of them says, staring at me.

"It is," I say.

"What are you doing out here?" the other asks.

Metal badges. They are cops.

"I work at the sideshow. I was just going for a walk," I say.

"All alone?" the driver says. He is young, midtwenties maybe, with a smooth, fat face and crooked teeth.

"My show is right there," I say, pointing down the midway. "There are lots of people inside."

"So what do you do for the show?" the driver asks as the passenger's walkie-talkie buzzes and he picks it up to listen. I want to hear what reports might be coming through, but I also

167

have the sense that I need to pay careful attention to the driver, who is paying careful attention to me. I regret that I am still wearing my shorts and cowboy boots, even though I'd put a long-sleeve button-up over the top of my costume. "I'm a bally girl," I say. "I eat fire, charm snakes, escape from chains, that sort of thing."

"Well, well!" the driver exclaims, smiling. "What sort of chains?"

"Handcuffs," I say, reluctantly. As my eyes adjust to the dark I can better see his face. His smile makes his cheeks stand out like two glistening lollipop heads.

"They aren't real," I add. "The handcuffs."

"Are you sure, now?" he says.

"They're called Siberian handcuffs. They're—"

"Because I've got some right here," he says, patting his handcuffs on the side of his belt, "and I'd really love to see you in these."

I laugh in my best good-natured way, trying to channel a polite Ohio girl, someone who would remind the cop of his sister or wife, someone he wouldn't want to either arrest or make sex jokes to, whichever is happening here.

"Well, I'm quite sure that's beyond my skill set," I say, smiling and intoning my voice in a way that I hope implies I am exiting the conversation, but he interrupts my goodbye.

"No, really, try these out," he says, a little louder. "Wait, we'll make it even better. I'll lock you up, and then throw you in the trunk of our car out in the parking lot," he says. "That way, you'll have to escape twice." He laughs hard and loud. "Come over here," he says, and his voice changes, drops a register. "Really. Tell me your secret. I'm not kidding, little girl. Come on over here and I'll lock you right up."

His partner is still fiddling with his radio, not paying attention to us. This, suddenly, in the few weeks I've been with the sideshow, is the most scared I've been of another person.

"It's getting late. I've got to get back," I say. "How would

168

you like your daughter to be alone on the dark fairgrounds with a cop joking about locking her up and leaving her inside the trunk of a car?" I don't say. Without waiting to hear their response, I turn to go.

"Anytime you change your mind, escape artist," the cop says, "I'll be waiting for you." The golf cart doesn't drive away. I can feel it behind me, the metal, the eyes following me as I walk quickly away, the stone in my throat growing smaller and smaller the farther I get.

⚡

A tire blows outside South Bend, Indiana. After Ohio we headed for a couple more small county fairs in Illinois as holdover stops before we reach the meat-grinders of the season: the big state fairs. Playing them grinds you up into little pieces, the hours are that long—8:00 a.m. to 2:00 a.m., often, because the audiences are huge all day every day, because the fairs are two weeks or longer. We won't get to them for a few more weeks, but I know they're out there because the seasoned crew talks about them as both a cure for these dopey little fairs and a curse on your sanity.

We've played only two fairs so far, but this life is becoming familiar so much more quickly than other kinds of lives I've had. It is so packed full all day, every day. I've escaped from handcuffs over a hundred times on that bally stage already, eaten fire nearly as many, I've unrolled and rerolled the banners every morning and night day after day, and now, just over a month into the tour, it is starting to feel as if I've always been here.

This isn't the season's first blown tire. On the drive from Florida up to Pennsylvania for the first fair, the tire on our semi blew, and a piece of the rubber spun around and cracked the truck's battery. We pulled off at the next rest stop and started calling

169

around for the cheapest, closest rig mechanic out in rural West Virginia. The pool of battery acid beneath the truck grew drip by drip.

"Get comfortable," Tommy said. "This'll take a while."

We trudged into the rest stop and slouched against the walls. "Of course this would happen," Sunshine said. She explained that the show never had enough money, and year by year it made less. Smaller crowds. Cheaper tickets. More people who believed it was politically incorrect to gawk, or gross, and then went home to reality TV shows nobody watched them watching. So each time the semitruck wore down its tires, Tommy, per instruction from the owners, took the worn front tires and rotated them to the back, where they were less important for traction, then bought newer but still used tires for the front. This is why the tire blew, I heard. It's old, cracked, worn well beyond its life. Nobody said anything else, and we settled into a card game.

"Are we playing Poobah's rules?" Sunshine asked.

"Of course," Spif said, and started dealing.

"Remember a few years back when Poobah got so pissed at Chris Christ?" Sunshine said, laughing as she organized her hand. "He hid behind one of the semi's tires with a knife. He'd decided to stab him. So when Chris walked by, Poobah lurched out from behind the tire but somehow missed Chris and slashed the tire instead. That's why we had the blowout," she said. "The stabbed tire probably got rotated into the wrong spot." Nobody looked up or asked if the story was true. Nobody sought clarification. The truth, I've learned, is less in the particulars of the story and more in the fact that there is a story at all. Somebody threw a joker.

With our second blowout, we wait inside a gas station for a few hours while it's repaired, sipping the local root beer sold at the register for a dollar each or Special! $2 for 2, which tastes exactly like every root beer I've ever had, though the bottle has

170

a handwritten label that promises Grandma's secret recipe.

We write postcards, walk the small aisle of trucker amenities, and touch the camo steering wheel covers. Staring at the hot dogs juicing on their spigots, I casually mention the creepy cops from a few nights earlier to Tommy and Spif. They stop gazing at the dogs. As I talk, they cross their arms over their chests and start shaking their heads.

"Motherfucking cops," Spif says.

"Tess, you should never be out alone on the fairgrounds at night," Tommy says.

"Or even in the day," Spif says.

"Get pepper spray or a knife. I'm not kidding. All the girls carry them," Tommy says. I know this is true, but don't want to accept its necessity. I've lived plenty of other places people thought were dangerous—New York City for two years, West Africa for a year—and I never carried weapons. "And listen." Tommy beckons the others over. "Here's the new thing. Anytime you need to go out of the tent at night—to the bathroom, to smoke, whatever—you bring someone with you. Preferably me or Spiffer. I know you girls are tough, but it's just not worth the risk. Wake me up anytime, seriously, I don't care, just don't go out alone. Okay?"

We nod. I understand the concern—not just for the cops, of course, but all the incidents over the years. There'd been a brutal rape on one of these fairgrounds last year. But I feel two things— angry that it is necessary to protect women who just want to go pee at night, and relief that there are willing allies. We are all in it together.

The July sun is gaining relentless heat.

The July sun is gaining such relentless heat that nobody wants to walk back out to the van to retrieve their backpacks for entertainment while we wait, so we sit around a sticky plastic table beside truck parts, watching a staticky, muted episode of *Judge Judy* on a small TV mounted in the corner.

By the time we get to the Kane County Fair in St. Charles, Illinois, the news station releases a heat advisory for the whole forthcoming week. The newscasters suggest that all vulnerable populations in Kane County—the elderly and children, two of our primary audience types, in particular—stay indoors in air-conditioning. It is a health risk to be outside at all.

Our show is set up in the center of a pool of black asphalt. By the third morning, everything is melting. I apply a few dabs of foundation, which turns into thin tan water and runs to my chin. My liquid eyeliner won't make a straight line because there's so much sweat pooling in my eye sockets. Cassie and I take turns getting ready in our bunk, the space in there only big enough to fit one body at a time, and too hot to stay for more than a minute. More layers of makeup do not make it stick. There is an actual wet stain on the ground from the sweat dripping off our bodies, and my hand slides when I try to steady it against my cheek to swipe on the mascara.

We decide on a new plan.

Makeup bags in hand, we slide out of our trailer and book it down the midway and into the presentation hall. In here, children's paintings of their dogs and a church group's prize quilt are displayed beside unusual vegetables lined up in a row. They're all awaiting judgment. We stand in the holy air-conditioned public bathrooms and draw on our faces.

Just an hour later, onstage, my makeup is completely smeared off, my costume is soaked all the way through, and my cheeks are bright pink. Tommy's face is completely reflective, a mirror made of sweat, and I think that this might be the end for me, for all of us. My head feels full of air and then pummeling stones, and my vision seems to be getting a little fuzzy around the edges. It is 106 with 90 percent humidity. Nobody is out on the midway but us.

"Tommy, tell me more signs that a person might be leaving."

"Why, you gonna leave me, Tess?"

"I wish I had the strength to leave," I say, joking, but that rings so true to me as I say it, I almost cry. Would I leave? Could I? I think about a trick my high school cross-country coach used to tell us. When you're on a long run, if you think about how much longer you have to go, especially when you're climbing a big hill, it feels insurmountable, too hard. You'll want to stop. If, though, you make small goals ahead of you, that tree at the bend, the crest of this small hill you can see, then reaching it feels, though still hard, within your grasp. And by the time you get there, the hardest part might be over, and you've worked hard to get to that point anyway, so you might as well keep going.

And then I think about my parents, and wonder whether, if I left now, I could get to them in time to see them once more. If they make it through the train journey, that would be something. And then the ship across the Atlantic. And then the ten-day waiting time in London. And then the ship to Italy. Then the travels between Rome, Florence, Venice, and back to Rome. Then the ship again. The train across the country.

My cross-country coach's trick didn't work. Each step felt infinitely more insurmountable than the last.

"The signs are all around," Tommy says. "It used to be that the sideshow was a community for all kinds of displaced or rejected people to find a home."

"Is it still?"

"Sort of," he says, spotting a mother and her three young children way down the midway and trying to get their attention. They turn into the air-conditioned presentation hall. "But not really."

"Why not?"

"This isn't a place where anyone can make it. People aren't used to the amount of hard work that goes into making it here. I mean, Snickers only lasted a week and a half. I guess it shouldn't be surprising. Many people just can't handle how demanding it is. Physically. Mentally."

173

In front of us, the black asphalt looks like a river as sheets of heat rise up from the ground and make waves. What was once solid ground is now part of the liquid world, and the cosmos is melting, too, and the inside of my body feels like it contains nothing but boiling water, a fat meat sack of boiling water, and it occurs to me that I might die. Here. Today. And that would be fine.

The few scattered people across the fairgrounds are taking momentary respite in faraway shade between air-conditioned buildings. A loudspeaker announces, "Welcome to Senior Citizens Day, sponsored by Miller's Funeral Services."

"Be right back," Tommy says, and darts offstage. I remain, the smaller of our two snakes, whom we have named Pandora, in my arms. I try to focus on something besides the heat.

Boa constrictors range in size from three to fourteen feet, with hearty tan bodies that have distinctive dark brown and white saddles across their backs, increasing in proximity closer to their red-brown tails. The females are bigger—"heavy-bodied snakes," Wikipedia tells me. I've been trying to read about snakes on my lunch break so that this beautiful creature becomes less an anonymous symbol of danger and more a complex, important creature of the larger ecosystem.

Pandora senses heat with her lips, and moves her mouth up and down my body, flicking her tongue along the back of my neck. She is active today, writhing all the time, never settling around my neck or waist even though I try to convince her I am just a friendly tree. As she swings her head close I can see that her eyes are again starting to turn a milky blue, opal-colored almost. She is readying to shed.

Since the tooth scrape incident, I've been reluctant to let her face near my body without my hand supporting her head and neck, just in case. But it is so hot today, and I've made a terrible mistake this morning in trying to wear my hair down. It is wet with sweat and clumped down my back, a nest of sorts, and Pandora keeps diving back there, probably for a respite of shade, and her body is clammy because I keep setting her back into her box into which we've hosed some cool water so that she can regulate her body temperature. She's heavy and sticky and diving her face back behind my head even though my loosely open hand supports her neck and tries to guide it back to the front of my body, where both I and the sparse audience can keep our eyes on her.

A few sweaty kids and their brave parents are down the midway at a lemonade stand. One of the kids spots the snake and points, and the whole group, reluctantly, slowly emerges into the sun and walks toward our stage. Once the boy who pointed is close enough, I parrot what Tommy usually says about the snake.

"Do you think you can be hypnotized by a snake?" I ask the boy. He shakes his head no and walks a little closer. "Many people believed snakes have the power to hypnotize, so come close and look right into Pandora's eyes," I say, which is my cue to guide the strong, heavy snake's head out toward the willing participant so he or she might gaze into the pools of her eyes, but when I start to pull her head, she won't budge. I try again, gently still, smiling at the boy who is waiting to prove me wrong. The little boy has a bright red shirt a few sizes too big, and buzzed blond hair, and I can see his teeny rounded teeth inside his open, expectant, lick-lipped mouth as he looks from snake body to my face to see what the damn holdup is.

Which is an excellent question. What the hell is happening?

I pull at her neck, trying new angles, grabbing different sections of her thick body to extract her, and each time I do, she does not slide any farther out, but I can feel a hard pull on my hair. She's stuck in there. Tangled deep, deep in my sweaty, curling-ironed hair.

The little boy is still staring up at me with a slack jaw.

"Can I see the snake?" he finally asks, as if that weren't clear.

"Of course you can," I say, holding a great fake smile. "She's just being a little shy, but I'm trying to coax her out for you."

175

I try pushing this time, thinking that perhaps the tangle is one-directional, and like a child with her finger caught in Chinese finger trap, if the snake can only relax and move opposite her intuition, she can be free. She will not budge. Despite her thick, muscled body, with each pull or push I imagine the skin twisting just past its threshold and tearing open, guts and blood and the rat we fed her two days ago, hair mostly gone now and eyeballs out and body coated in some white and pink gooey slime, a whole package of horror bursting out of her body and sliding down my skin, down into my dress and tights and splashing onto the little boy's face, the giant limp body still stuck to me for all eternity, the snake carcass my Sisyphean boulder.

The little boy has now looked back to his parents for instructions, as the adult world isn't operating according to promise. They're looking at me with that same wide-jawed expectancy, but I can see in the mother's face that she understands something of what is happening here, a recognition of my panic or the potential for violence and she says, "Honey, looks like maybe the snake is too shy today," and walks toward the little boy, her arm toward him but her eye not leaving me, but the boy doesn't budge, stays firmly planted two feet from me in the hot, hot sun, his pink cheeks and little teeth still gleaming in the afternoon's brightness.

It doesn't matter how forcefully I try to pull her, the only pull I feel is on great patches of my scalp. As she's gotten herself farther in, her body has pressed against the back of my head, forcing my chin down to my chest, straining my neck. The mom reaches the boy, her hand on his back, and I look at her, mouth *sorry*, look at the boy and say, "I'll be right back," and turn and exit the stage. Big, Big Ben is working the ticket booth and hasn't taken his eyes off his phone's screen, where he's rereading the Harry Potter series.

"Ben," I hiss, but he doesn't move. "Ben," I say louder, and he grunts without turning around. "Ben, I need your help," I say louder, still trying to keep my voice out of the register that the family pacing in front of the bally stage might hear, but loud enough to draw him out of Hogwarts. He turns around, annoyed.

"What's the problem?" he says.

"The snake," I say in my most serious but not hyperventilating panicked whisper, "is stuck. In my hair." He takes a long second to look at me, longer than a quick moment of assessment, longer even than his usual longer processing time, or maybe it was just one second, but the snake was surely strangling in my ringlets so everything felt like forever. Finally, a half smile passes across his mouth.

"The snake is stuck in your hair?" he asks, and the half smile turns into a big-lipped, full-toothed grin, the brink of hilarity, my inadequacies a comedy club. "Oh man," he says, laughing, and turning back to Harry Potter.

"No! Ben! Please, this is serious!" I say, and he turns back to face me, still smiling.

"I really don't want to help you," he says.

"No, please," I plead. "Because it's way too funny."

"I know."

"To have a snake in your hair."

"It is. But she might be hurt! Please," I say.

"To have the snake trapped in your hair, now that's funny," he says, laughing, slapping his knee.

The family lingering up front loses patience with the sun and spies the shaded pig races down the midway and wanders off.

"I really don't want to help you," he says, reaching up toward my hair. I spin around, still clutching the larger section of her body in my hands and letting Ben's hands follow her neck up through my tangles, letting him part sections of my hair to see where she is.

"Oh man," Ben says. "She's really stuck in there."

"Is she okay? Is she alive?"

"No. She's not okay. She's stuck in your hair. I mean, she's fine, but there's a lot of hair wound around her body," he says, and I'm thinking of a spindle and then a hot dog in a hairball and a host of other inappropriate images, because it's really hard to picture a giant snake wrapped in human hair. "Hi, beauty," he says to the snake.

"Just get her out, Ben. Whatever you have to do," I say.

He glances around for something to help, but there's nothing close, no scissors or knife as far as we can see, and so he begins trying to wriggle her out. Both of my hands are behind my head, a few hairs being pulled out as he loosens tiny portions of her at a time.

"This is probably gonna hurt," he says, eyeing me.

"I don't care," I say. "Just please get her out."

He reaches both hands back again and I feel a series of small tugs and then one giant rip and sting and he grunts and my head is throbbing, but in his hands is the beautiful brown girl, eyes milky blue and unblinking, a sleeping bag of blond hairs circling her body. I reach back to touch my head, surprised that a large portion of skin isn't gone, surprised I'm not half-bald. In the stinging area, the hair feels thinner, but it doesn't matter.

Ben is still laughing to himself as he holds the snake, gently peeling the hairs off her body as she slowly climbs across his arms.

"Thank you, thank you, thank you," I say, welling up with relief.

"That was funny," he says, and I set Pandora down in her box to cool off, run backstage for a hair tie, put my hair in an ugly half bun without care for showmanship, wipe off the rest of my makeup with a baby wipe, come back onstage, and, not knowing what else to do, open my arms again to the snake.

EMERGENCY

Day 29 of 150

WORLD OF WONDERS
JULY 2013

Steve, the new burly working man, is holding his belly and moaning softly. It's our third night at the Kane County Fair in Illinois, and Steve asks Tommy to come offstage between ballys to talk. Steve's been with us for just over a week. They whisper together under the ticket awning and then Tommy comes onstage and the working man disappears.

"What's wrong with him?" I ask Tommy.

"Bellyache," Tommy says, eyes locking in on a young family vaguely looking in our direction.

An hour later, a medic approaches our stage in the middle of a bally asking for the boss. I take over, telling the crowd about the snake in the box in front of me as Tommy hops offstage and takes the medic to the side. Sometimes the added attention of emergency workers, who also come sometimes after we get a fainter—a falling ovation—can be a draw, a suggestion of danger for a show that already looks like something might imminently, violently fail. But this time Tommy takes him aside and, after a quick chat, whispers to me from the side of the stage that he'll be back. He follows the medic down the midway.

Cassie pops onto the stage to continue ballying shortly thereafter, and we finish out the hour without more information. A little while later, Tommy and Steve come back, Tommy walking quickly in front with a thin-mouthed grimace and Steve dragging behind, holding his side. They pass by the stage, making no eye contact with anyone as they round the edge of the tent and turn back to our bunkhouse.

Tommy comes back out a few minutes later alone.

"Everything okay?" I ask.

"We need a new working man."

"Where is he going?"

"On the bus back to Ohio."

"What happened?"

"Said his cannon fire stitches had burst open and he thought his guts were going to spill out. Wouldn't stop crying."

"And? Were they?"

He snorts. " 'Course not. I had him lift up his shirt to show me."

"Oh."

"He bought his own bus ticket home."

"Well, shit," I say.

"Oh well. Out another guy," Tommy says. "Couldn't hack it."

"Couldn't hack it," I say.

⚡

The fair is slow.

I crouch low from the bally stage to look through the entrance and see Pipscy inside, bouncing as she talks the bed of nails act for just one single person all alone in the audience.

There were stretches out on that bally stage, weekdays during the daytime especially, when nobody at all would walk by for twenty minutes, thirty, an hour, the absence finally punctuated by a young mother and her two small kids waddling past who, despite our best attempts to lure them in with a snake and magic and sword swallow, continued straight on without giving us more than a glance. I wondered, of those people who would walk straight past fire going into my mouth or a sword going down Tommy's throat, if they didn't believe what they saw. If they were too skeptical, too sure that whatever appeared to be happening was not in fact happening at all.

There was a tradition in the sideshow of things appearing questionable, controversial. P. T. Barnum took great pains to promote the dubiousness of his oddities' authenticity. Instead of concentrating on the authentication of his Feejee Mermaid as a real, genuine specimen, for example, he sent letters penned as a variety of authors to newspapers with doubts about the creature's very existence. Surely someone could discern whether the creature was cast from a mold or pulled from the sea? Whose eyes were sharp enough, whose wits quick enough? The only way to find out was to see it for yourself. It brought the audience into the act, charged each member with the role of scientific explorer, investigator.

After a long, long stretch with nobody walking by our stage, a boy of about eleven or twelve is running past when his eye catches one of our banners. On it, a headless woman's bloody neck is fitted with machinery. He stops running and assesses a few of the paintings.

Tommy asks, "Do you think you can be hypnotized by a snake?" The boy shakes his head no.

"Are these things real?" he says, pointing to the banners. "Oh yes, those are a hundred percent authentic banners," Tommy says with a grave nod.

"No," the boy tsks, "the stuff inside. Is it real or not? This is a freak show, right?"

Tommy bends forward a little, bringing his face closer to the boy's as if the midway were filled with marks who didn't deserve to know the secret he was about to reveal.

"You be the judge," he whispers.

The Laestrygonians are evil cannibalistic giants from Homer's *Odyssey*. The Kappa is a Japanese water demon made up of

181

the body of a tortoise, a beak, and the limbs of a frog. He eats disobedient children. Mermaids lure fishermen to drown. Monsters, giants, cyclops, centaurs, vampires, werewolves, griffins, minotaurs, sphinxes, satyrs. Many of our stories are made up of creatures who are partially human, who frighten us with what is both recognizably like us and different. They are us and not us.

We've changed our ideas about who, and what, makes a "freak." The medieval and early modern idea that a non-normative body was supernatural, some kind of omen or warning from God, has been gradually replaced by a belief that all bodies come from within the order of nature, but that natural order can be internally disrupted. The range of what occurs in nature both makes the idea of natural diversity more concrete and therefore wonderful, and seems to present an example of something that must be outside it. *Deformito-Mania* was the term coined by the magazine *Punch* in 1847 to describe the contemporary fascination with so-termed human curiosities.

Freak has been used for those who were born with, or who through an accident or illness acquired, a nonnormative body. Before adequate social services and advanced, widely available medicine, performing in a sideshow was one of the only ways for a "freak" to make a living. By contrast, a "geek," or working act, was a person who, from a wider range of options, chose to manipulate his body to make it nonnormative. Because of medical advancements, increased services and financial support, and declining social acceptance of "freaks" within freak shows, most of the performers on the circuit today, and largely those with the World of Wonders, are geeks. But there is a real awe for traditional freaks within our show. Stories circulate about past performers who were the show's brightest stars. There's buzz about a performer who'd be joining us later this season.

The language used to describe people and things within

a sideshow has continually shifted. In the Victorian era, the word was *curiosity*, used in Charles Dickens's freak-obsessed work, *The Old Curiosity Shop*. P. T. Barnum, in the late nineteenth and early twentieth centuries, called the people who performed in his shows "curiosities," the same name he used for taxidermied oddities on display in his museums. Around this time, too, the term *freak of nature* was commonly applied to something that had developed "abnormally." It is from this term that the idea of the "freak" performer is derived, and the term, while not common anymore, is still used to describe nonnormative performers. Many performers on the sideshow circuit now embrace the term, for the same reason as some in the LGBTQ community have reclaimed the term *queer*—to take back the word's power.

But *freak* has meant many different things in our last American century, as has other language used to describe those with different bodies. As early as 1908, *freak* applied to a person obsessed with something, originating with *Kodak freak*, a camera-obsessed person.

Monsters and *monstrosities* were the standard medical labels for people with physical differences until the early twentieth century.

In 1945, *freak* was used to mean "drug user."

In the 1960s, *freak* was claimed by the socially dissident hippies, who chose to participate in activities like eating LSD, which made them "freak out." This freakiness was self-proclaimed and self-made.

In 1990, Digital Underground released the song "Freaks of the Industry." Here, the rappers call themselves freaks for their sexual prowess, and the women they're with are freaks for the same reason, and together, they're "freakin'," meaning, having sex. As a strange counterpoint to all that, when I looked up the words to the Digital Underground song, they scrolled across the screen on top of a still image of Schlitzie, the pinhead from the 1932 movie *Freaks*. In Tod Browning's pre-Code horror movie, deemed too shocking to be released, the characters in a freak show are played by real freak-show performers, though the true monsters of the film are their foes, the norms.

⚡

The mermaid can't hack it.

I learn this on the toilet. Sunshine walks with me on the long trudge down the midway, up a hill, right beside the slushie truck, and down the next midway that runs along the goat barn, to the bathrooms. It has been a week since Steve went home, and we're at another county fair in Illinois just a few hours from the last. Sunshine and I go inside separate bathroom stalls, and in the momentary silence, she says, "How would you like to become an inside performer?"

As we walked into the building, I'd glimpsed myself in the mirror and noticed that my skin had taken on a purple hue. Five weeks of twelve hours a day in the Midwest summer out in the direct sun meant my body was taking and taking in the heat, skin pulling in all the sun's offerings, the hair I'd dyed dark brown before joining the show faded first to a mousy brown with blond streaks and then blond-blond, and I loved it at first, felt like a solar panel, charging myself on the sun. But the heat built fast and woozy hour after hour, the sweat pooling in my corset, my vision getting blurry. And the color of my skin, which always gets to a dark olive tan in the sun, had gone beyond that into some sorts of navy and purple and was probably a dermatologist's nightmare. And so, at the moment, this question sounded like a dream.

"You could learn all the acts, not just the bally acts. It would give you a chance to try out every position here. What do you think?" she says, coming out of the toilet stall.

"I think yes," I say. "But what happened to Pipscy?"

"Pipscy is homesick, she misses her boyfriend, blah blah

184

blah. We're gonna be hiring new performers for the season's big fairs anyway, and it's easiest to hire bally girls, since they don't really have to be able to do anything already, and you know the show now, how things work."

It was still a surprise, given how uneasy I was to begin here with almost no skills, that no skills are needed to be a bally girl. The idea of joining a show as a performer with nothing to perform is strange. And yet, it makes more sense the further along we are. How after just one day of performing, I had those acts down pat and, in the scheme of things, one mediocre day of figuring it out didn't matter.

Pipscy has done a very decent thing, Sunshine explains, and told the bosses of her departure in advance, a week and a half or so. The ads have just gone up on Craigslist for temporary performers to join a traveling circus sideshow. What would it be like to come across that by accident? I don't know if I would have believed it was real.

"I'm in," I say, ready for the next chapter.

There's that one inside act I've had my eye on since the beginning. It sits on Red's stage, separate from the main stage, and amazes me every time I glance inside and see Pipscy performing it. The electric chair. Red flips a switch and the electric woman, seated on the chair, is filled with electricity. She lights bulbs off her fingertips and tongue. I don't yet know how it works.

I'm in a sitting-in-the-electric-chair daydream onstage later that day when Cassie asks a woman emerging from the tent whether she likes our show. Cassie often asks customers what their favorite part of the show is as they walk out—as long as they don't walk out shaking their heads or looking upset. It gives her the opportunity to repeat into the mic what they say, adding enthusiasm, offering a teaser.

"It was boring," the woman says.

Boring?

I flip through my first experience watching the show, trying

185

to imagine if any of it was boring. A little corny, yes, not always totally believable, but never boring.

"We were hoping for blood and guts," the woman says, slowly walking away. She looks incensed, with a pinched expression that Sunshine calls a fart face, as if she were smelling something wretched. Sometimes you'd see those faces out in the audience, supremely unimpressed by whatever you were doing. But to be so vocal about the show being boring baffles me. Is it unclear that these are real human beings inside the show made up of actual blood, actual guts, some of which they are showing to the audience for two dollars?

"We didn't see anything cool, no extreme gore at all."

Cassie turns toward the other people gathering near the stage. "And there you are, folks," she says into her mic. "Proof of the harmful effects of television's desensitization. Come inside the show right now and interact with real human beings with real human blood and guts and see them perform real human feats of wonder."

The woman walks off.

"What a dummy," I say.

Cassie assures me that the giant state fairs we're headed into will have fewer idiots to think our show is boring than there have been in some of these smaller fairs, but then she corrects herself and says there'll just be too many other people for them to stick out much.

"It'll finally be time for this," Sunshine says, sticking her pointer finger out at me. There are four letters tattooed along the side of her finger closest to her thumb: GTFM.

"What's that mean?"

"When people outside the show ask what it means, back at home and stuff, I tell them it means Get That For Me. You know, as stage manager, I'm always pointing at things and bossing people around."

"But it doesn't?"

186

"GTFM is carnie code. It's about the bottom line. About doing whatever you have to do to get by out here and make it worthwhile. GTFM: Get the fucking money."

⚡

A few months after my interview at that fancy private high school, I'd received a letter letting me know I was on the waiting list. The scholarships were limited and the application pool unprecedentedly large, so I'd just need to wait.

My mom opened the school's most recent newsletter. "Look, their play opens Friday. Why don't we go to it?" she said.

"Don't you think it's weird if I show up since they're still deciding if they want me?" I said.

"I'm calling now to buy the tickets." When the play was over and the lights rose above the audience, she stood me up and pointed across the crowd. "There," she said, "is your target."

A man was just standing up, chatting with and smiling at those around him.

"The headmaster," she said. "Go."

"What am I supposed to say to him?" I asked.

"It doesn't matter," she said. "Introduce yourself. Say you're on the waiting list. Say that you see yourself here. That this is your place."

I looked around the theater with its plush emerald seats, big wooden stage, and lights. It wasn't my place, not yet, but I could just glimpse the roughest edge of a fantasy where it was. Getting there took more courage than I had.

"No," I said. "I don't know what to say to him." I started to turn around and walk out.

"Tessa," she said, slowly. I didn't move. "Sometimes you've just got to do the hard thing." She stared me down. Then, she grabbed my hand and pulled me over to the headmaster, introducing us both. She explained to him how I saw myself there.

A week later, I received another letter. I'd been accepted,

with a full scholarship. On the bottom of the letter was a handwritten note from the headmaster. *It was so good to see you last week. The kind of interest and dedication you showed by coming to the play are exactly the kinds of characteristics we look for in our students. We honor perseverance. Welcome!*

FRESH MEAT

Day 39 of 150

WORLD OF WONDERS
AUGUST 2013

As unofficial alternate shuttle driver, I am tasked with heading to the airport and bus station to pick up the new performers. We are getting four at once, three who will be with us for one month and one who will stay for just two weeks. Other performers will join later in the season, as we go.

There are three new bally girls, all of whom have some performance experience, and one new inside performer, who has an act he's been doing for years. Francine comes in from Oakland, a beautiful pinup burlesque performer who can eat fire and has dreamed of working with our iconic show for years. She arrives with armloads of boxes and suitcases, unpacking beautiful beaded tassel bras and belly dancing skirts and different-size hot rollers and feather boas and scarves, a glamorous tattooed beauty moving into a dirty truck. She is not thrilled.

Rachel flies in from Pennsylvania and has attended Coney Island sideshow school. She immediately demonstrates her human blockhead act, jamming a screwdriver deep into her nostril. Before she joined us, she ate glass for one of the touring nightclub shows and stays pretty quiet most of the time, though she also arrives with some amazing costume pieces.

The third female performer is Jessie, a local girl, who will be

189

with us for just two weeks and looks like a mad scientist drew a sexy cartoon—with fire-engine red hair and tight-fitting white tank tops over too-tight black bras. It is immediately clear she knows some tricks that I have yet to learn about how to get things from the carnies. Most nights she strolls backstage with a foot-long corn dog or giant turkey leg that some carnie has given her just because.

The one new male performer is Brian, a lanky young guy in a bowler hat who walks out of the airport with a backpacking rucksack, a wooden board in one hand, and juggling clubs in the other. In addition to juggling acts, he also performs the rolla bolla, a balancing act where a short rectangle of wood is set on top of a cylinder, and the performer balances atop the board as it rolls around. On top of the rolla bolla he ties balloon animals or puts his body through a hoop or juggles. He walks outside first thing in the morning, hair pointing every direction, and, in his undershirt and boxer shorts, begins juggling the way another person might stretch or brush his teeth.

There is not enough space for the new performers to have beds in the back of our truck. Sunshine unfolds cots in our main backstage area with sheets hung between some of them at night for privacy. New bunks.

A flat wooden board is set on top of a lighting rack, a thin camping mat laid across it, and Brian's room is formed. Other mats are rolled out across the stage, and people find places to sleep wherever they need. In truth, there is so little time spent sleeping, and we are so exhausted when that time comes, the accommodations almost don't matter.

It feels good to have this fresh blood among us after the same faces day in and out for nearly forty days. But I also feel wary. Maybe Tommy or Red will take to one of them; maybe they'll prove their worth here quickly and make my presence unnecessary. I keep a little distance, watch them carefully.

The first night, we all head to a carnie bar just off the fairgrounds. It's packed with loud, chain-smoking men and women, most of whom are obviously people who spend all day outside, who work with their hands. The crew who have been out with World of Wonders for previous seasons greet the carnies, laughing about stories from past years, lamenting those who've been lost since then.

"I love Francine," Cassie says loud and often, hugging and kissing her. We've found a table on the back porch that most of us are sitting around. "I'm so glad Francine is here, she's just so hilarious and fun." The other new arrivals quietly sip their beers. I'd started being snappy with Cassie lately. She is so loud all the time. So quick to say something mean to someone on the crew, though she is always joking. So fast to say how much she loves people to get what she wants. There is such volatility, and I am getting too tired to be good at holding on for the ride.

You're a nice person, or you *could* be a nice person, I tell myself on the walk back from the bar. Mean people are usually hurting more than the rest of us, I try to remember. Be kind to Cassie, I try to remind myself. But a shadowy golem in my head asks whether niceness is really what is going to keep me afloat out here, or anywhere.

Yes, it is, I think. Right?

⚡

The human teeth clink like gentle bells. In a small glass in the van's cup holder, they are a shadowy white nearing gray and look fragile, almost hollow. They have failed to keep themselves inside their human mouth despite their rooting and pinching and grabbing.

The teeth belong to our current working man. Every few hours, since he'd started with us two days before, he'd swear and spit and another hard object would fall out of his mouth and into his hand.

Drew was hired from bum tryouts. After Cannon Fire Steve quit, we went without a working man for the next ten days to save a little bit of money, which meant that Big, Big Ben had to do twice his regular work—both acting as a ticket man and doing all the repair and labor jobs. Before we showed up in Wisconsin for the first meat-grinder, Tommy had posted an ad on Craigslist, and a handful of down-and-out-looking folks seeking temporary employment—under the table, no questions asked—showed up. The boss chatted with them, asked them to help for an hour or so with setup to see how they moved, checking if anyone looked tired or like they thought the labor was difficult, which it was. He'd given each of them ten or twenty bucks for that hour of work and then hired the one who looked like he had the most staying power. Drew looked promising. He had worked hard and kept quiet and barely broken a sweat.

The first day, he claims bad allergies as he grinds his knuckles into his eyes again and again like he can force the irritant out of himself. Allergies are the reason for his narrowed eyes, he says, and also the reason why whenever we pause our labor, he falls asleep.

He looks very tender asleep. Most of his neck and arms and hands are covered in tattoos, many of which look homemade, like he was a pad of paper on the lap of a child who kept doodling spiderwebs and skulls and unintelligible words. I have always loved people who fall asleep at unexpected times, or in surprising places. On a bus, midtest at a hospital. I like the idea that the brain can't quite keep control over the body, that the body gives up its defenses. That they suddenly rejoin the world of the awake with wonder.

The second day, Drew arrives forty-five minutes late, sweating, puffy-faced, a red rash across his cheeks, swaying, his eyelids barely open.

"I'm sorry," he says to Tommy. "It was my daughter. She couldn't sleep last night. Sick." He rocks gently back and forth, his hunched shoulders making little empty caves in his collarbones. Damn daughters.

"What happened to your face?" the boss doesn't ask Drew,

but I wish he had. Instead, he whispers "strike one" as Drew passes, but his tone is almost apologetic. Drew goes right to work, hauling wood behind the show that needs repainting, hustling behind Big, Big Ben even as Big, Big Ben very openly rolls his eyes at the tardiness and excuses.

"I don't do drugs," says Drew, slurring. "I used to have a problem, but not anymore."

His face is so red and swollen, it looks like he has been beat up pretty badly or caught a serious case of poison oak, all in the eight or nine hours since we'd quit work last night. As the first hour passes, the puffiness doesn't go down at all, and it is hard to tell if he can see anything out of the slits between the meat puffs of his eyelids.

It is opening day at the Wisconsin State Fair, and I am taking one last shift on the bally stage with the snake, waiting for the crowds to flock. The late morning sun is growing hotter, and Drew is in the ticket booth nodding off. Ticket taking is the working man's other duty, the only requirement for which is to stay awake and be able to count out change. I can help him with one of those.

"How old's your daughter?" I ask him.

"Three," he says. "She's a princess." I nod, make eyes at a passerby. "Or four," he says, moving his lips suddenly into a tight circle. His tongue is moving against his cheek on the inside of his mouth. He lifts his hand to his lips and spits out a tooth. "She's four."

"Where is she right now?" I ask, trying to eye the tooth. This is not my business, but these are the kinds of details I can't help but barrel toward. The intricacies of other people's lives. Their confessions.

"My mom is looking after her," he says.

The tooth is dressed in a sheen of spit and lies nested in his half-closed fist. "I'm making money so I can help her out. Take care of my little girl myself."

His eyes begin to close but he jerks awake. "She's a real cutie," he says, sitting tall on the stool and continuing to talk like he's been telling the same story in his sleep and just keeps on telling it. But it doesn't take long—fifteen or twenty seconds—and his eyelids slide closed again. He works for a few flutters to pull them back up toward his brow, to continue his story, until the words slur and the fight against gravity becomes too much for his upper lids and they find the lower. A few more words come out, impossible to understand, and then a few seconds of total rest before he nods back awake, still talking. He manages to not fall off the stool.

Lost tooth as wishing stone.

The evening before, after setup, a few of us loaded into the van and went to a sandwich shop. Drew headed right into the bathrooms. Cassie and I ordered and sat down at a booth, where I tried to scooch far back into the bench to make evident space beside me. We ate our sandwiches, and after coming out of the bathroom Drew ordered, keeping his voice low and soft, keeping his teeth in his mouth as far as I could tell. He sat at the booth behind us.

"Do you want to join us?" I asked, but he shook his head.

"That's okay," he said, and the purple crescent moons beneath his eyes caught a glint of neon light from the window's sign. He was quiet despite my continued harassment, carefully pulling a chip at a time out of the bag and eating it in small bites until, half a bag in, he said he was full. The sandwich remained untouched.

Driving back, Drew slipped the teeth out from his pocket— where they might have felt sharp against his thigh, or where he might have been afraid they'd break even further, if something like that would even be a concern—and dropped them into the water cup he'd just finished drinking from. He was in the front seat, and held the cup in both hands for a minute or so, looking down the clear plastic tunnel like some prophecy lay

194

inside. I hoped those mangled roots and ground white edges weren't his future. He sighed, jammed the cup into the small storage pocket on the passenger door and left it there when he climbed out.

"What's Drew's thing?" I asked Cassie later that night.

"Methadone," she said.

"Meth?"

"No. The drug they give you to get off meth. And heroin. He's a junkie."

I looked across the tent to where Drew sat on the edge of the stage, waiting for the boss, staring off into the darkness with the two eternal sinkholes of his eyes.

The next morning, I decided I'd ask him more about his daughter, because maybe talking about her would give him some sort of spirit he might have been having a hard time finding lately. Because all the men on the road with us had little daughters they'd left somewhere, and I wanted to believe, had to believe, that the idea of their daughters had the capacity to rouse some love or healing or determination in them, something. I wasn't ignorant enough to think that it could cure Drew of a drug addiction, or that I could really help, but I still wanted to try. To focus on someone else's suffering.

I waited, thinking nothing of it when a few minutes after Drew was supposed to arrive passed and he didn't show up. Then a half hour, an hour, two. Ben was back in the ticket booth. By the end of the day Drew had still not shown up, and that was that. He never came back.

I thought about all the questions I'd asked, the stories I'd tried to pry out of him in the three days he was with us, and wondered if instead of bringing him closer to some nebulous state of peace, I'd actually done the opposite. Maybe he looked at me and saw who I really was: a person who had chosen to run. I was not working to care for my loved ones like he was. I had said goodbye and flown thousands of miles away. My head played the recursive loop of leaving: flying to California to see my mom for a few days, then flying back to Alabama for a few weeks, thinking of her constantly, calling Davy all the time—Davy, who was wildly stressed and depressed and barely hanging in there himself. I had left, and then left, and then left, and then left. And while I was away from her, I made it through the day by imagining that she was already gone.

How might my mother have healed if she'd had my love constantly by her side to buoy her in the months and then years after her massive stroke? Would she have regained her ability to walk? To talk? What if there'd been a chance, however improbable, of her waking up one morning and writing *take me to the beach*, and all of us bundling her and supporting her on both sides as we crossed the sand and stood at the rim of the Pacific, putting our toes into the cold water and letting that sun warm our faces? It's impossible to listen to all the echoes of what of might have happened without going deaf from the cacophony.

A few weeks later, Sunshine is in the passenger seat and notices them, their brown and gray and white roots.

"Gross," she says, pulling the cup of teeth from the door. "This is disgusting."

Tommy grins and starts drumming on the steering wheel with excitement, holds his hand out for the cup. He dumps the teeth into the palm of his giant hand and turns them around in his fingers like golden coins. He is laughing, this high-pitched *tee-hee-hee* he lets out whenever something deeply delights him.

"Anyone else?" he asks into the rearview mirror, holding the teeth in the air. Everyone shakes their heads. "Your loss," he says, still giggling. "Thank god for junkies." He pours the teeth back into the cup and plants it in the dashboard's drink holder, where it remains for the rest of the season, adventuring with us across the country.

THE TITANIC WAS
CHILD'S PLAY

Two and three-quarters years after the stroke

---

10 DAYS INTO MY PARENTS' TRIP
AUGUST 2013

My parents' train derails somewhere in Nebraska. Or just out-side Chicago. Or in the Sierra Nevadas. It happens suddenly in the middle of the night, throwing the passengers out of their bunks and onto the floor, against the wall. The force throws my mother's whole body up from the flat plane of the bed and into the air, freeing her limbs from gravity, from paralysis. Imagine it, the body loosed and airborne, the soft angle of a shoulder floating through space. Like a woman underwater. For the first moment, at least. Before the body's smack.

In my dream, the train crash isn't beautiful. I want to remember it beautiful, to put lightning bugs out in the cornfields, to see the egg-tip of moon up in the sky and the blues of the night fingering over one another like Van Gogh's starry night. But it isn't. The dreams are brutal.

The next dream has them in the small room they'll be living in while they take the boat across the Atlantic. It is Davy this time, dead on the ground while my mom sits beside him in her wheelchair, the pee collecting beneath her, her cries collecting in the room, staring at him for minutes, hours, days, unable to

197

know how to get help, what to do, unable to do anything. Just watching while possibilities for help fade away.

These aren't dreams I have at night. I am too tired by the time I lay my head down to think about anything much at all and my subconscious seems to feel the same. I fall right asleep, sleep through the night, wake in the morning to do it all again. Some mornings I wake and wish so deeply to be waking, instead, in a room by myself with a locking door and a few hours to do as I wish. But when I play that out—what I would do next: read? cook eggs?—the action inevitably turns to doing something to keep my mom safe, to helping Davy, and again, as it's been for two and a half years, I don't know what to do. Here, I get up out of my bunk and know exactly what to do.

Many of the nightmares are actually waking daydreams. I want to believe they bubble up out of my subconscious, as dreams do, but I think, mostly, they are conscious attempts at practicing for the worst. They happen as I sit backstage between acts, staring out the trailer's back end into the late morning sun on the pig races next to us, the little pigs' pink skin becoming the purse of the woman who happens to walk under a window in Italy and smell something foul, who happens to know the old woman who owns and rents out the little apartment where she smells the bad smell and whom she accompanies to check on the current renters, an American couple, one handicapped, who have been quiet as little mice and are now two rotting corpses.

"You know what's really neat? Watching the color of the rocks change as you move across the country," Davy says. We're on the phone, finally, a few days into their journey. I'd called and texted a few times, and he hadn't responded. Too busy, he said. The train had stopped over in Chicago and they'd switched trains and now they were in New York and things were FINE.

"They go from gray to almost gold and then you get the red rocks, which have orange in them, and then granite in some places. It's just really neat to see," he said.

"How's Mom?"

"Na na na na," she says into the phone.

"Great, she's great," he says.

"And you?"

"Great, too."

"Great."

"Well, the train car was a little small," he says. "We got bumped around in there quite a bit, trying to get to the toilet."

"How bad?"

"Not bad."

"How bad?"

"Just some bruises. No big deal. We're going to Times Square tomorrow. Mom wants to get a hot dog from one of those vendors on the street. And then we're gonna sit out there and people watch. I'm sure she'll want extra relish. My pickle girl."

"Na na na na," she says.

"Well, we better run, cutie," he says.

"Na na," my mom says.

"I love you, too," I say. We hang up.

For the next part of their act, if you can believe your eyes, the two great American daredevils will board a ship and set off across the Atlantic. For nine days, they'll be aboard the vessel with no phone service and expensive Internet. Don't expect to hear from us, they say. They'll be too busy fighting for the best view of the dolphins jumping alongside the ship.

"Mom got a set of paints and a notebook and wanted to record street life in New York," Davy says. "She wanted them for the ship, too. We're going to find a little table next to a window that looks out over the water, and she's going to paint and I'm going to whittle and we're going to just sit there. We haven't had time to do anything like that in a long, long time."

"She was a very serious little girl," my grandmother told me once, of my mother. "She turned into a funny woman, but when she was young, she was very serious. Two things happened at around the same time. First, she realized how much she loved to draw, and second, she started believing in Jesus. She'd sit at this little desk in her room for hours drawing excruciatingly detailed depictions of Jesus on the cross. Perfectly shaded thorns on his crown, spherical droplets of blood hanging by a thread from his palms and feet. Picture after picture she would draw, like she was trying to exorcise something out of herself. Like there would be some truth, or salvation, if she could just get the angles right.

"The rest of us weren't very religious. We'd go to church on Sundays, I mean, like all good people from Oklahoma were raised to do, but she was the one in the family that took it to a new level. Went to a camp for Christian kids, then became a counselor there as a teenager. She loved it, was gaga for Jesus. But one summer, when she came home, she said that was it. That she'd never go back again."

My mom had told me a story about this, once, with some sadness. After the first session ended, there were a few days before the new campers arrived when she and the other counselors had meetings and planning sessions. One of the primary topics was how to get the campers to have a moment of salvation or, for those not devout enough, who'd been sent there by worried parents, maybe, to feel some sort of light godly pressure to convert. That was what many of the daily activities were structured around, the pressure to show other campers you'd found God.

This was crushing. All those years of believing that finding God came from somewhere beautiful, somewhere inside, now seemed a sham.

When she believed in something, she wanted to believe in it all the way. For its beauty. For the way it felt true inside. But she never wanted to be duped. Never wanted to seem like she wasn't smart.

She stopped drawing Jesus and became a hippie instead.

Some of those ideas, some of what Jesus taught, some of what the free-flowing skirt people taught, were the same. And these were the things she carried with her. Kindness. Sacrifice.

Driving in the car to a soccer tournament when I was thirteen or fourteen, she'd made two pieces of toast each for us with mayonnaise and sliced garden tomatoes, big thick red slabs. I ate my two, scarfed them down the way a teenager would, and she'd just finished her first slice.

"Here," she said, "eat my other one. I'm not hungry anymore." We had hours and hours ahead of us on the foggy soccer fields. I knew it wasn't true that she wasn't hungry, knew it wasn't a nice thing for me to do, but I gobbled down that other piece of toast, too, licked the mayonnaise from my fingers, and, later, tried not to look at her much from the other side of the field where I sat on the sidelines across to where she sat on the sidelines, chatting with one of the other moms probably wearing pearls, knowing not to wave at me, but watching me. We watched each other a lot. She wanted something from me. She was desperate with how much she wanted it. I thought it was success, to have a daughter who did all the things she hadn't done—go to college, have a career, achieve financial stability, be a person other people called smart. Find a job with health insurance. Dental insurance. Move forward in the world with a paycheck. She believed in art but wanted desperately for me never to be an artist. It took me a long, long time to figure out that although all that was important to her, it wasn't the main point.

"There's one thing missing from my life," she told me when I was twenty-one. "One thing that has been the biggest heart-break of my life. The biggest hole. It's you. It's that you don't love me."

I didn't say anything back.

I knew this was the wrong thing to do. This was a moment where she was reaching across our chasm and all I had to do was say what was true, which is that there was always love,

201

even if it sometimes felt like a broken train, like a suitcase of weapons, like a sick dog. Even if I didn't always believe my love was true.

I like to think that if I'd known that in five years we'd never be able to have a spoken conversation again, I would have grabbed her hands and, tears cresting, told her that of course I loved her then and always had, that I was so sorry I'd been cold and distant but that I'd felt hurt by her for so many years and it seemed like distance from her made the hurt feel better. And maybe now could be a time we could start again and get to know one another.

But I didn't know the future. I only knew I had a little power. I stayed silent. It was one step kinder than what I'd said to her in the past.

MONSTERS
Day 49 of 150

WORLD OF WONDERS
AUGUST 2013

One afternoon, I see the boss laughing and chatting with a short guy who is gesturing around our stage with great familiarity. His head darts back and forth, scanning the tent like he's selling hot watches from his trench coat. I lose track of him while I perform, but when I return from my act he's waiting for me backstage.

"Hey, can I talk to you?" he asks me. Eyes the other girls. "Privately?"

We walk out back as I hear the guillotine music begin, which means I have about four minutes until I need to slide into the headless woman's chair. A few carnies are walking in a cluster along the dirt road we're parked beside, an entryway to the back alleys of carnietown, and I can see my toothpaste spit from that morning drying in the dust.

"I'd love for you to get eaten by a monster," he says, grinning. I'm silent. Interested, obviously, but wary. "I make these movies," he says. Tommy had told me that a guy named Raymond would show up at the fair, and that he was eccentric and hyper and made some adult movies, and that he was a friend of the show's. "There's a monster named Vore I've built and you'd be tied up and eaten by him. If you agree, after the fair closes one of these nights, I'll pick you up and bring you to my studio, and we'll film you getting pretend-eaten by a huge papier-mâché monster, I'll give you a hundred bucks, and bring you back. Sunshine has already agreed. She'll be the dominatrix. I'm going to ask Pipscy, too. You two will be sidekicks. No nudity, no violence, nothing you don't want to do. Just getting eaten. Oh, by the way, I'm Raymond. How's that sound?"

Three nights later, Raymond meets us as the show is closing at midnight and leads the three of us, each carrying a bag with costume options and a makeup case, down the darkening midway. I would never do this alone, but I trust these women, and they seem to feel just fine about going with Raymond. The lingering carnies wipe down the counters in food trucks or hang new prize stock in their game stands. I expect a big truck or old Chevy convertible out in the parking lot. I am surprised when Raymond unlocks the door of a midnineties Honda, the back seat sprinkled with Cheerios and a baby-doll bib beneath a car seat.

"Wanna see pictures of my niece?" he says, and begins scrolling through a series of photos on his phone: the baby behind a plate of spaghetti, the baby tottering across a wide, open field.

"Raymond? We should get going if we want to get back before we open tomorrow morning." Sunshine nudges him.

"Oh, right," he says, "that's good. You should keep me on track. Whenever I start to lose track like that, just say, 'Raymond! Stay focused!' And I'll try to get focused. I'm just"—he stops to giggle for a moment— "so easily distractable."

Twenty minutes later, we pull into the driveway of a suburban brick house. The kitchen windowsill is covered in owl figurines; crocheted pot holders and sunflower dish towels hang from the oven. There are checkered drapes by the windows and the smell of years of pot roast and rhubarb pie baked into the Formica. I don't even know what rhubarb pie smells like, but still I believe it's what the kitchen smells like, the idea of rhubarb, the idea of readying for a picnic in the shade on a June day in the Wisconsin suburbs.

"I got the call when I was with the World of Wonders," Raymond says, tossing pink puzzle pieces back into a box. "My mom had just died." The fridge hums behind his whispered explanation as he gets up and searches one of the cabinet drawers for pens. "I left the show, came home right away. That's when I started making movies." For four years since then, he's been living in this house with his dad, who's getting on in years. He helps his sister, who lives close by, with her daughter. He makes his movies down in the basement.

"Here we go," Raymond says, setting down three stacks of paper and three pens in front of us. "A contract?" I ask.

"To protect the adult entertainment biz. So that actors can't have some come-to- Jesus moment later in life and ask that their kinky porn be taken down by the production company."

I can see the words *Moral Consent* printed along the top of the paper.

"Driver's license?" he asks, holding his hand out.

I'm surprised by the formality surrounding this papier-mâché-monster-fetish-movie-filmed-in-dad's-basement, but it also feels somehow good to be bound to this. To have no option of backing out. Aside from agreeing that Raymond can use any video or audio he takes at any point tonight for any purpose, there is no more information about a binding "moral code," what it means to give away the rights to one's own future moral perspective. There are plenty of contracts to be locked into—loans, cell phones, insurance claims—but they are all uninterested in the kind of people we will become. This contract asks that my judgment at this moment be forever binding. How much do I trust myself right now? I sign.

Raymond has requested bare legs, so I peel off the fishnets I've been wearing for fifteen hours. Per usual, I have the distinct imprint of diamonds down my legs, something reptilian or fishy. I have on bicycle shorts beneath my velvet flapper

205

dress, and heels. Because it is already the end of a fifteen-hour performing day, I look like I'm at the end of a fifteen-hour performing day. Sweaty. Makeup a little smeared beneath my eyes, glittery on the bluish puffs, and the black specks of fallen mascara on my cheeks. I take out my makeup kit and try to do some of the fix-its I've learned on the road, dotting concealer under my eyes, adding another, darker line of liquid eyeliner on top of the fading, smudged one, applying new lipstick. I'm getting better at burying who I am.

Two steps down into the basement and I stop. Must. Scents of the other world, of families, of my grandmother's basement with a furnace that would whoosh on, its starving mouth full of fire and malice, this American middle-class suburban basement smell that, though I've only been on the road for two months, feels alien in its suggestion of permanence, the possibility of generations living together under the reign of mothballs.

It's hard to miss the monster in the basement. He is huge, rounded, about four feet by four feet, big enough to eat a whole human, green, made of papier-mâché and foam. Before we start shooting, Raymond brings his can of green spray paint over for some touch-ups.

"Try not to touch the monster except for when you're being eaten," he says, touching Vore. He pulls his hand away and it's covered in green crumbles. Vore is decomposing.

"What's he made of?" I ask.

"Lady bodies," Raymond says. He moves quickly around the basement, setting up his tripods and framing images from behind the stairs, on top of the box of Christmas ornaments, his flip-flops thwacking against his heels as he steps. I haven't seen him hold still for more than two seconds since I met him.

"Okay, here's the plot," he says. "Tessa and Pipscy are chained up, back to back, over here. You guys figure out why," he says, nodding over to us. "At some point, Sunshine will come into the frame. She's your capturer. I don't care who throws who into the monster, but at some point, you will escape or be

206

released from the chains and then each be thrown or fall into Vore, or he will decide to eat you himself and his giant pink tongue will capture you. Sound good?"

We nod.

"Don't worry," he says, spray-painting the sections of Vore that just crumbled off. "We'll make it look good. I like taking advantage of creative inspiration as I go."

"Well, let's go quickly, Raymond," Sunshine says. "It's already one forty-five and I want a cigarette."

"For the record," Raymond says, suddenly serious and standing up straight, "I don't know why this turns people on. The monster thing." He looks from one face to another with some hint of apology in his eyes for just a flash, but then it's gone and he's back to arranging optimal locations for the camera.

"Don't look at the camera, and kinda overact," he says. "Big gestures play well. Thrashing and struggling. That's what makes the hits."

There's an old exercise bike in one corner of the basement, boxes of seasonal decorations in another. In between, shelves and piles and stacks gather the physical refuse of a loss, the banal items that you somehow don't seem to have enough authority to get rid of. I know about these items. Picnic baskets. A waffle iron.

He places Pips and me on a crate, back to back, our arms crossed behind our backs and touching one another, then takes a long chain-link metal rope, wraps our wrists individually and then together. He's crouched low between us, giggling as he goes.

"It's the strangest thing," he says. "Right after my mom died, I made this animated short of a monster eating a girl and put it on YouTube. Just for fun, you know? It got a hundred thousand hits. Blew me away. Too tight?" he asks.

We wriggle our wrists.

"Not tight enough," Pips says, then lets out a long, low evil-villain laugh. Her eyes don't have that sleepy tilt Sunshine and

207

I both have, and it's true she's younger than me by a few years, but there's something else. Being here seems to have sparked some fuses that cause her to light up. Plus, she only has a few days left performing with the sideshow, and then she'll make her way back down to her home in Florida, though nobody is really talking about that.

"I'm not gonna tie the ends of this chain-link," Raymond says. "I'm just gonna tuck it behind your hands so when I tell you that you've struggled enough and can escape, you can just shake this off. That'll be a funny joke. Right? Don't you think that'll be a funny joke?"

Pipscy starts thrashing around in rehearsed panic. By virtue of our attachment, I do, too.

"Can we be funny in this?" I ask.

"Oh sure," he says. "As long as you also fight the chains and monster. But just know I might cut out some of your dialogue."

"I make a very good angry hero," Pips says.

"I can't wait to feed these girls to the monster," Sunshine says, eyes not leaving her phone's screen. But she smiles, a lovely, genuine, private smile that breaks my heart a little with its tenderness, with its purported disinterest in what we're doing but clear love for being down here together, for performing. Maybe even some love for us.

We begin filming, Pips and I tied up and bantering about escape plans. When we say something that Raymond thinks is particularly clever or actually seems to advance the improvised plot in some way, which is nearly never, he yells, "Pause!" and moves the camera to a different angle, and has us repeat the same line again. I suppose this is a trick of the cinema, to emphasize a line of dialogue by changing camera angles just before the line, jarring the viewer almost imperceptibly.

We finally break free from the chains by using our wits and are bickering about how to next escape from the room when suddenly Raymond yells "Freeze!"

He uncoils a long pink cloth that he hooks inside Vore's mouth, unstretching it all the way to Pipscy's waist. "Hold this," he says, placing her hands against her hips as she holds the tongue in place, "and hold still." He runs back to the camera, takes a few seconds of film, and returns to Pipscy, wrapping the tongue a little farther around her. He tells her to hold still, runs back to the camera, and repeats this series of actions until Vore has her coiled inside his tongue and pulls her into his mouth.

"I'll fix all this in editing," he says, "but for now, Pipscy, I need you to yell and kick and fight, flail your legs out of Vore's mouth as much as you can without actually breaking the monster in half, and when I give you the okay, slide down his throat." She obliges.

"Finally, she's dead!" I yell toward Vore's empty mouth when we begin rolling again. Sunshine's turn. You can hear her five-inch heels tapping and thumping as she enters the frame. She's in a leather corset and tiny black booty shorts and, in all ways, looks like she knows what she's doing. I keep hoping my years of school plays will become useful any moment here, but so far I'm relying on overacting and a poor imitation of whatever the other girls are doing. Luckily, my time is nearly up.

Sunshine backs me up with accusations until I'm just outside Vore's green, flaky lips. She pushes me in. Here we pause again so Raymond can best adjust the angles of my body for consumption. I am ready to be eaten by the monster. I'm ready to give myself an out, to take myself offstage, to enter a pool of monster stomach acid and let myself break down. When I slide down his mouth and arrive at the bottom, I am warned against hitting my head on the washing machine. I'm told to look out for rug rash on the belly from all that sliding. I'm told to go sit quietly in the back of the basement until it's time for my final shot, the one where all three of us tangle our bodies on top of a blue cloth and are digested together within the frame of the camera because it is not enough to be consumed, all evidence of life must also disintegrate.

At 5:15 a.m., Raymond drops us off back at the fairgrounds. He hands each of us one hundred bucks. He'll spend the next month or two editing our video before he releases it.

"I have high hopes for this one," he says as we get out of the car. "I think I'll make my money back in the first week. They're gonna love it."

I crawl into my bunk to sleep for two hours before we open again.

⚡

This is who I am now:

A headless woman.

A four-legged woman.

An inside talker for the bed of nails act, sitting on the strong man as he lies on the nails.

An inside talker for the contortionist act. This is my most important role. I am now a moneymaker.

My new world is full of boxes. The boxes I put my head inside, the semi's container we live inside. I run between acts as the show cycles through from first act to last every thirty minutes, the same pattern of movement between my four acts, so that already by noon on opening day of being an inside performer, I could have shown up where and when I was needed almost automatically, my feet moving by themselves.

I still don't have much in the way of actual skills to perform, not really, not like everyone else out here, but I know how to talk into a mic. I can look right into an audience member's eyes and, with a smile, lie.

When I am not talking into the mic, though, I present my

210

body in various forms. These, for example, are the instructions for losing your head:

Put on your hospital gown. Step quietly onto the rickety side stage and prepare to slide sideways into the chair. Try not to ruffle the curtains surrounding it. If you do ruffle the curtains, or even if you don't, a child or teenager or adult might pull the curtain away from the stage anyway, peering inside at you. She will catch you with your attached head right there, midslide into the illusion.

⚡

I slide off my mom's brace, the sock beneath. She is sitting on the bed, knows now, with practice, to let the muscles on the left side of her body flare then squeeze and hold the bones of her whole body together, an ocean keeping a tree upright, afloat, way, way out. It is the last few days before I leave for the sideshow, before the lovers will sail off into the Atlantic.

I unzip her vest, remove her glasses. There is much work to be done to keep up with the rush of life on the vertical plane, the y-axis. All the therapies, all the doctors, working toward that y. My mom peers past my busy hands to my face. She wears a grimace, a furrow of concentration. She isn't wearing a helmet today, not anymore, even though beneath her shaggy gray hair, her skull has a ledge. The absence of bone creates a canyon over a quarter of her head, where just below the skin's surface her brain is firing and firing and always still bleeding.

⚡

Ms. Olga Hess, the Headless Woman, is a miracle of modern science. When the curtain is opened and they look at you, the audience will see a full woman's body, arms and legs flailing, in a chair surrounded by plastic tubes that light up red and green and blue. Sparkly. They'll see the chest and collarbone of a

211

woman's body and then, apparently piercing the flesh, a metal pole where a head should be. You've entered into the world of box jumpers, women who run backstage between illusions, sliding their bodies into one box and then another—spider woman, electric woman, four-legged woman. You're all body. You are part of a long tradition of women who have lost parts of themselves. You will be whole only when nobody is looking at you.

$$\lightning$$

My mom holds my shoulder with her one good arm as we lean down toward the bed. I shift her hips, lift the right leg onto the bed, hear the crinkle of her diaper—a word we never use in front of her—her short baby-breaths, and a dog barking outside. Usually, this is where I tuck her in, kiss her forehead, and leave. Lace up my running shoes, move as quickly as I can on foot down the shaded streets of my hometown, breathing hard, trying not to notice neighbors who want to talk about her prognosis. Or I close myself into the kitchen to do homework, grade papers, or hustle around the stove to prepare a meal, or walk slow circles in the bathroom and talk myself out of taking any of the painkillers singing their siren songs in their orange dresses.

$$\lightning$$

If someone is holding the curtain open who should not be holding the curtain open, politely ask her to close the curtain. Change your tone as the day wears on and you become more tired, as the fair goes on. Use the loudest mean whisper you can muster. Say, *Shut the curtain*. Then, use only your arm when you see a peeker, a fast, wide swipe across the air in front of you toward their body, a warning, and then, as you are into hour fourteen of performing, month four of being on the road, say nothing at all. Kick hard and fast toward the body of the person staring in at you. Try to avoid contact, but don't worry if you don't succeed. As you slide into the chair sideways, your body tipping low and back, there's a moment of vulnerability where you cannot yank the curtain shut or make contact because you're lying too far back. To get flat is dangerous.

⚡

Instead of leaving, I lie down. I am tired. I hold open the covers and slide in beside her. Why this time? She turns to me, takes that one good hand and places it on my cheek. It is warm and dry and gentle. We have left the vertical plane where I hold her up and wipe her crack. We are horizontal people now, and somehow that shift has reorganized the nature of how and who we once were to each other. Her hand on my cheek, my hair, is the move a mother makes to her child. She slides her fingers along my neck, runs them, very softly, through my hair. It has been too many years since I have felt this much tenderness, and I don't have a place for it anymore. That's the awful price of coping.

⚡

The metal post, as big around as a flagpole, sticks down a foot from the wooden box you need to slide your head inside once you sit in the chair. Crane your neck around the pole. Do not hit your head or you'll make a noise. Scooch back against the chair and straighten your spine and stretch your neck all the way up inside the wooden box, mirrored on the outside, tight and hot on the inside. Drape the blanket across your lap to look like what a sick person should look like, and arch your back. Sit straight up so the metal pole presses its angled tip against your breastbone, into the freckled hollow between and just above your breasts, press into it hard enough that this spot will, for

213

the next three months, be a little bruised in service of the illusion. Hunch your shoulders forward to cover any space behind the box, and ready your arms to grasp out wild and blind once the curtain is pulled. Never reach your hands higher than your shoulders, never try to touch your own headless head, or your hands may shine back in the mirror to the audience, and then what miracle will they believe in? Instead, spread your fingers wide and keep them low, parallel to the dirt, reaching for the earth, shaking and alive, very alive, trapped in this headless body, escaping into the greatness of your own illusion.

$$\lightning$$

We are two soft horizontal bodies breathing. Other mothers and other daughters in the world and in time lie side by side and pass on the secrets of the universe. My mother's waved, soft gray hair falls across the missing chunks of her head. Does she think about what is gone, or what remains? I want to reach my hand out and trace the edges of her missing skull, but I am paralyzed. No, she is paralyzed. Half of her is struck still. With the other half, she is running her fingers through my hair. Tears are pouring out the corners of my eyes and my hands are moving up to catch them, because we've been warned by all the specialty doctors that we may not cry in front of her, may not show her our sorrow for fear of killing her hope.

$$\lightning$$

Hope there is not a yellow jacket stuck inside the small wooden box your head must stay in for the duration of the act. Hope it is not 107 degrees, and hope you don't faint with your face in the heat box, your body under extra blankets and costumes. Hope you'll be able to regain your head after the curtain closes and you slide sideways out of the box, hope you won't have to kick any strangers on the way out, hope your shoes are where

214

you left them and haven't fallen behind the stage, hope your makeup hasn't melted completely off, hope you're suffering enough to begin to understand the suffering of others.

When you move between the worlds of head and no head, know that you must move parallel to the earth. You must change your plane, reinvent your orientation until in front of you is sky and below you is the black earth, and that is your passageway—sister, mother, box jumper—you are your own door into a world of a different kind. You x-axis. You flattened miracle.

PREMIUM FOOTLONG CORN DOGS

Day 54 of 150

I'm sharing an uncooked, soggy corn dog with Pipscy, who is a vegetarian. She eats away a few inches of the corn batter, rotating the dog horizontally in front of her mouth like a spitted pig, then hands it over to me. I chomp the exposed dog. Hand it back to her. Like this, we make it through three corn dogs.

We ten performers are standing in a downpour. It is 4:15 a.m. Rain has been falling steadily since we began teardown at 10:00 p.m., first as sprinkles and then moving to the giant drops that explode on the pavement when they hit, the kind of rainstorm that lures children to play in it, their arms wide and wild like whirling dervishes. And for just as long, the rain has been pooling into the box of extra dogs a carnie threw out from his food joint, rising around them like a soup, as if they were foam noodles floating in a swimming pool.

"How can you eat that?" Francine, the vegan burlesque dancer, says to our grease-smeared cheeks.

We have been working straight through since 9:00 a.m. the day before, setting up and then performing all day and then beginning teardown. That's how, we don't say, instead taking bigger and faster bites.

We have survived our first meat-grinder. Or, we are close to surviving, once we finish teardown here in Wisconsin. Two swelteringly hot, long, exhausting weeks with full tents and the regular performers plus newbies crammed into the semi and all we have to do is finish packing the show away and we will get to sleep. For a few hours. On our way to the next show.

But we are stuck. That's why we're taking the corn dog break. Our two-foot- long tent stakes, which closely resemble railroad spikes, will not budge from their burrow in the asphalt.

At this mega–state fair there are no grassy lots. This fair is four square city blocks of smoothed asphalt. We'd jackhammered holes into the ground and pounded the stakes the rest of the way in. There they stood for the two weeks we've been here, reassuringly unbudgeable, but now we have to get them out.

The stakes will not move. Not with the regular crowbar we used, not with the metal extender, not with sledgehammers or jackhammers, nothing.

If we are not set up in time for opening day at the next fair, we'll incur a huge fine. If we incur a huge fine, the show will likely shut down—it's a struggle to pay us week by week, and the bald, patched tires on our semi continue to explode on the highway. But more important than the money and the comfort, I'm certain everyone agrees, is the fact that if our show shuts down, there is no longer any American traveling sideshow left.

We can't leave the stakes in the ground because we need them to hold the tent in place at the next fair. Also, this fairground board levies a huge fine for leaving any equipment in the asphalt.

And so it is 4:15 a.m. and twenty-eight stakes are still stuck in the asphalt. We are standing in the downpour, trying to figure out what to do, stuffing our faces with corn dogs. Tommy decides we'll wait until 8:00 a.m., when we can hire a forklift.

We wake to a forklift, two long metal prongs sticking out the front, and all the men leaning in close with great tenderness to watch the driver try to jam an edge of the fork under the exposed small circle of metal, the stake's top. It looks so inconsequential, that small bump nearly flush with the asphalt—doesn't hint at the two feet below the surface its body reaches.

The rest of us are finishing the final teardown details, hauling the last poles, coiling electrical equipment. I am on ropes. There is a special crochet system we have for each of the ropes that turns the long two-rope pulleys into short, neat, foot-long grubs. It took me a few setups to understand the pattern, but now I can knot and twist and pull the inch-thick ropes with speed, and I understand how helpful it is to keep tools organized and ready to use once we begin setup again at our next spot, which will hopefully, hopefully, be later this afternoon.

One of the forklift's prongs is against the edge of the stake's head, pressing with the full force of its machinery, trying to make a little space under which it can sneak and pull, but this stake will not budge. The driver tries different techniques, the fork's side edge, the armpit, and finally the very tip. This is when he finally manages to insert a small edge under the metal. He is pressing harder on the throttle, and there is some excited chattering from the crew around the stake.

"Stand back a few feet," Tommy says. "It might pop into the air."

The forklift driver presses the throttle farther, and the giant metal fork begins to bow. It's beautiful, the small arc, like a long slice of rusty melon. All eyes are on the stake and the bent forklift, all voices exclaiming how amazing it is, to put that much force on something and for it to hold utterly still, and then, all at once, the tent stake is gone.

The sound it made.

That's what people talked about after.

The quiet *whoosh*.

At the moment before it finally breaks free, I turn my attention back to the ropes in my hand. I see nothing, but hear, from every person within earshot, a collective gasp. I look quickly to those near the forklift and see all their faces turned to the air.

218

See all the necks cranked all the way back, faces looking high, high in the air, like some form of group worship.

Of course, this is where we use phrases like "Time stands still," and "Each second stretches to eternity," because time extends here in ways it is hard to articulate.

Time stands still. Each second stretches to eternity. All those necks looking to the sky. I would move my neck to the sky, too, but before I can even begin, all the heads are moving, lowering, turning. The chins are coming back toward their chests and the necks are swiveling, and before I have a chance to look up I realize that all the faces I can see, each of them, are looking at me.

I feel a shadow.

No. I see a shadow.

Is that real?

I notice a suggestion of shadow.

The shadow comes from the stake, which blocks the sun for just a moment as it comes down upon me.

The stake's sharpened tip scrapes the end of my nose.

This is where it is falling. Forty feet up into the air hurling through space and then down on me.

It grazes my nose and then falls past my mouth and chin. It whirs past the fragile pumping of my heart, inches from the skin.

My elbows have been tight against my body, my hands pulling the ropes into taut braids, my left hand covering the right as I tighten the knot.

The metal stake finally lands, the full force of its fall, on my hand.

How safe is your body right now?

The force knocks the rope from my hands, shoving them down to the ground, and the tent spike falls with an ear-splitting clang onto the asphalt below.

There is screaming.

It isn't me.

Where is the worst moment of this story? Just after, with

219

the havoc of pain? Or is it the moment before, the days, weeks, years before, before the illness sets in when there is still the possibility of learning the ingredients in her famous Moroccan carrots, about why she'd had that spell of zealous Christianity, and why she'd lost it, about what word I said first as a baby, if it was her name. When there is still a chance to make amends, but I don't take it.

I look down at the stake for a second, two, the sounds from the rest of the world gone except for some distant buzz. I pick my hands up from my side to look at them, because I feel some sensation there, though I cannot tell what that sensation is. I look, thinking it's possible that my hands won't be there. I'm not sure why. I'm not sure what has happened at all.

But there they are. Both hands. Ten fingers. No exposed bones. A big smear of dirt where the stake hit my left hand.

I crouch down to pick up the rope and resume braiding.

As I stand, sound comes back. There is some loud human voice somewhere, or a few of them. There is the blur of bodies moving toward me very quickly.

Nothing that isn't a complete catastrophe really matters at all.

"Are you okay? Jesus Christ, are you okay?" say the voices I hear.

I look up.

Cassie is standing right in front of me, taking the rope out of my hands.

"Stop, dummy, put this down," she says.

Tommy is right beside me then, too. "Tessy? Are you okay?" he says.

"I'm fine," I say.

"You're fine?"

"I'm not even hurt," I say, starting to shake.

He is staring at my face, studying it, shocked, it seems, that I am not covered in blood, that my brain isn't sticking out of my skull.

220

"Where did it hit you?" he says. I raise my hands from my side, and they float into the air between us like new balloons.

"Shit," he says, gently grabbing my wrist. I can see it now, my left hand. There is no blood, no bone, but my knuckles are growing bigger and bigger, they are pink and going purple, a few fingers are doubling in size, and there is a lump like a marble sticking out from the bone. My right hand feels tingly, but the left was mostly shielding it.

"Move your fingers," he says. "Can you move your fingers?"

I do, a little.

"Not broken," I say.

I look at them, these hands, this noncatastrophe. I look at them, and more performers gather around and all the world's sounds are back to their regular weird selves and there is the morning sky with clouds and there is the life that has happened so far and whatever else is ahead and everything is the same as it was before and maybe always will be. I start to cry.

Not a lot. I'm not a goddamned baby. Just a little.

"You're in shock," Tommy says. "Jesus, Tessy. Poor Tessy. Here," he says, pulling Cassie right into me, forcing her into a tight hug against my chest. "Take her to my trailer," he says to her.

"I've got to keep working," I say, reaching for the rope. My fingers won't move much.

"Take a breather," Tommy says.

"I've got to keep going or I won't hold it together," I snap back.

Sunshine appears beside us. "Tessa," she says in her stage manager voice. "Come with me. Now."

"There are frozen grapes in the freezer. Put them on her hand, sit her in the shade," Tommy says.

Sunshine nods at him, takes the ropes I'd managed to pick up and drops them to the ground, and pushes my back until I start walking. She runs my hand under a cool spigot of water, rubs my back. Gives me frozen grapes.

221

Every day we put fire and swords and electricity into our bodies, throw knives at them, contort them, wrap them in snakes, and every day we wake up sure those things won't harm us but also sure that there is so much else that will.

I start to feel a deep throbbing in my hand. I'm not sure if it's a feeling I should care more about. Red catches my eye as I walk past. He holds it. Makes his mouth into a grimace and shakes his head, an acknowledgment of what has just occurred. Perhaps I've passed some test here, taking in pain and carrying on.

"Damn, Tessy," Tommy says a little later. "In my nine seasons with this show, that right there, hands down, was the scariest thing that has ever happened."

But isn't this our collective deceit?

Can one moment, the happening of the event, be the worst moment of our lives? The truth is that the worst moment is always still waiting. The next fair. The next stake ripped from the earth. The next phone call from your stepdad where he's crying and you're telling him, *Calm down calm down calm down just tell me*, until he does, and then you are rocking and crying, too.

I don't think our former working man Steve, the moment he came to after shooting himself in the stomach with a cannon, actually thought the worst was over, that he'd succeeded in reaching the most awful moment of his life. That from there, life would be easier. Or the carnie I met in Butler, who woke up from some dream to his toes chewed off and in the mouth of his Chihuahua, believed that he'd found the worst moment of his life. Or the junkie Drew, whose teeth fell past his lips and onto the dirt like magic beans each time he snapped awake. Or even when I learned about my mom's stroke. That wasn't the hardest part, that singular moment. There was always more.

This is one of our collective agreements. To tell each other how bad things could be, how bad something was—really shitty, awful—and move with the dimming sun toward night as if this is the truth, as if we've seen the worst even as we ignore

222

the quietly waiting future stretched out ahead like a long, long tongue leading into an open mouth.

⚡

In the moments surrounding the tent stake incident, I wasn't thinking, of course, about my mom. I wasn't thinking about the way the stake must have looked at its apex, splitting the blue, blue sky in two like the hemispheres of a brain.

But here's a story I learned:

In 1848, Phineas Gage was working for the railroad, blasting rock with a work gang in Cavendish, Vermont. The gang would bore down into the rock, fill it with blasting powder and a fuse, and then pack it in with a tamping rod before lighting. Distracted by something the men behind him said, Gage turned to look back at them over his right shoulder and, for reasons that have never been pinned down, a spark ignited the blasting powder and it exploded, shooting the big metal tamping stick directly into Gage's head, point first.

Reports say that the rod whistled as it flew.

It entered just below his left cheekbone, scraped the back of his left eye and tore through his brain's left frontal lobe, exiting near his front hairline. Three feet seven inches long. It passed through a man's head and then sailed through the air, landing straight up like a fencepost twenty-five feet away. It was greasy, one of the other men there said, and had streaks of blood. The force of the blow knocked Gage over, but he never lost consciousness. He twitched a few times on the ground, then rose and continued chatting with his crew as if nothing had happened.

Can you imagine? I mean, triangular fragments of his skull were sticking out around the hole like a crown atop a head.

Gage lived for twelve more years, though Gage was "no longer Gage," according to Dr. Harlow, who followed Gage's case. This is the part of the story that has had lasting scientific impact and wildly different interpretations. Prior to Gage's accident, nobody quite understood that different portions of the brain served different functions. There's not very much direct evidence about what kinds of personality changes Gage underwent, but reports mostly suggest that he became much more profane, lost his ability to manage his money, was prone to changing his mind often and completely, and in general let his animal instincts, the papers reported, take over from his former civilized self. What were they? Humping? Howling at the moon?

This misunderstanding of neuroscience was the root of some real problems, like the use of lobotomies in the mid-twentieth century. And the belief, for example, that all our amoral behavior is housed in the frontal lobes. That anyone who has an injury there, a stroke, for instance, is necessarily going to revert to animalistic behavior. Untrue. But we have learned that there *is* some degree of our impulse control housed there. A person with a compromised frontal lobe may not know, for example, where it is or is not polite to scratch in public, or how one might or might not use a spoon when faced with a bowl of cereal.

Based on Gage's personality changes, which grew over time, the rail- road would not rehire him. Dr. Harlow wrote that the balance between Gage's "intellectual faculties and animal propensities" was gone. Gage worked a stint in P. T. Barnum's New York museum, where audience members purportedly paid to part his hair and see his pulsing brain.

He carried the tamping iron around with him for the rest of his life.

Is it ridiculous for me to associate this stake event with what happens in a stroke? Is a stroke a weaponized event, a kind of warfare? An injury? An accident?

There are two main kinds of strokes. In one, your brain bleeds. In another, your brain clots. My mom had the bleeding kind. It's called a hemorrhagic stroke, and only 15 percent of strokes are this kind, but they kill a lot more people than the other kind. They're the serious players.

The main risk factor for any kind of stroke is high blood pressure. Other risk factors include high blood cholesterol, smoking, drug abuse, obesity, diabetes mellitus, and a few other things.

She didn't have any of these.

Half of people who have had a serious hemorrhagic stroke live less than one year.

In the corridor and waiting room outside the ICU, where we spent weeks and then months, I read a lot about strokes. Websites, pamphlets, books, essays, research. I was given a book by one of the neighbors called *My Stroke of Insight*. It's written by a neuroscientist, a young woman, who has a stroke. The book recounts, in as much detail as she can recall, what it actually physically felt like to have the stroke, the way language and meaning slipped away from her, the way the panic of what was happening flitted away, too, gone down the stream like everything else. The way, for months, she was in some calm, peaceful, timeless float, and how it was actually quite pleasant. I loved that part, thinking that my mom might be somewhere outside time and stress, maybe not even aware of what was lost because of how beautifully things were gained.

But then the book shifted. This scientist recovered. She regained her speech, and her ability to walk, and she eventually went back to work as a goddamned neuroscientist and wrote this really interesting book about the whole thing and is quite Zen about the experience, like she's grateful she learned how to slow down in that peaceful golden field of the brain's nether regions. Maybe, in fact, all the people with serious left hemisphere strokes were in there together, spread out in a field of soft grass and low golden dusk light, running their fingertips across daisies and very sweetly smiling at one another when they passed. But the neuroscientist left. She recovered. Like, fully. I mean, it's great, it's amazing, good for her and her

225

family, yada yada, but she became the story of the person who went all the way to the edge and then came back; she left my mom in that field all alone. And what about the rest of us? For those who never quite leave the field completely? Why aren't there more stories for the other side?

I'm just scared for her there, in that field, all alone. She probably can't watch out for snakes anymore. Doesn't even know what they are. I just wish I could be there, on the edge even, behind a tree so I wouldn't upset her peace, with a loaded shotgun. I'd have binoculars and ammo slung across my chest and I'd scan the horizon, scoping out the enemy.

WORLD OF WONDERS
AUGUST 2013

Between two meat-grinders, we have one small county fair in Wisconsin, a holdover, and it's time for Pipscy to go. She asks to be dropped off at the bus station before we begin setup, but there's no time.

We do not all stand around wishing her well as she gets ready to leave. Many in our crew don't say goodbye. We start unloading the truck and then she is sort of just…gone. She had called a cab to come pick her up at the fairgrounds, apparently.

To leave before the agreed-upon time is to become a deserter, a status made permanent by the Sharpie marker that lives in the back end of the semi. On the walls, which form the borders of our backstage area and living space, the backdrop to our lives at all hours of every day, her fate, along with the fates of many others, is written:

PIPSCY
Couldn't hack it

Those words mesmerize me. *Couldn't hack it*. It isn't just that there is an action you aren't completing—it doesn't say *abandoner*, or *left early*, or anything that externalizes the events. Instead, it is a simple statement about you, your capacity as a person, what you are made of, if you have any guts. Can you do this thing or not?

TESSA
Couldn't hack it

The possibility is devastating.

The ship arrives in London, and Davy sends an update.

"Something extraordinary happened last night. I don't know exactly what it was or even how to describe it, but at 4am Teresa grabbed my hand and started 'talking.' Not words, but stringing together sounds which she had previously only made one at a time and with some concentration. Now they were flowing like a dam had burst. She went on for about 45 minutes. Her tone was excited and happy! She indicated that she wasn't in pain and didn't need anything. She was just talking and singing about stuff. We fell back asleep about 5 and slept until 9am.

"This morning she indicated that she remembered what had happened the night before and it seemed that there was no particular sensation associated with it. So it is a mystery now. We'll see how it goes today."

I don't know if Davy's interpretation of her actions would be the same as mine if I had been there— did she really string sounds together for an hour, or did he just want her to badly enough that he interpreted a few sounds that way?—but reading this still makes my gut feel like it is filled with moths, then stones. The idea that she might talk is overwhelming in its beauty, in how desperately I wish for it, have wished nonstop for it, until I remember that even if it were true, I would not be there to hear it. They are gone. Maybe she will talk again. Maybe being on the road will enable her to find the words she hasn't been able to find since her stroke, and maybe Davy will

228

get to hear them and know what she thinks about the sound of the rain on the cobblestone streets, but I won't. They're gone.

In Minnesota, there was a dangled carrot. It glimmered, all rooty and infused with beta-carotene dreams, and we wanted it because we were starving.

After the two weeks at the Wisconsin State Fair and a week at the small Wisconsin county fair, we'd moved on to the biggest meat-grinder of the season: the Minnesota State Fair. And Tommy knew just what to say to keep our gears turning.

"Finish setup early," Tommy said, "and we can take a little trip over to the Mall of America." The idea was astonishing, a vast lighted complex smelling of perfumes and soft pretzels and the starchy carpet-scent of cheap clothing made overseas. Indoor plumbing. The chance to buy new underwear or soap or a bra or a costume piece that didn't come from Walmart. Forty-three million people per year come to this mall, the largest in the United States, and our presence there, however fleeting it might be, felt like a necessity and a glorious extension of the America we were learning through the fairgrounds. We'd just be regular shoppers, strollers, eaters, not on display any more than everyone else.

We hang lights at double speed, leap off the ladder halfway up, and unfurl the tent's sidewalls with a mania that I usually only see when it seems like a neighboring crew has scored something really good. But we had the mall ahead of us. America's mall.

"You have an hour and a half. Meet back here at seven. We'll leave without you if you're not here," Tommy says as we emerge into the clean, climate-controlled palace. The only places I've felt air-conditioning in the sixty days I've been with the World of Wonders are Walmart and the occasional fair building I sneak into, so the idea of being left here is intoxicating. I could sneak into the Applebee's at night and gorge on fruit that's not deep-fried. Could sleep on a nest of hoodies

229

in a toilet stall—my own toilet stall, with walls. Could find a mall boyfriend to hold hands and share an Orange Julius with. Once I made it past the preteen years, malls had never been places where I'd wanted to spend much time. But I have never been so overcome with a desire to purchase everything within my sight until now. There is a store called Journeys, full of hats and fat sneakers, and I want to put on each of them. Nearby, several tables seem to be piping the overly sweet smell of fake apple pie and vanilla from candles that sit grouped together in small waxy armies.

Because we've been paid only in cash, I have a huge pile of ones and fives. I didn't count it out, just grabbed a big handful from the envelope where I keep all my cash, stashed deep in my duffel bag tucked under my bunk, which always makes me nervous. I've heard about plenty of carnies getting robbed, but the number of us crammed into one truck means there's always someone around to keep an eye out.

Spif and Sunshine immediately lock arms and skip down the tiled hallway, the blinking sale signs they pass on each side like an enchanted forest they can't wait to explore. They laugh at each other. I take a sharp turn and disappear into the maze of H&M, touching every piece of clothing I pass—tankinis, bralettes, wispy purple scarves, plastic heels, boho sweaters with tassels to the floor. I narrow in quickly on the racks that hold clothes in blacks and grays, torn and tough. Much of the rest of the cast dresses like they're in a hardcore band when we're not performing, and I don't want to stick out from them, for them to comment anymore on how square I look, how like a sorority girl. I grab a cheap necklace made up of four or five gold chains loosely braided together, imagine myself a Hells Angels biker, and head for the register. I buy an Orange Julius, which I drink, alone, wandering the corridors. It is strange to be under evenly lit halogen. It is strange to be inside. I wonder if people can smell me as I pass, as I linger beside soaps not tested on animals, then hundreds of Lego animals. I want each thing.

230

But as I keep walking, I enter fewer and fewer stores, gawk at the prices in those that I do, am less sure that the items could fit in the life I'm currently living.

I round a corner and find myself staring at a giant roller coaster. Though the Mall of America is the number one tourist destination in the Midwest, though on any given day the mall becomes Minnesota's third largest city by population, though it is 1.15 miles around each level, when I find the roller coaster, I also find Tommy, Cassie, and Ben. I join them as we watch kids screaming past, and then Sunshine and Spif skip up, and we all stand there in a row, listening to the sound of wheels on the tracks, to the click of the pulleys hauling the carts uphill, the symphony of our lives, the screams of our dinner sound track, the smiling whiplashed faces and flying hair of our most familiar neighbors. Sunshine breaks our trance.

"I'm going," she says.

"Me, too," Tommy says.

"Me, too," we all agree, and march over to buy tickets. Everything smells of chlorine and packed dirt from the fake stream and planter boxes used to make the place feel like a real, wild, out-of- doors carnival somewhere.

"Are you all in a band?" a young guy asks Spif as we wait in line.

"Nah, man. We're a freak show," Spif says.

We hand over our tickets and climb into the plastic bucket seats like we are weary travelers finally come home. We're off. Rattle up a hill, whip down it, all of us riding together like some normal group of friends delighted by the uncommon pleasure of a roller coaster. We scream. Throw our hands up when we want to seem brave. Our direction, our speed, our pleasure—out of our hands.

We drive from the great gleaming mall across the highway overpass and into a giant parking garage outside the airport. Tommy parks the van, kills the engine, and turns back to us.

"Sunshine, you're with me. The rest of you, don't move."

Like most times, I have no idea what's going on. I know, vaguely, that we are getting a new performer soon, but I didn't know it was now, today, if it is. I know as we head into the next meat-grinder, more performers means more bodies to fill in acts onstage, which means a slightly longer show, which means slightly longer breaks between acts, potentially, like four minutes instead of two, and so I'm delighted. Nearly two million people come through the Minnesota State Fair. On our last Walmart trip, Tommy instructed each of us to buy a plastic container with a screw-on top that we could use as a pee jar in our bunks for the times we wouldn't be able to make it to the Porta-Potties between acts. I choose an extra-large plastic jug of trail mix.

We wait in the van for ten minutes, twenty, thirty. Finally, about an hour later, Tommy and Sunshine emerge from the elevator area pushing a luggage cart, atop which sit several pieces of luggage and a man.

"What's up, everybody?" the new guy says as he opens the van door. His arms are tan, muscled, and he reaches both of them into the van, grasps onto a lever beneath the seat with one hand, a handle inside the van with another, and pulls himself inside. He is wearing a black cowboy hat and black T-shirt, and his body ends there.

"Everyone, this is Short E Dangerously, the world's shortest daredevil. Short E, this is everyone," Tommy says. Short E uses his hand to throw a death metal devil horns into the air but does not turn around to look at any of us.

I'd met Short E briefly at the Florida fair the evening I'd spent lurking around the tent and trailers, trying to get in with Chris Christ. He was smoking on the backstage steps and made the mistake of making eye contact with me. I barreled over. He watched me approach, squinting his eyes like an old cowboy though he was no older than his early thirties, and as soon as I could see his face clearly enough under the shadow of his hat, I blushed a little. He was very handsome.

232

He obliged me in some of my questions about life on the road, and his acts, and when it was time for him to go onstage again, the Big Boss Chris came back out.

"Watch out for him," he said, nodding at Short E as he retreated through the stage curtains and onto the stage. "He's a merciless flirt."

On the van ride back to our show from the airport, Short E chats with Sunshine and Tommy up front about the last few months of his life and his international tour with a magician, in which he took part in the grand finale act. The magician saws a man in half, clearly pulling the blade all the way through the man. Not a new act. Where Short E and the magician brought the act to a new level was that at this point, the top half of the man, Short E, jumps down from the table and is able to walk on the floor with his hands, breaching all possible explanations for hidden limbs or contortion or mirrors. He swings his torso back and forth while holding himself up with his arms, and there is no way, it is not possible, for legs to be hidden anywhere, and it never occurs to the audience, because why would it, that the man onstage didn't have any legs to begin with.

"You perform one, maybe two shows a day. Don't have to be anywhere until evening. You can party hard all night. People loved us in every town we came to, wanted to chill. I had a lot of long, long nights with those Brazilian women," Short E says, smiling.

The idea is almost too much to bear: one performance a day. I'm not sure I am going to know what to do with myself when the season is over, and the momentary daydream of free time almost sends me into a panic.

The next morning, a car pulls up behind our tent and Chris Christ, the Big Boss and World of Wonders owner, climbs out. He still has the two dark trails of snuff running from the corners of his mouth, and the few patches of hair still on his head are wild and wiry like those of a mad scientist. He approaches

233

our crew with a hunch, a shuffle, and a subtle smile as we are cleaning some of the freakatorium pieces.

The seasoned performers—Tommy, Sunshine, Red, Cassie, and Short E—take turns giving him hugs and hellos, and then he gives a wave to the greenhorns. A truck pulls up hauling another small trailer, which it drops next to Tommy's trailer, where Chris will stay for the next two weeks with our show while we are in the heat of this meat-grinder.

"I'll work the bally sometimes," he says. "So Tommy and Cassie don't blow their voices." I can't wait to see the legend play.

"What are the hours at this fair?" I ask Tommy later that night.

"Nine a.m. to midnight weekdays, nine a.m. to two a.m. weekends, plus work call an hour and a half before opening and the work after closing. For two weeks."

"Oh shit."

"Exactly."

⚡

"I was a Navy SEAL," Red says. He's sitting in the front seat of the van. He bought new bright lights for the tent, but they're the wrong wattage, and Tommy has sent us to Lowe's to exchange them.

Aside from that morning backstage, this is the first time I've been alone with Red, and my heart is pounding. I don't have much chance to interact with him aside from when he directs action during setup or teardown, much of which I flub since I can't remember exactly how each different piece of vinyl siding is folded, for example. And we don't interact during performances, since he has his own stage—on which also sits that glorious, gleaming electric chair—and his own code of conduct he's developed after enough years on the road.

"The thing is," Sunshine had told me, "he's been doing this

for so many years, and seen so many people come and go, that it's sort of pointless for him to remember names. Especially at the beginning. If as the season goes on he sees that you're gonna make it, that you can hack it, the likelihood of him knowing you drastically increases."

If he knew who I was, if he—dare I dream it—respected me as a performer, then I'd be a real part of what was happening here, a GTFM showperson earning her keep. And if I understood who he was, maybe some secret of the show, of life on the road, of bravery, would be unlocked.

When I ask Red about how he started performing, he begins with his time as a Navy SEAL.

"In Vietnam, I was on a team that snuck in to rescue people. Generals and POWs. I always either headed up the platoon or was in the very back. One day, my commander was up front, leading, and I was bringing up the rear. We hit a field of land mines. Booby traps."

He pauses, takes a sip of coffee from the plastic Big Gulp coffee cup he holds between his legs. In the tight confines of the car, it's impossible not to smell him. He smells like an old, important costume piece. Not a new, fresh sweat, but an older, deeper smell that has settled permanently into fabric or wood or air. It is the kind of smell that never lets you forget how long he has been working hard, and how hard, which all makes you think about why. Why has he done this for so long?

"My commander stepped right on a land mine. He knew it. We knew it. He didn't move. Held it down with his foot while the rest of us passed by. We were just a little ways past him, and I was in the very back, when he thought he could get away in time. He thought he could leap off it. He tried, but he didn't move fast enough. The bottom half of his body flew into the air and landed right on top of me. His knees knocked me to the ground.

"When I came to, I realized my mouth was open and I was screaming. I couldn't stop. The other guys from the platoon

235

were yelling at me to shut the fuck up. There were gooks all around, and they thought I might give away our position. I couldn't stop. I wouldn't. They dragged the commander's legs off me, but I just kept screaming and screaming. I'd cracked.

"Someone in the platoon pinned me down and held his hand over my mouth. Then they got tape. They taped my mouth shut to mute the sound of the screaming, and then when that wouldn't work anymore, they knocked me out.

"I got sent home not long after that. And I decided to kill myself. What else was there to do? But I thought that I'd do one last thing before I offed myself, and that was go to Woodstock.

"There, I met people who had a way of explaining things about the world like I'd never heard before. They gave me some peace.

"So I went home to the carnival. I'd been there before, from when I was fourteen on to when I joined the SEALs. When I went back, I learned to be an electrician, light up the midway. Did that for a while, then worked as an electrician on the Lakota Indian reservation. Learned about things in the spirit world I'd never even dreamed about. And from there, I went back into sideshow work. Performance. I met a fakir I studied with who taught me to control my breath and heart rate, to slow it down almost completely. To control pain. Those things are all related—the people at Woodstock and the Lakota Indians and the fakir. It's all about your mind. And your mind's control over your body. Once you achieve that, you are free."

$$\lightning$$

"When I was in my early twenties and living in Carmel," my mom began in my memory of the telling, the first line of a story I had often begged to hear. We were sitting in the bathroom as she combed my hair after a bout with lice. It was late at night.

Sometimes a story suddenly changes. It was one story, meant one thing. And then, boom. The story becomes newly clear.

I had stories I held on to about my mom, but the longer it had been since I'd talked to her, the more the ground shifted from beneath those foundational ways I thought I knew her. Or, really, how I thought I'd lost her.

"I shared a house with my friend Tweedy. She worked a nighttime waitressing job, and I worked a daytime shift for a travel agency. When I was alone in the house, I started hearing strange sounds. Doors and windows would close on their own, and something that sounded like footsteps in the attic. I thought we had raccoons or possums living up there, even though I knew the weight of the steps meant something heavier. I ignored what I could, afraid to think too much about these kinds of things. But the sounds kept happening. Finally one day, I asked Tweedy if she'd ever noticed anything strange in the house when I wasn't there, and she eventually told me she'd heard a lot of creaks as well, and that the cabinets in the kitchen would sometimes slam. She heard the same footsteps, too."

"Then what happened?" I asked. She liked to be goaded.

"We didn't really know what to do," she said. "It felt good to know she'd been experiencing these weird things, too, because it meant I wasn't crazy, but it also made everything scarier. The next night, while Tweedy was at work, I went to bed and tried to think about other things. I heard the footsteps again, upstairs, and this time they were right above my bed. They stopped. I rolled over so my back was to the door, convincing myself to remain calm and that probably these were just animals. Then I heard the bedroom doorknob twist. I heard a creak. The door slowly opened. I was too scared to turn toward the door, so I just lay there, staring at the wall. My heart was pounding. I heard the faint sound of footsteps walking across the room. And then, and this is the sensation I'll never forget, I felt the weight of the bed shift, as if a person sat down on the edge of the mattress. I was petrified. I couldn't move."

I sat rigid in my chair, heart thumping.

237

"Finally, after I don't know how long, a minute or two maybe, the weight let up and whatever had been pressing down on the bed lifted. I heard steps back across the room, and then the bedroom door shut. As soon as I could move my limbs, I got up and out of bed, and went to spend the night at a friend's house.

"The next day, Tweedy and I decided we needed help. We searched the newspaper's classifieds until we found an ad for a woman who specialized in dealing with the dead. When she arrived at the house, the woman said she was a medium and could communicate with spirits. As soon as she stepped inside, she took a deep breath and put one hand on her heart. 'I feel the presence of someone with unfinished business,' she said to the room. Then, to us, 'We are going to need to perform an exorcism.'

" 'Why us?' I asked the medium. 'Other people lived here before and we never heard anything about this.'

" 'The spirits choose who they think will be open enough to communicate with them,' she said. 'They chose you.'

"I wasn't sure if I believed the medium, or even *in* the medium, but I didn't know what else to do. We told her to go ahead with the exorcism, whatever that meant.

" 'Can it hurt us?' Tweedy asked the medium.

" 'No, probably not. Most spirits aren't able to harm anyone, and don't really mean to be frightening the living. They're just stuck here and sometimes need some help to move on.'

"The medium turned off the lights, lit some candles, and got herself into a trance. 'O spirit,' the medium said, 'we mean you no harm. We will not hurt you. We are here to help you. Are you with us right now?'

"We were frozen, listening, but nothing responded.

" 'Spirits, we are here to help you,' she repeated, 'we mean you no harm,' and as she was talking, the shutters on the windows started opening and closing. 'Let me know what you want and we will try to help you, as best we can,' she said, and the coffee table, I kid you not, started shaking. I was getting scared, very scared, wondering if we'd gotten mixed up in something we shouldn't have. I wanted to leave but knew, somehow, that it was necessary for me to stay. That this was a moment to face the thing that seemed so far beyond my control.

"The coffee table's shaking got more and more violent, and finally, incredibly, it lifted into the air. The medium was yelling and turning herself all around the room, directing her voice at any place the spirit might be. The table was five and then ten feet in the air, still shaking, but completely and totally elevated, unmistakably floating. The shutters were still slamming and the candles were flickering and the whole thing was so strangely like a scene from a movie that it was hard to tell if real life was happening. But my overwhelming fear had almost turned into something else. Some trust in the larger universe that whatever was happening was going to be okay.

"Finally, the table dropped back down to the ground and the shutters stopped slamming and the medium stopped yelling. The candles were all out. The medium turned to where Tweedy and I stood hugging each other and said, 'There is a woman in this house. She died here. She's missing something, and that is why she's still here. I think I know where it is.'

"The medium led us out the back door, to the small tile patio where we smoked our cigarettes. She used a hammer to swing at the patio tiles, breaking away small pieces at a time until she had cleared out most of the stone. About six inches under the dirt, we found a small wooden box. Inside were a few objects that a child might have collected—a glass bottle, some dried and crumpled flowers, a tattered white scarf.

" 'Do these things belong to the woman in the house?' we asked the medium.

" 'Her daughter,' she said.

" 'Now what?' we asked. 'What comes next?'

" 'Nothing,' she said. 'The woman will leave, I think. Maybe she already has. She just wanted these items back out in the world. She didn't want her daughter's treasures buried.'

239

"And that's the end," my mom said. "You can go to bed."

"I'm scared of ghosts," I said.

"There's no reason to be," she said. "If you don't want a ghost to come, close your heart to the idea of a ghost and it won't be able to communicate anything to you. Say, *No, ghosts, I won't hear you, and I won't see you.*"

"But you didn't."

"No, I didn't. I wanted to hear them."

"Why?"

"I guess I was just curious."

"What did you learn?"

"That the world is much more mysterious and magical than most of us think it is."

She'd said this before, when I'd asked, as a small child, if Santa Claus was real, why photographs worked, how cars kept running once the gas light came on. *The world is much more mysterious and magical than most of us think it is.* This was some basis of her great belief in how the world worked, a foundational mystery and magic that was beyond our capacity to understand but our great duty to explore. If we were ready for it. If we could open ourselves to the terror as well as the joy that comes with that deep unknown. I was not ready. Not then, not later. But she always has been. And maybe however her brain has rerouted in these last years has opened even more channels toward some new, deeply beautiful mysteries, and maybe sometimes when I feel disappointed that her eyes, which still haven't fully returned to green, are vacant when I'm telling her about our afternoon plans, she's actually in some dark living room in another lifetime, watching coffee tables shiver through the air and taking in the new map of the mysteries.

CASH MONEY

Day 67 of 150

Short E balances upside down on center stage.

He's doing a handstand, but his hands aren't on the ground. They are gripping a bowling ball, trying to keep it steady on the stage as he lifts himself closer and closer to a fully vertical upside-down position. The volume of the cheering crowd rises. He calls himself the human applause meter. Eighty people in the big red-and-blue circus tent clap and hoot and wipe the accumulating sweat from their upper lips. It is ninety-eight degrees. Opening day of the Minnesota State Fair. A little girl in the front row shrieks at the top of her shrill voice for him to go higher. He does. He wears his shoes, leather workman gloves, on his hands, and a black T-shirt with a picture of himself, tongue-out toward the camera. The ball wobbles, but the small jean shorts he wears loose from his waist still hang like a windless flag.

I normally can't see what goes on in any of the acts I'm not in. I can hear them, but the stage curtain separates the audience from our backstage area, and there isn't anywhere to go in the tent that offers a view of the stage without being in view of the audience. And, this show is all about illusion.

Or so I thought.

241

A few hours into opening day, Chris Christ hulks up the backstage steps and into our small metal world. There are a number of fold-out chairs on either side of the container, but there is no way his body could fit in one, and besides, something so regular as a fold-out chair seems too banal for a man who has spent so much of his life in sequins.

He clomps the few steps from backstage door to stage curtain and, in full view of the audience on the other side of the curtain, opens it a few inches. Short E is onstage, raising the bottom of his torso higher and higher into the air in response to the audience's clapping, both his hands balanced on the bowling ball, and I've maybe never heard the audience going this nuts and I can see why through the crack in the curtain that the Big Boss is holding open to watch Short E.

I watch Chris Christ watch Short E for five seconds, then ten, sure that at any moment he'll drop the curtains and seal the illusion back into its proper layer of reality, where we exist as our characters and not as people in cheap costumes who sit backstage and eat tuna from a can while scrolling Facebook.

But he doesn't. The Big Boss keeps the curtain parted for the duration of Short E's act, watching the world's smallest daredevil and the audience's reaction to the world's smallest daredevil and also the audience's reaction to the Big Boss giant's face peering from between the curtains behind the balancing man.

"Why's he doing that?" I whisper over to Sunshine. "Doesn't he care that the crowd can see him?"

"I'm sure he doesn't," Sunshine says. "One crowd, one show, doesn't matter. I'm sure they were more interested in what Short E was doing anyway."

Short E is the only performer we have whose natural body is part of his act. All of us—Short E included—manipulate our bodies for the audience. Though the cast has a great display of tattoos and piercings, Short E is a freak performer in the traditional sense—a person with a different kind of body who

242

displays that body—while the rest of us are geeks: those who enact performance and illusion to wow the crowd.

And he is good.

Very, very good.

He speaks into the mic like an announcer at a professional sporting event, with the rhythms and cadences in his speech that clue the audience in on an imminent spectacular spectacle.

Aaron Wollin, aka Short E Dangerously, is thirty-five years old. He is thirty-three inches tall and weighs seventy-two pounds. Story goes: after twelve years as a strip club DJ in Daytona, he retired from one kind of spotlight to pursue another. "My dad was worried when I first joined the sideshow," Short E says of his first season with the World of Wonders in 2012. He tells me his story in fits and starts between acts, on the folding metal chairs that make up our living area. "He thought they'd keep me in a cage or something." It was his first venture into performing.

While I go out to perform, Short E drives a race car on his phone, a cigarette hanging from the corner of his mouth. "I love the cheering here. All these people are cheering for me," he says when I return. I raise my eyebrows at him. The cigarette ember matches the hue of the flames tattooed around his arm. "When I was born, my dad didn't even think I would be able to ride the Ferris wheel, and here I am," he says, gesturing out the open door to the whirling lights, the screaming teenagers grabbing one another as they shoot toward the sky.

Born without the lower half of his spine, Short E's atrophied legs were amputated when he was two and a half years old. In elementary school, he was strapped into a big bucket with Velcro straps over the shoulders and prosthetic legs attached to the base. He used crutches. Then he moved into a wheelchair.

"But I'm stuck in a wheelchair with these goddamned fake legs and everyone else is outside having fun," he says. "I got rid of them." He's been walking on his hands ever since.

Propped in his DJ booth at the strip club one night, he met

243

his girlfriend. "She was onstage and did this move where she kicked her leg behind her head. I looked over at the owner and said, 'I think I'm in love.' " She moved in right away. Her two boys did, too. "They respect me," he says, after telling a story about when they found his gun and shot a hole through the wall, about when they shoved the air conditioner out the window. Drank his bong water.

Short E's mom, a Lutheran minister, died eight years ago. "She tried to raise me to have a normal life," he says. He pays his bills, rent. Vacuums his apartment. "The only thing I wish I had legs for was to drive a stick shift."

Short E's act ends and Chris drops the curtain. Short E comes backstage.

"That's good stuff," Chris says. "Real good stuff. Come with me into my trailer. I have an idea."

"See?" Sunshine says. "Chris had the curtain open for like three minutes watching Short E, and it gave him an idea for something that I'm sure will be crazy and very Chris-like. And it doesn't matter about the audience that one time around."

"Because they still had a good time," I say.

"They did or they didn't. But we tried."

$$\mathbf{\frac{\textstyle /}{\textstyle }}$$

Do you know what feels good? Dollar bills in your underpants.

"Do you have a script for the blade box I could look at?" I ask Tommy.

I am to be the new inside talker for the blade box. This means the person with the mic who brings the crowd closer to the act, tells the story of the rubber girl or Gypsy magic or whatever tale I come up with while the audience watches sixteen blades slide into a rectangular box a bit smaller than a phone booth. The performer is locked inside, contorting her body around the blades. The talker tries to get the audience to pay an extra

244

dollar to go around back and see her inside the box. It's called a ding, and it's a big extra moneymaker for the show.

"Say whatever you want," Tommy says, and of course I know this is the answer he'll give, the answer for everything, but I wish for something else. He must see some panic in my eyes. "All right. If you want to watch me do the first couple when we open so you can hear what I say, that'd be fine."

When I visited the sideshow for the first time, I remember the talker telling the story of a poor Romanian woman, Sunshine, with a young daughter at home. The Romanian, the talker said, wasn't paid for her role in the sideshow but survived solely off tips. She was sharing her family secret, and shouldn't we reward her for that? I remember falling for it hard, seeing her huge, sad eyes, and thinking about the monsters who wouldn't pay her for her work in the show.

In previous iterations of the act, the blade box was laid down on top of a table like a coffin, the scantily clad girl laying herself down into her own shallow grave. An assistant would stand beside the box, sliding the blades into precut holes on the top and pushing them through until they emerged on the other side. The audience could wonder at both sides of the blade, imagining the shape of a contorted body inside or the tricks that might be at play without being able to see the exact constellation of the blades.

Inside the tent, where the audience's skepticism and search for the nuance of deceit is always present, the visual assurance of both ends of the blade does a lot of work. When I'd first seen this act in Florida, I'd invented elaborate ideas about the hoax involved, the sword, for example, breaking off when it enters the box, holding to the box's exterior by magnets, and another piece coming out the other side, plans that would have involved a significantly higher budget than we ever had.

I watch Tommy talk the blade box act twice, and when the third cycle of the show comes up, he asks if I am ready.

"Maybe? Probably not," I say.

"Great, you'll be fine," he says, handing me the mic. He has the bally stage to talk, and other performers to manage, and money to deal with, and talking an extra act—a long one at that—isn't something he can afford.

"I'll stand next to you this first one, as your assistant, just in case anything goes wrong."

We walk down to the separate side stage where the stand-up blade box reaches high into the air. Sunshine presents herself, and I start talking— "There are sixteen slits and slats into which we will be placing these blades," I say—and she climbs in. Sort of remembering what Tommy had said, I throw in little details I'm not sure he'd said or I am inventing, and I stumble over words, repeating things I don't need to repeat. The crowd has thirty or forty people in it. The blades are all in. And then I get to *the* moment.

"So this is where our act usually ends. We get the blades out, take Ms. Sunshine out of the box, and bring our next performer onto the stage. But people keep coming up to us here and asking, What does she look like in there? Can I see her? And today, Ms. Sunshine has agreed to share with you her family secret. She's agreed to let you see her inside this box, and if you'd like to see Ms. Sunshine today, there are just three rules.

"The first rule is she asks that we make it happen quickly and in an organized fashion, because we don't want to leave her in there any longer than is necessary. So you're going to make one line starting here by me and going back straight in that direction to see Ms. Sunshine today."

The audience lines up quickly, still looking at me. Excited.

"The second rule is we ask that you not touch Ms. Sunshine, for her safety. And third, because this is Ms. Sunshine's family tradition, and it has been the way her family has made their living for the past five generations, Ms. Sunshine asks for a small donation today to see her inside this box. Now, she'd take as big a donation as you'd like, even one hundred dollars, but

246

she does ask for a minimum donation of just one dollar per person to see her in the box today."

My sequined dress is soaked beneath the armpits. My voice is shaky. I am sure these nice fairgoers will see me for the sham that I am. Why on earth would someone hand me extra money?

I look at Tommy, who is looking very seriously at me, nodding along.

"So if you'd like to come on back and see Ms. Sunshine, I'll collect your donation for her here, then you'll go back around behind the box, look through those viewing windows, and exit on the other side."

The first person in line reaches into his pocket, pulls out a dollar, and hands it to me. The others behind him do the same. I have to pinch myself to keep from smiling. It is working. I am making it work.

"Ms. Sunshine thanks you. Go on back and see her now," I say, collecting the first dollar, and the second, collecting dollar after dollar until most of the people in the tent have gone through.

Backstage, I sit beside Tommy as we count out the dollars in my hand. Twenty-eight. "Shit, Tess. Best turn today. You're a natural."

I beam so bright I think my eyes might shoot off as stars into the sky.

In Minnesota, three weeks into talking this act, I want to be better. The best. I practice timing out the story I tell about Sunshine as the blades go in, looking momentarily concerned at the box if I see the audience's eyes wandering away from me so they think that something especially dangerous, especially wonderful might be happening this time, and *this time only*. I learn how important the first few people in line are, that if they decide to come on back, many others will follow. If they don't, more in the back will think it's a scam and not come back either. I must win them over. Group psychology. Make them

247

believe not only in the magnificence of this particular feat, but also in Sunshine's unique familial treasure. Make them feel sure they aren't being swindled.

Every single time it's a brand-new puzzle to solve. It keeps me paying attention. Making real money for the show. And it's the first act I've done here that I'm legitimately good at.

A couple of days into the fair, I turn away from the crowd, pretending to sneeze, so they won't see me stuffing the wads of dollars down my tights because my hands cannot hold any more money. The crowd is gigantic. They all want what I am selling. The bills bloat my sequined shorts, a brimming black rainbow around my crotch as the dollar bills create padding, the coins already warm from the hot air and the hot hands of the audience and now only slightly cooler than my body. Speak to me of power and political ambition and I'll remember the press of paper and metal against my bare hips.

I spin a story to a crowd.

They buy it.

"We can only keep Ms. Sunshine in the box for one more minute," I say into the mic, trying to count by fives the line still waiting in front of me. I don't know if people really buy that this is a family secret she's deciding to share just this once, but I think the teensy sliver of possibility that that could be true is enough for them to fork out the dollar to come see.

At first I was afraid of lying, and then I wasn't.

Well, sort of.

When I was very young I loved lying. It was so easy.

In first-grade show-and-tell: "My daddy gave me this necklace," I said, touching the necklace I was wearing, "because it was my birthday this weekend. And he threw me a party and we had a cake." I am looking down at my beautiful plastic beaded necklace and up at the wide-eyed jealous faces of the children sitting cross-legged in the circle around me, who were not nearly special enough to have been gifted beautiful things.

248

Sophie's eyes across from me, perfect circles beneath her black eyelashes, are stuck on my jewels. We are going around the circle with special things we've brought in to show, or stories about our weekends that we want to tell. But I'd forgotten, and had nothing to show, nothing to tell. Or that's what I thought until, when my turn came, I remembered the plastic necklace I was wearing.

I looked back at Sophie, ready to further impress her with the glory of my weekend, but then there was a movement behind her. I looked up. Never look up. There she was. A classroom helper for a few hours that day. I'd forgotten. My mom. There she was with a look on her face, a certain twist of her mouth, a certain flare of her nostrils. More than disappointment, a confusion. That I was the kind of person I was. She was learning it right that moment. I couldn't shut up. I felt my cheeks go red and had to pee. "All my cousins were at the party," I said. "My one older cousin, too, and I'm his favorite. I'm his favorite and also my dad's favorite. He gave me other presents," I said, but I could see her moving over toward me. It was too late.

I hadn't seen my dad in months.

As the crowd hears and believes in Sunshine's story, some people smile, look me in the eyes as they hand me their dollars, our fingers touching, like this handshake buys them a real secret. Others hand their money to me with great reluctance, don't make eye contact, or, if they do, scowl like I am forcing them, cheating them. Which I am not, and also am, both. Sometimes one will pay and the rest gather round on the other side of the platform, waiting for the chosen member to walk through, to snap a picture and come back to show the rest. But we don't light the backside and pictures are hard to make out. They are more of an appetizer than an answer. What the audience sees on the backside of the box is Sunshine, on tiptoe, her knees and hips and back and arms and neck bent in such a way that she fits around and between the blades. Her torso is curved in, her knees bent, her body one large S. Once you see her there, you can make out her body's path on the other side of the box, between the handles of the blades.

"Is it worth it?" other people from the audience will holler to someone coming out. If we are lucky, the kid nods her head in astonishment, an assertion of wonder. Other times, a woman shrugs her shoulders, taking huge wet bites of her foot-long sausage, gulping beer while she surveys our magic and, shaking her head no, heads for the exit.

A young woman stands in line with a frayed shirt, three kids, one of whom is in a stroller with a broken wheel, and they have little dirty faces, or maybe my memory is adding the dirt beneath their nostrils, the brown collected in their snot so that their faces resemble the portraits of Depression-era Dust Bowl babies. They come forward with dollar bills in their hands and the mother stands back—she's twenty-five at most maybe, looks closer to sixteen—craning her neck around because she wants to see what's behind the trick as much as anyone. And aren't we lucky to be filled with that wonder? She has pulled dollars from her pocket and straightened them out, and there are two bills left and three children, and she hands the dollars to two of them old enough to walk so they can come see this wonder whose story I've just spun, and the other little one, left behind, is squirming in the stroller, crying, and the mother is staring at the other kids in great anticipation.

I wanted to whisper to just the kids to sneak around back and peek, to let the mother behind, too, and the little stroller kid, but it was rare I could swing it. Usually, I had to just take their dollars.

Those were the hardest. Not because I thought glimpsing Sunshine uncomfortably posed around the blades wasn't fun to see—it was—but because it filled me with this sudden moral dread. Is it okay to lie in service of entertainment? Okay to spin a story that causes someone to give you what seems like much-needed money?

250

I had to find my own moral line. I found, quickly, that it was easy to stand up in front of an audience and tell them about Romanian secrets and family tradition, to tell a backstory that made people more excited to see her. In my moral world, it was another thing— shadier, more deceptive—to say she had a child at home and this was her only source of income. Why was the second story so much worse? They were all lies, of course, and probably the one with the child would have been more effective, would have collected her, and by turn us, and me— because as a ding talker, you took a cut of what you brought in, 10 percent for the blade box—more money. But something about that felt like it pushed us over into cheats. Pulled too hard on easy sympathies.

I settled on a story that fit into my continually shifting moral guidelines.

"Ms. Sunshine comes from a Romanian circus family. And this is an act that her family has been performing in this same traditional way for the last five generations. She learned it from her mother, who learned it from her mother, and on and on up the family line. She's been doing it since she was only four years old, when they brought the act from where they'd toured in Europe over to California. She's now the last person who can perform this kind of contortion act today."

I knew that other performers—the owners, Ward and Chris, for example—didn't agree that there was any difference between the kinds of stories we were telling out here. They didn't tell me so, since I was bringing in good money, but Ward famously said that the thing to remember about the term *show business*, was that *business* was the longer word.

When I come backstage after the biggest turn, with money shoved down my shorts, dollars in my tights and jammed into my corset, filling my hands and the little change bag I carried, I stand in the middle of all my fellow performers. Standing there is unnecessary, but I want them to look. I reach down into

251

my shorts and, handful by handful, dump the money onto the broken wooden floor of the truck backstage. I bend over, pull my corset away from my chest and dump coins, reach down and pull out the dollar bills that are still stuck to my breasts and stomach. Beneath me, a pile of sweaty money grows across the floor. I make sure all the eyes are on me. I make sure they all see what I can do.

Short E gives a few slow claps. "And there it is, folks," he says. "GTFM. Get. The. Fucking. Money."

It's the first moment since joining the show—maybe even since my mom got sick—that I feel like I nailed the thing I'd set out to do.

Chris Christ catches me as I am walking backstage the next night.

"You're pretty good at talking the blade box," he says. "You have the kind of voice people listen to. It's unusual. A little bit too rough," he says, "and a little bit too high. Almost unpleasant."

"Thank you?"

"You don't sound like a showperson. That's perfect for turning a ding. Do you notice when you turn the biggest crowds?"

I think about this a moment. I'd just perfectly recounted Sunshine's story. Spoke quickly and with a great rhythm, I thought, remembered all the major events of her life I'd invented, felt smooth and confident. I'd turned only three people.

"Not that last time," I say.

"Why not?"

"I don't know. I thought I had the story down pretty good."

"Think about it. People don't trust a used-car salesman who is practiced and smooth, someone whose job is obviously to put a veil over their eyes and best them," Chris says. "There are lots of styles talkers use, but think about this: less polish. It'll give them the illusion that this isn't something you do professionally, that you're not out here twenty times a day giving the

252

same speech, taking money from people over and over again."

"That they are in on something special," I say.

"It's a game you're playing. You both know the other one is smart. Let them think that they are a little bit smarter. That they will be the ones, the only ones, who might see behind the veil."

We are walking back toward his trailer, parked beside our semi. His steps are slow and lumbered, the way it seems a real giant would walk, and I wonder if this is a by-product of being so tall or an act assimilated into every facet of his life after so many years of embodiment.

"Anyway, you're good at this. And I bet you're good at a lot of things you try. You're going to do good things in your life, whatever you do," he says. "You're so young still."

"I'm not that young."

"Oh Christ," Chris says. "Be whatever age you want."

⚡

By the fourth morning of the Minnesota State Fair, nobody is speaking.

We are up for the 8:00 a.m. work call, all in a row along the front banner line while we hoist and tie, but there is none of the usual chitchat or shit talking. There are a few sounds, Spif grabbing the rope from one of the new bally girls as he says, simply, "No," and does the task himself. The sound of Big, Big Ben testing the speakers out on the front stage. The soft thwack of Brian the Juggler's clubs landing in his hand just outside the bunk doorway as he practices in his boxers, hair pointing every direction. Francine the burlesque dancer sweeping the dirt and bugs from the floor beneath her bunk that have accumulated since the day before. The quiet gurgle of our mini-coffeepot as it brews Folgers. And finally, the *swoosh* and shuffle of everyone transforming in costume and makeup. Their voices are too tired to come out. We finished last night's performance just six

253

hours ago and have fifteen hours of performing ahead of us.

Though our crew is made up of very different people, we move like one large breathing organism. Somehow we decide on this silence, pledging ourselves to it for the full hour before we open, letting the first words spoken happen onstage in front of an audience.

The other sound this quiet morning is the hose, always hooked up just down the trailer's steps. Short E is down there, taking a shower. The bathrooms are far and take too long to get to, he says, so he stands out there in his boxers or swimming trunks with his bottles of shampoo and body wash and lathers up. It looks dreamy, really. The day is getting hot already and the hose water is always cold after you run it for a minute. I fantasize about that cold hose water as the day goes on and I put on the extra costume for Ms. Olga Hess, the Headless Woman (hospital gown) over my own costume, or for Ms. Vickie Condor, Four-Legged Woman (vest, skirt, and knee socks, plus scarf around my head). I think about it as I grow light-headed from the heat, come back to the main backstage area, and press my face against the single box fan we have there to cool us. Greedy, I stand so my face is right against it, blocking the air for a moment from everyone else. It feels like there is no other way to survive. But then Short E, back from his act onstage, will do a handstand in front of it and cool the length of his upside-down body, cool his ass, and I begin to boil at the injustice of it if he stays longer than five seconds—how dare he block that air from us! Can't he see how many of us back here need it? Require it for survival? But the next time I walk anywhere, I press my face or chest right back to it.

The meat-grinders last a month in total. Two big, huge, giant, long, massive, thrilling, nasty GTFM state fairs with that smaller county fair in the middle just to tide us over. Even if you slept every minute you were off work during the meat-grinders—between 12:15 a.m. and 8:00 a.m., or 2:15 a.m. and 8:00 a.m., you could not get enough rest. The full month of

August. And then the extra performers we picked up will hop back on buses and planes and trains and return whence they came. And we will barrel on.

I wonder how full everyone's pee jugs are.

"Listen," Chris Christ says to me as he comes backstage with Short E. "We're adding a ding that we think is gonna be a real moneymaker. We need you as Short E's assistant. Okay?" I nod sure, because of course it sounds alluring, though in truth, adding another act to the others I already do is not what I want—those backstage moments to sit or sprint to the closet toilet between acts are precious. I won't get any cut of this ding, Chris Christ says, but I will get to help Short E. And walk among the crowd. I'm still unsure, until they explain the ding.

It's brilliant.

Short E walks out onstage and tells the crowd that he wants to share a special story with them.

"My mom was a preacher," he says. "And I grew up going to church and listening to her preach. A couple of years ago, she died of cancer. It was the hardest time in my life, but right before she died, she said she wanted to give me a gift. I want to share with all of you what she said, and what she gave me. It's this," he says, pulling a small gold object out of his pocket. "The world's smallest Bible, for the world's smallest daredevil."

The Bible is about two inches by two inches, a teensy paper book with print so small it requires a magnifying glass. It slides into a gold plastic case bedazzled with red or blue sequins. The whole thing is very ornate and gaudy, and an exact replica could be purchased by the audience for just one dollar.

Or two dollars.

Or three dollars.

Depending on how God-loving the audience seems. How willing to part with their money for a little reminder of the Lord's words and the story they'll be able to tell their other good Christian friends about the no-legged man they'd

255

helped by purchasing the Bible from him in his dead mother's honor.

"I'm going to bring my assistant out now," Short E says, and I come through the curtain with a sweet smile on my face and Bibles dangling from my fingers. Did I mention that the Bibles were also keychains? So that the Good Word can come with you wherever you go?

I walk across the stage and down the steps into the crowd, swinging the little dazzlers from my fingers as I weave through the audience, smiling my best sincere close-lipped smile, which I hope erases the memory of me from just a few moments earlier, when I was asking them for another dollar to see a girl bent like a pretzel.

"You don't look like a freak to me," one Christian in a lime-green collared polo shirt whispers to me after I sell him the world's smallest Bible. I can tell he is a Christian by the tenderness with which he clasps the gold book I trade him for two dollars. Also by his haircut. "In fact, I think you're beautiful," he says.

"Okay," I say, and consider marrying him and moving to a condo, but the music cue for the guillotine act starts, so instead I walk up the steps and part the curtain and sit in my backstage chair for four minutes until I become a four-legged woman.

Another night, a man in wraparound sunglasses and a sleeveless orange T-shirt asks if I like being an entertainer.

"Yes, it's pretty great," I tell him, trying to let the sheen of my blond hair blind him into purchasing five Bibles.

"Well, baby," he says, "I'm an entertainer, too. I'll entertain you all night long." Each of my fingers has a Bible dangling from it, like a mobile of holiness. I look over at the woman standing beside him. I'd assumed she was his wife. She smiles a wide grin at me. Her cheeks are shiny and hot, hot pink. My Bibles clink. They buy seven.

When the act is over one night, and Short E and I count out the money we've made him—he gets a percentage of this ding, like I do for the blade box—the Big Boss sits between us.

"Who sells more, Short E, you or Tess?"

"Tess, usually," he says.

"That's what it looked like to me, too," Chris says. "It's too bad. Back in the day, the crowd would only buy whatever ding we were selling from the freak. Wanted to support him directly, give him business. Wanted to be up close and shake his hand and look. Nowadays, people are too scared."

"Sometimes they come up to me to buy one, take a picture with me," Short E says. "It makes sense. I'm the biggest star in the show."

"People are mostly chickens, now," Chris says, ignoring Short E's last comment. "Want to sit on their fat asses and see freaks on TV and not have to actually be face-to- face with them. Too scared to see them as people. Easier to only consider them from afar. Chickenshit."

"Chickenshit," Short E says, and we tear into another plastic bag of Bibles, ready them for the next act.

WILDEWOMAN

Two and three-quarters years after the stroke

---

25 DAYS INTO THE TRIP
AUGUST 2013

I get a photograph of a towel folded into a swan.

There's another, folded into a dog.

The towels are crisp, white, stiff. They are perched on the end of a finely made bed. These, I learn, were waiting for my mom and Davy each day, after their small cabin on the cruise ship was made up, and wasn't it pretty funny?

It was pretty funny.

There was another one, two legs out to the side, some kind of tail, maybe, and an oversize head, but nobody could figure out what animal that was supposed to be.

Then there's another photograph.

The background is black night sky. There is the faint hint of a recent sunset from a deep red stripe across the horizon.

Davy posts a photograph of my mom from the ship on the blog he's keeping. The caption beneath the image reads: "On the deck, singing."

If this were a painting by one of the masters and not a quickly captured cell-phone snapshot, we'd discuss the brilliant use of light to illuminate the face, a bright wash across all the skin so it seems to glow. Not the kind of light that has been still, like

258

an ever-glowing constellation, but instead a kind of light in motion and a face that has just moved through darkness into the light.

The background's tinge of red is just enough to bring the color out on her cheeks and a rose flush for the lips, enough to remind us with just a glimpse of her pink, pink tongue that she is vibrantly alive.

There is wind in her hair, that wild silver mane, raised to the heavens and tossed to the side, a Wildewoman out at night on the deck of a ship somewhere in the Atlantic.

And her eyes. They had been the gray slugs of illness for those first months after her stroke. Unrecognizable. And then they'd come back moments here or there, but they seemed to gray over again when stimulus was too overwhelming.

But here, in this photograph, they are two gorgeous moss pools—almost green? could it be?—and glittery and focused, sharp, and she is looking at the camera, at her husband, and she is on her way to somewhere.

I want to feel terror. I do feel terror. I fear that all the bad things I can invent will happen. But then there is this photograph. She is sparked.

And her mouth is open.

In motion.

And there is song coming out.

There are things to say, and there are so many ways to say them.

THE SWORD SWALLOWER

Day 71 of 150

Chris Christ is hunched on a stool with hands as big as truck tires and his two continual streams of black snuff running from the corners of his mouth.

"Tess!" he shouts. "Time to learn!"

He knows every act backward and forward and is a former chimp trainer and knife thrower.

"Stand here," he says, pointing beside him. His legs are stretched straight and wide from the stool. Maybe this should be a moment of hesitation. I do not hesitate.

He puts one hand on my clavicle and one hand on my forehead. Presses.

"Stand up straight," he says. "Straighter."

It's early evening and there's a pause in our regular day: a storm. Lightning nearby. It has temporarily shut down the fair.

He pushes my head back until I am staring straight up into the eye of our tent's center pole.

"You've got to be lined up perfectly straight," he says, "or you'll never get the sword down."

In India, fakirs, beginning as early as 2000 B.C.E., swallowed swords and walked across hot coals, handled snakes and

260

stepped on broken glass as ascetic tributes to the divine, as assertions of power, connection, and invulnerability. What is a body if you take its power over you away?

In 1912, there was a Dutch fakir, Mirin Dajo, who asked his assistant to pierce a metal foil all the way through his body. It went from the center of his back through his organs and came out the front. He appeared unharmed, creeping up to the edge of the stage for his audience to inspect the foil and skin that the metal came through.

This was not an act of trickery. Dozens of doctors examined him, X-raying his body, asking him to perform various tasks to see if they could spot the illusion. He even jogged around the building. He wanted to prove that his feat was possible only through his ability to withstand the pain.

The doctors decided that he was able to create scar tissue in his body over time by slowly inserting the metal and allowing it to partially heal before inserting it farther. Between performances, he walked around with metal tubes through the holes. A secular stigmata.

Eventually, as the audience's need for shock increased, he was impaled by three hollow tubes at once, and had his assistant pump water through the tubes so the clear liquid poured out the front of his body, splashing the crowd.

Human fountain! people chanted.
Human fountain!
Human fountain!

After swallowing a sword that nicked his heart, Mirin Dajo died of an aortic rupture in 1946.

The way pain works:

When a sharp object presses against our skin, receptors send electrical signals through nerve fibers to the spinal cord and then up to the brain. Some of these fibers run like insulated telephone wires and carry the signals rapidly; others move through weblike neural connections and travel more slowly.

261

The signals move to the brain's thalamus, which acts as a relay station and directs them to the sensory cortex. The signals are then interpreted by the brain as a sharp pain. The slower impulses, traveling through the weblike neural fibers, become a throbbing ache.

Our brain has total control over our pain signals. When it believes we are in extreme danger, the brain turns the pain signal down so that we are not hindered by relatively minor pains instead of fleeing greater danger.

To train the body not to feel pain, to control thinking about the pain, then, does your brain have to believe itself to be in a constant state of life-threatening crisis?

Loose carnie children, dripping rainwater, peek under our tent's sidewall. It's pouring. The fair is closed until the storm passes so that nobody gets struck by lightning at the top of the Ferris wheel, so Chris has decided it's time for me to swallow swords. It's one of the only acts I haven't yet learned, but we all need to know every act in case anything happens to anyone, the Giant says.

It feels good to put the blade in my mouth.

But good isn't quite the right word for how it feels to have the metal inside—it isn't complicated enough. It feels dangerous and important, one of the pinnacle sideshow acts. And it hurts. Something jammed in the throat leads to gagging and the rise of bile. There are three sphincters to pass in the throat and esophagus—a body's emergency brakes. Do you want to know the secret to all the sideshow acts right now? Ready? Untrain your instincts. Unlearn self-preservation.

There are five big caged lights hanging from the tent's center poles that emit a soft buzz against the storm-dark. The wet earth smell has, for a moment, overtaken the funnel cake and corn dog grease that hangs in the air all day.

A wrong wrist twitch and the sword inside might pierce my lungs. Might nick my heart. I feel some relief as I stop imagining the pain of others and, instead, live inside my own potential for catastrophe. As I look for the divine.

"Think of the blade going down your throat like it's a big stiff prick," Red, who swallows swords in the inside show, tells me. He can slide twelve down his throat at once. He holds seven Guinness World Records. It says so on his van.

"And the gag reflex, think of that as just the pubic hairs tickling your throat," he says, winking. Tommy has folded a coat hanger into a sword for practice, which he made by straightening a wire hanger all the way out, doubling it, then twisting a handle. Mimicking him, I lick both sides and tilt my head back, let the metal rest on my tongue. I choose a little danger.

Anything can happen to anyone. Last season, the knife thrower flung his blade at the board and it landed in his long-time partner's thigh. She was taken to the hospital for stitches, but thirty minutes later, when their act came around again and she was still gone, another cast member had to go stand on the board. She had to know how to go stand on the board as if she didn't know how blood looks falling down the angles of fishnets. Had to know how to immediately erase memory. That's the predictable kind of crisis in this business, of course, and the predictable victim. But there is a whole carnival of bodies being whipped through space on big machines and sex and meth and the momentary elation of being the object of attention under those bright stage lights, and the truth is, there are potential crises all around at every minute.

I heave. My throat's gag keeps catching and I cough hard, waiting for the vomit to rise. When I pull the sword out the quarter inch it's gone down, the metal has flecks of white and clear fluid on the tip.

"Relax your throat," Chris says.

"Some people are naturals," Red says. He watches me attempt a few swallows and cough. "Some people aren't," he says, staring me down. Rain is falling up from the ground.

I've tried and coughed the hanger sword out twenty times.

263

It's hard to tell how far it's gotten, but I don't think I've even passed by the first gag sphincter.

"This is the one," I say. I lick, puff my chest as I lean back and the tip hits my sphincter and I keep shoving it in anyway, and then I feel something rising and pull the sword and double over and retch.

"Half-inch down," Chris says. I try to high-five him still buckled over, but my hand doesn't even reach his plane of vision.

An hour earlier, state police had come into our tent and ushered the last lingering audience members out.

"When the lightning hits, the last place I want to be is at the top of the big wheel," one of the cops says. "And the second-to-last place is in this circus tent."

It's true that tents get picked up in storms, tossed around like a flap of loose skin and deposited far away. It's true that there are all those tent stakes holding the thing in place that could also get tossed into the air and land on any person at any time doing anything.

"We're about to get a real bad one," the cop says. "I'd put your people somewhere safe," he says to Chris and Tommy.

"Girls," Chris says as the cops leave, "I want you all in your bunks. Stay in the trailer. You'll be safe."

"Chris—" Sunshine starts, but he holds up his hand to her.

We wait in the trailer for a few minutes, the lightning and thunder getting louder and closer, the men's voices coming through the slits in the trailer's walls. They are closing everything up, getting the insides of the tent and backstage storm-ready. I eye my empty trail-mix jug, feeling glad that earlier that day, though I'd started to squat over it beside my bunk to pee, I'd decided to just stop drinking much water in general, and held it.

We stay put. Well, briefly. But then Sunshine goes into the tent where there is more space to make a phone call, and Cassie

264

goes to show Brian the juggler something on her phone, and pretty soon we are all back in the main tent, the rain coming down and the thunder cracking outside.

And that's when, giving up on his initial directives and finding ways to pass the time, Chris tells me it is time to learn how to swallow swords.

Tommy folded the hanger sword for me a few weeks back, and I've practiced based on his instruction, the tips he gave me while we stood out on the bally stage on slow days, but I haven't practiced much because there's so little time for anything. Plus, it's not a thing that's easy to explain, or read about. It's something you just keep doing until you get it. I'd think about it during the day, while I was onstage inside one of the illusions. I'd fantasize about being center stage with a sword deep in my body and a wowed audience instead of sitting on a chair as a four-legged woman while they looked at me, annoyed. Doing something that the audience would find so attractive and repulsive both, doing something memorable. But by the time the show closed at night and I'd been performing for sixteen hours, I had no desire to practice new acts.

"Don't worry, Tess," Tommy says later, patting my shoulder. "It took me years before I could get the sword all the way down."

Story goes: as a high school student in New Jersey, Tommy decided he wanted to be a circus performer, but at six foot two and possessing little grace or flexibility, his options felt limited. He didn't come from a circus family and didn't have the physique of a typical aerialist or tumbler. What he wanted most of all was to wrestle an alligator. When he learned about sword swallowing, he thought it could take him to the circus, the gators.

He checked out a bunch of books on swallowing swords from the library and spread them across his bed, desk, and floor. Their illustrated pages provided step-by-step how-to

265

instructions and detailed accounts of some of history's most famous sword swallowers. He got to work. For three years he practiced every day, sticking a folded coat hanger down his throat to replicate a sword. Though his classmates began heading toward jobs as accountants and roofers, Tommy kept shoving the metal down his throat. An angry girlfriend once screamed that she thought Tommy loved practicing for his sideshow fantasies more than he loved her. He agreed.

Tommy's short stint in college to study biology—the closest he could get to those gators—was over after he enrolled in the Coney Island Sideshow School. He joined the World of Wonders shortly thereafter.

"I'd do anything to keep the sideshow alive," Tommy says. "I know it's my home."

Have you ever stuck your finger deep in your mouth? Tried to make yourself puke? Touched your uvula? That's what sword swallowing feels like when you first stick the sword in, but then, instead of heeding your body's direction and removing the object that's causing you to gag, you override the system. Stick it in a little deeper. Wait until you actually feel your insides rising to chase out the foreign object like townspeople chasing out a wolf, but instead of feeling grateful to your grandmothers and granddaughters for their good, safe work, you call back the wolf. Make his teeth a little sharper. Force him in.

Sword swallowing is one of the most iconic sideshow acts, something I thought I might see people practicing the first time I'd visited Gibsonton the way other people in other towns might practice baseball. When I pulled into Gibsonton that first time, what I first noticed was that the gas station had an amazingly long line of people buying beer. I had come down to meet Chris Christ and his partner, Ward Hall, right after I'd first learned about the World of Wonders. Just down the road a drive-through liquor barn sat next to half a dozen adult bookstores and strip clubs. Huge trucks hurtled down U.S. 41, Gibsonton's main street, which stretched long and flat for miles, north toward Tampa, south toward beach towns like Bradenton and Sarasota with their Easter-colored vacation homes. Palm trees and swamp grass waved as truckers and tourists rushed through, always on their way somewhere else.

They say at one time the town had the world's only postal counter designed for dwarves. That conjoined twins ran a lemonade stand on the side of the highway. That the town had permanently altered its legislation to allow for elephants and tigers in every front yard, their trainers throwing knives around unblinking women in sequins when the mosquitoes weren't too thick.

Story goes: a few performers were on their way to Sarasota, Ringling Brothers' Circus's winter headquarters. In the batch were "the giant" Al Tomaini, who claimed to be eight foot four, and his wife, Jeanie, "the half-girl," born with no legs. They noticed how peaceful a certain patch of swamp was and decided to stop right there. Not too close to cities and gawkers, not too far from the rest of their circus folks. They set up camp by the river and opened a little cookhouse. Once they and a few of their friends settled in, sideshow performers from a range of shows came quickly. It was a place for the winter months, when carnivals take a break, where the unusual would be usual. A rest stop. A retirement destination. A new home.

By the time I visited Gibtown, the town's very small sign stood overgrown by thick vines at the base of a bridge spanning the Alafia River. Passing through, you might miss Gibtown's history, unless you notice the Showtown Bar & Grill, a grimy brick building that once served performers amazing enough to inspire the murals coating the walls. The paint is faded and peeling, the acrobat by the door nearly invisible.

And yet, Gibtown is still the home of the real American sideshow. I forget, forget often, that these folks I'm working with, this show, are such legends. These three men teaching

267

me to swallow swords hold various Guinness World Records, perform on all sorts of TV specials and movies, are the titans of the industry, even if the industry is mostly a ghost of what it was fifty years ago.

"Okay, me, too," Francine, the burlesque dancer, says, walking over to us with her sword. She brought a real one with her and has been trying to learn the right technique for years.

"You're new, right?" Chris asks her. She smiles at him, nods. "And you're not staying the whole season?"

"I would if I could," she says, "but no. I'm leaving after this spot."

"Then no," Chris says.

"No?"

"No, I won't teach you. Only skeleton crew gets to learn. You gotta do a whole season to have free classes on everything."

"That's not fair!" she says.

An explosion of spit and booming sound bursts from Chris's mouth as a laugh.

"Sorry, Francine," Tommy says. "Tradition. For part-time performers like you, you get a discount on classes if you ever want to take one, but you can't learn here."

"I really can't believe that," she says. "It's kind of bullshit."

Chris stops laughing and looks at her, and the few hairs on the sides of his head might be waving a bit like a cartoon man preparing to explode with anger, his lip trembling.

"Fine, okay, sorry," she says, skulking away.

Chris turns back to me. Dumb, unskilled, slow-learning me. "Tell me, Tess," he says. "What did your mom think when you told her you were going to run away with the circus?" He's instructed me to take a break for a few minutes while the bile retreats and my eyes stop watering.

I could answer this truthfully. I could tell him the story, tell all these folks I've been working with for months now the truth, the whole thing, the mess of it. I've mentioned once or twice

268

to a few of the other performers, Sunshine and Cassie and maybe Spif, that I have a sick mom. And they've told me about their lives. But life moves so quickly here, when it's not moving painfully slowly. And when I think about trying to tell someone the whole long arc of the drama, I feel exhausted. I'm already exhausted. I look around me at all these tough folks who have had hard things happen in their lives and continue on, and it makes me want to do the same. To harden my gut. And then ready it for swords.

"My family thinks it's great," I say.

"They do?"

"Sort of. Well, they said it sounded fun as long as I promised not to ever try sword swallowing."

"Ha," Chris says. "You're not very good at keeping promises."

"Right," I say, and study the coat-hanger sword in front of me, hoping for some trick to reveal itself. Knowing it won't.

"You know why I invited you to come join the show?" he asks me.

My heart stops. I do not know. I have no idea whatsoever. I have kept myself from even thinking about it, let alone asking anyone. I am scared of the answer. It will somehow further illuminate what a fraud I am here, what a fraud I am in how I obsessively think about my mom but don't obsessively act to help her. I'm also desperate for the answer. I manage to nod my head.

"You seemed genuinely interested in this world. You came to the show, looked me in the eyes, and I could see something about you there. That you'd stick around. Plus, I think you're a good person. Someone like that should witness this."

So there it is. Tapped to step into another world as witness. To stick around. To watch. For a moment, the fact of my outsiderness doesn't seem as alienating. There is something I can do as an outsider. Something only I among us can do. I can bear witness.

269

"Thank you," I say, overwhelmed, surprised.

"Are you having fun?"

"Yes, definitely."

"Good."

"Well, yes and also no."

"No?"

"I've never worked this hard or been so bad at so many things. It's kicking my ass."

"Ah," he says. "That's normal. It'll do that. Just remember that no matter what, we're always playing. It's all just playing."

THE ANIMAL UNDONE

Day 76 of 150

WORLD OF WONDERS
SEPTEMBER 2013

How to take the animal apart:

Tough pants, hard-toed shoes.

Some of the first steps are easy. We unsnap the velvet curtains around the headless woman's chair, locking the wooden wings that spread wide from the mummy cases, unsnap the hard vinyl belly cloths from the stage, its skirt. Close the sword cases, dismantle the electric chair, untwist its screws. For a moment, then, as we do our work, my hands touch items that amaze the audience. Many of the acts I'm in now—headless woman, four-legged woman—get a lot of groans. The other acts I talk—bed of nails, blade box contortion act—position me as the hype woman, a necessary conduit to focus the attention on the wonder taking place just beside me. The closest I came to making the amazement happened before I became an inside performer, when I was eating fire on the bally stage, or holding the snake, but those small miracles are cut down quickly by how easily new bally girls are hired and trained, by my knowledge of the pecking order.

But I want more. I want to be wonderful. I want the electric chair.

It isn't the time to think about that now. Who I am here, in

271

these teardown hours, matters only in terms of my physical being and my being part of the group.

And so:

Earlier in the day, we'll have taken any hanging items down from the walls. We shove everything as far under the bunks as possible, to ready the bunk rooms to be stuffed with props.

We must take care not to puncture any surfaces when unhinging, unpinning, unclipping, folding, rolling, twisting, or stacking. Not to contaminate any of the fragile parts with mud, feces, or blood. When we bleed, we wipe our own blood on our pants to keep our precious gear pristine.

Starting with the tent's central entrance across from the stage, we peel away the skin, clip by clip, from the bones. The live animal of the tent is dismantled. The junctures have the most resistance. It may hurt, pressing our fingers hard against the metal to release the vinyl, pressing until the skin on our fingers is marked. We do not fall off the top steps of the ladder as we reach way out to push and unclip and pull.

Once we have peeled away the tent's skin, we continue slipping it off the body as we work our way around until we have the fully separated hide of a flayed animal. It is now three hours into teardown. The tent walls fall to the ground in huge wrinkled piles like skin we must preserve. We keep on.

We prepare each piece of the loosed vinyl tent on the ground for curing by hosing it down if it needs to be hosed, by dragging it along the ground until it is perfectly straight and flattened and then begin, yellow by red, yellow, red, yellow, red, folding and smoothing the creases. We tuck and pull, two of us crouching together for each fold so we move simultaneously, so no extra creases form beneath the folds. The vinyl tent must slide perfectly into a canvas bag, which must fit perfectly in a stack of other canvas bags, which must fit perfectly between Queen Kong and a light box in the meticulously organized truck container. All of this care. The minutiae inside the wild animal of sideshow.

Five hours.

We look at the tongue, our stage, that expanse of wood we've been parading across for ten days. We see the eye, that single doorway behind the curtain into the backstage world, into the animal's brain where we live and work and sleep and eat and fight. This face will be dismembered last. Once all traces of the former animal are tucked inside, we hoist the stage up until it tucks flat against the side of the semi container, closing its eye until the next unveiling.

Beside us on both sides and across the midway, carnie crews are leaping between sections of their rides, yelling, killing their animals, too. I wonder about wandering down to carnietown once teardown is done, to see if there are any special celebrations that go on before they load back up and move on to the next town.

Seven hours.

There is too much work to be done.

And what is that bloody meat beating in the middle of it all?

What keeps pumping when the bones have been released from the skin, when the skin has been folded and tucked away, when the mouth has been shut? What else is still throbbing? Do we hear that humming? Don't we hear that music? A low drumming? Teeth, somewhere, hitting against a glass?

I can hear it still, even after the semi is hitched and pulls the container onto the next grounds. I hear it when the lot is empty except for piles of hot-dog containers and a broken Octopus ride, and I hear it when we are barreling down the highway with the dead animal all packed away in the truck just ahead, I can hear it. Ravenous. Thrumming. Desperate to come alive.

⚡

The trailer behind the van is fishtailing. It's a heavy, old trailer, and though the van was upgraded a few seasons ago, it isn't hauling the trailer in a straight line. The trailer swerves to one

273

side, pulling the van along with it. It's throwing us over the lane dividers on the freeway, hemming us right up against the semitrucks throttling alongside us. We feel the blowback of the trucks' wind pressing our trailer toward the other edge of the lane, a seesaw we can't ever stabilize.

We've unloaded the temporary performers. We dropped the last three off at the bus station and airport after teardown in Minnesota.

Big Boss Chris has left, too. We are back to our skeleton crew, plus Short E, who will stay with us for most of the rest of the season. Well, our skeleton crew minus Pipscy. We are very quiet. It feels like the whole thing should be over, like we've survived the hardest part to survive and therefore it is time for a big break for everyone, margaritas by the pool, but we still have two and a half months to go.

I had a text from Pipscy saying she'd made it home, saying it was wonderful to see her mother, her boyfriend, saying that she had found a job in a bar as a mermaid, one of those girls who swims, in a bikini and tail, in a giant tank behind the bar. She also had a mermaid gig lined up for the next Renaissance fair, too. Mermaids fill her future.

We point the van toward Hutchinson, Kansas. But we don't make it far.

The van keeps skidding across the road, fishtailing back and forth. We pull over to check the tire pressure, fill the gas tank, change the oil. Nothing works. Hours pass, our caravan swaying gently back and forth across the highway lines while our performers inside all sit straight up on the bench seats, fists taut around the ceiling handles.

A blue Honda is on the shoulder ahead of us. Our trailer sways. We can just make out the blur of several arms waving frantically from a pile of humans beside the blue car. We swerve, and Sunshine keeps her hands on ten and two at the wheel and says, "Oh shit, Oh shit," and we're all staring at the commotion beside the road, and suddenly, thankfully, we're

274

beside them and not directly upon them, we're barreling past and we see two adults waving their arms madly around and a woman between them, her mouth open in a wail we cannot hear, and in her arms a child's limp body.

Somebody else's catastrophe is unfolding right now, right this very moment, right beside us.

We barrel on. Say quiet things to ourselves like *oh shit* and *that sucks.*

At the next exit, Sunshine veers off the highway and I think it's maybe to call for help or to go back and help, but we don't. Instead, we pull into the parking lot of the Kansas Star Casino, a massive reflective tomb surrounded by a mostly empty asphalt parking lot and, beyond that, fields of corn as far as you can see in any direction.

My heart is beating fast, both from the caterwauling van and the emergency we passed, and the feeling is familiar, the panic, the danger. The taut faces that signaled distress.

"Fix this fucking trailer problem," Sunshine tells Tommy, who has swung the semitruck around in the parking lot and, sighing, gets into the van's driver seat.

"Everyone out," he says, and we pile out onto the empty parking lot, the sun a low gold ball above the cornfields. We hear sirens in the distance. I imagine the people on the side of the road hearing the sirens, too, believing that there might be time for what has gone wrong to be made right again.

Spif walks toward the casino to pee and walks back several minutes later. They wouldn't let him inside.

"What are you going to do?" Ben asks Tommy, eyeing the trailer, but Sunshine leans over to him.

"Shut up," she says.

"What Sunshine said," Tommy says. "She's in charge."

Tommy leaves all of us and drives the van and trailer out of the parking lot and down a road whose horizon disappears between golden fields of corn.

We get comfortable on the asphalt, leaning against one

another. We sit in the sun, wondering aloud how close to the next fair we're going to get that night, whether we'll have to sleep in the unplugged bunkhouse in an empty lot on a back road or in a Walmart parking lot, whether we'll pull in somewhere at an hour when anyone who has someone to call can still call them. We roll small stones between our fingers. We are chatting or silent. Some are on phones. Someone passes out gum. People lie down. Someone yawns and we talk about yawning. Pebble tossing. Shoulder massages. Clouds move across the sky in the shapes of fat horses, and then are gone.

In between emergencies, there's the regular, boring muck.

An hour later, the van and trailer pull back into the parking lot. Tommy rolls down the window and shakes his head at us. Smiles. He holds up one hand with a screwdriver clenched in his fist.

"The trailer won't fishtail anymore," he says.

"How can you know?" Sunshine asks, jumping up. Her huge blue eyes squint against his confidence, always testing him.

"The tank," Tommy says under his breath.

"Oh god," Sunshine says. "Sewage? I thought you stopped using the toilet after we couldn't get it open to dump anymore."

"Well, I stopped shitting in it."

"Oh my god."

"It was full. That's why you were fishtailing. The sewage tank was really heavy on just one side of the trailer."

"Thomas," she says, slowly.

"It was the meat-grinder," Tommy says. We all understand what that means. The busyness of Minnesota didn't allow for Porta-Potty breaks, and there were too many carnies and kids wandering back behind the midway's bright lights to allow for peeing against the trailer's tires, a move I pulled on other darkened fairground nights in smaller lots.

"So you got the latch open with that screwdriver and dumped the tank?"

276

"I still couldn't get the latch open," Tommy says.

"This is disgusting," Sunshine says. "What are we supposed to do?"

Tommy smiles a long, flat grin. He holds the screwdriver up again. "I stabbed a hole through the side of the trailer into the tank. I dumped all the year-old piss into a sunflower field a few miles down the road."

Back down the highway, maybe near the yellow sheets of sunflowers, the family has probably left the side of the road. Whatever emergency has happened is likely still happening and will probably continue causing a wake for a long time. The ripples will travel and travel and eventually, hopefully, it will be the strangest thing, when suddenly that child will find herself looking at the clouds, no longer measuring time by proximity from disaster.

⚡

One and a half years after my mom's stroke, her brain was suddenly bleeding again. Too much. We didn't know why, or how, but the drain had stopped pumping and so we had a problem.

I shouldn't say that her brain was bleeding again, because it is actually always bleeding. It is never not bleeding. It hasn't stopped since that first stroke. Not really. The liquid space around her brain is constantly gaining volume. When she first came into the hospital, the emergency-room doctors cut away the skull on half of her head, and it cannot fit back on there. It won't take. They kept trying to reattach it and the body wouldn't have it.

To reduce the fluid, they surgically implanted a drain that sucks the liquid, blood and fluid, and carries it down the inside of her neck and dumps it somewhere in her stomach, where her body digests it like it processes everything else.

But the drain stopped working, and everyone was moving very quickly.

She was in a rehabilitation hospital that did not have the capacity to deal with this. I was standing in the back corner of the room with my limbs and stomach and butt and throat sucked in as close as I could get them, trying not to be noticed. It was the family members, usually, who wailed, who asked questions, who tried to touch when touching could not occur—they were the ones who were asked to leave. I stayed quiet.

The EMTs were young men, three of them with close-cropped hair, boys still, who left high school five or fewer years before and probably played beer pong on Thursdays. I wanted to play beer pong on Thursdays. I wanted to go to their beach parties. To do something that didn't mean anything.

They slid her onto the gurney and wheeled her into the hallway. There was oxygen over her nose and her eyes were closed, then open and looking at people on some other plane of existence, and then they closed again.

We waited outside the room while arrangements were made at the hospital. Would she die this time? The question never changed. We called the aunts and uncles with news of the new emergency. Davy wailed in his car.

She was released from the hospital ten months after her stroke. Then she had an infection and had to go back. A month in the hospital. Then out. Three days in. Out. Three weeks in. And out, and back, and out. And in. Et cetera. Would she die?

I was beside the gurney, and her eyes were opening and closing—did she know what was going on? Was she in pain? Could she see the tiled ceiling and soft pastel bouquets lining the walls in this world?

There was one EMT standing at the head of the gurney, waiting for instructions. His hair was dirty blond and parted loosely in the middle like a teen heartthrob from the nineties. I stood by her shoulder, on the side, holding her unresponsive hand, which was cold and dry and had longer fingernails than I'd ever seen on her.

"She your grandma?" the EMT asked.

278

"Mom," I shot back quickly. "My mom." I was terrified that she'd heard that. The question would not have been well received in the past. But I also felt, shamefully, embarrassed for her, on some vain and irrelevant level, given the crisis at hand.

She did look old. The previous year and a half had put her body through so much that her skin sagged away from her bones. She was very skinny and frail, her hair gone further from gray toward white.

"She just...It has been hard lately," I said.

"Sure," he said. "I bet. Sorry for your loss."

I couldn't believe he said that: my loss.

My loss. It was a loss. Is. But nobody had said that word, would say it, or could—because she wasn't technically lost. Here was her body, right here, alive, and to say *loss* would imply that she wasn't working as hard as she was to remain here in this world. Which was hard. So. Fucking. Hard.

As long as she was alive, the conversation with medical staff and family had to remain firmly about recovery and progress, about indicators of forward-moving time without the recognition of the past—of who she had been to me, to my brother, to her husband.

"Has she made any progress?" the EMT asked. I thought about the first weeks when she was in a coma, of the following weeks when we first felt one hand squeeze, when she began, from time to time, to make eye contact with us, to breathe, to get to the point where she could sit propped up for ten whole minutes. To move the one leg, the one arm. To go through painful physical therapy, occupational therapy, speech therapy. To get to the point where she could eat and drink on her own, where she could look us in the eye sometimes and laugh, touch our hair like it was nothing, where she was strong enough to be released from the hospital.

"No," I said. I wanted more sympathy from him. I was desperate to hear someone talk more about the loss.

She punched me in the nose. No, I only wanted her to punch

me. I wanted her eyelids to peel back, for her to look at me with condemnation and accusations, with disdain, but she didn't move. I flooded with guilt.

The other EMTs gave a signal and we loaded into the ambulance.

$$\maltese$$

Someone removed my eyeballs from their sockets and soaked them in hot sauce. They blew insulation in through one ear and it filled all the space in my head, forcing my brain out the other side. And my bones were replaced by the steel poles we used to build the tent, which were so heavy and hard to move that my whole body started scraping the ground every time I tried to walk anywhere.

I couldn't remember the last time I'd slept more than five or six hours. We'd been on the road two and a half months, though it felt like years. We were never more than a few feet from one another, even sleeping, with our bunks stacked vertically, and the thin boards that separated the beds horizontally thin enough to hear someone cracking their toes in their bed inches from your face. It was getting ugly. I was. Everyone was taking little stabs at one another to try to deflect some of the knives outward. Eyes were red. Little veins across the balls.

"I've never wondered how folks here get so into uppers," Spif says. "I don't do that shit, but I almost wish I did."

So did I. There was weed around, and booze sometimes, but our crew, as far as I knew, stayed away from any harder drugs. But I wanted some. Something to cool the brain, to wake the body. I was too scared to ask around for it, but I looked longingly at the folks grinding their jaws and walking quickly between machinery fixes. There hadn't been a drug test since that first fair, and the lack of regulation was obvious.

I'd been exhausted before—after long nights studying or worrying about my mom. I'd felt moments of this tiredness in fits and starts, but never as this total takeover, like some other being was creeping out from its shadowed cave and speaking for me, thinking for me.

It is late, and we're on the jump to Kansas from Minnesota. We left the sunflower fields hours before. Motel for the night, cheapest thing we could find, because there was no suitable place for us to park and sleep in the bunkhouse and then go on to setup tomorrow. The few hours in the motel, though it is dirty and stained and noisy, is pure luxury. Warm showers. Bed. Even with four of us to a room, which we'd been sure the clerk couldn't see, the space feels infinite. Though I want to slide into that bed the moment we check in and never emerge, it is 11:00 p.m. and most of the crew hasn't eaten, and Tommy and Sunshine, the only other two who can drive the van, are quickly out of sight.

"I'm gonna teach you fire breathing in Hutch," Short E tells me. "You know how to do everything else now, and even though fire breathing isn't in the show, because the flame is too big for the tent, I'm gonna teach you."

Unlike fire eating, where you extinguish a flame in your mouth or perform tricks with a torch, fire breathing involves spitting a mouthful of gasoline onto a torch in order to create a gigantic flame ball.

Short E, Cassie, and I are at a fast-food chain. There are burgers and fries in front of us, and drinks, and many weeks left in the season.

"Be careful with fire breathing," Cassie says. "We don't wanna hurt anyone's little faces."

"It's not dangerous if you're careful," Short E says.

"It's always dangerous. You're spitting gas out of your mouth and creating a fireball," Cassie says.

"If you do it right, it's not dangerous. Trust me."

"Are you kidding me? The wind can change in a second, which is totally out of your control, and the fireball will shoot back and eat your face. That, in my definition, is dangerous."

"Whatever," Short E says.

"I just wish Elton were here to teach Tess. That's as undangerous as you can possibly make it."

"Fuck you."

"Fuck me?"

"Whatever."

"I'm not saying you're a bad teacher, I'm just saying that Elton is the best teacher," Cassie says. "Don't be upset."

"It doesn't matter, guys," I say, trying to put a little neutrality into this conversation that is clearly heating up too quickly. "We'll see when we get there."

"I'm just trying to help," Short E says. "I've been fire breathing for a long time."

"Not as long as Elton."

"These fries are so good," I say.

"Stay out of this, Tess," Short E says.

"I'm just worried 'cause—" Cassie starts, but Short E shushes her.

"Just stop," he says.

"Don't shush me," she says, in a very low tone.

"Shhhh," he says.

"Do. Not. Shush me."

"Sssshhhhhhhhh," he says.

Cassie's hand flies from her lap across the table and knocks Short E's basket of fries and burger onto his lap. The fries rain down all over him.

Without a moment's hesitation, Short E picks up the basket, which still has some fries in it, and hurls it across the table into Cassie's face. It lands right on her forehead, salt and little hard chunks of fries coating her hair, and she is instantly fighting tears and clenching her jaw and balling up fries from the table and throwing them at his face.

Both are moving quickly, and I'm sitting still like a dumb doll, waiting for them to break into hysterics over the ridiculousness of this, but the only breaking is the fries under the shaking, furious fists as they are thrown back and forth. Smashed potato is ground into the table. Clumps are stuck to both their shirts. Arms. Mine, too.

There are only a few other customers in the restaurant. Everything else is quiet, but Cassie's voice booms over the din.

"All I asked was for you to stop shushing me," she is yelling. And he is yelling, "You're such a bitch, you're a giant bitch," and their voices are escalating, each of them finding other things on the table to throw at one another's faces, salt and pepper shakers, napkins, each growing redder and full of tears.

"You're the fucking worst and everyone hates you," Short E yells.

"You're a talentless fuck," Cassie screams. "You're not a daredevil at all, you're just a little piece of shit. The only reason you're here is because you have no legs."

All eyes in the restaurant are on our table now, assessing Short E. Cassie gets up and storms outside. I haven't moved. I sit with Short E for a moment as he slows down his tirade. As our heartbeats slow. The employees resume movement behind the counter. We start cleaning up the fries. Get up, dump our trays, and walk outside. I drive us all back, in a long silence, to the motel.

SOUNDS PAST THE NOISES

Two years and eleven months after the stroke

In the audio recording, it's easy to make out a guitar and keyboard. There's occasional percussion, too, and two voices, one male and one female, singing in accented English. The first song is a cover of "Stand by Me," then some originals, some instrumentals, and I eventually pause the recording. It's twenty-five minutes long.

"This is one of the great things about Mom's chair," Davy says when I finally get them on the phone. I've asked how the trip was going, and by way of response, he has e-mailed me the file. "I can hide a lot of things on it that people don't notice. Like a small mic, which I can attach to one of the handles and get real close to the street musicians to record them."

"Why do you want to record them?" I ask, as if I don't know this answer.

"So that we can listen to their music whenever we want. So that when people ask what The Trip was like, I can let them hear it."

Davy was an audio engineer for years, first on tour with musicians and music festivals, then at National Public Radio, and then at THX for Skywalker Sound, George Lucas's sound company. He loves recording sounds. He loves hearing something, capturing it, manipulating it to make it sound like its best, truest self, and then letting other people hear it. There is no better way to replicate an experience, he thinks.

"So the great thing about street musicians is that you can hear all the other stuff going on around them at the same time, too. The cars honking, the people clapping, the kids chattering, the carts rolling by. There's this whole world that makes sense when you hear it with the music, and you can hear in the music that whole world, too. The rhythms and moods."

The young couple singing in the recording, he says, are these nice Italians who speak a little English and sit in the same spot every day, so my mom and Davy have added this into their routine. They roll up in the afternoon to listen to music, record, drop a little money in their case.

"How you doing, cutie?" Davy says in the recording, in a kind of soft voice that is not meant for outside listeners. Maybe they're sitting in the shade, beneath a tree, and maybe it is very hot and they've already had a long day. Maybe she's just up from a nap and still in the wet-eyed stare that usually follows. From what I can hear in the recording, she doesn't make any sound, and for a moment this worries me, listening as I am spatially and temporally removed from a moment that already took place, changed, and is something entirely else now. How was she? Why didn't she make a sound?

I love those sounds she makes. The hums. The little songs she sings into the phone, into my ear when I lean in close to hug her.

The human brain is bilateral in structure. While the left hemisphere has zones connected with language, analytical processing, time sequencing, and so on, the right hemisphere has regions governing musical ability, humor, visuospatial skills, and so forth. The left hemisphere of her brain was severely damaged in the strokes, but the right side, the music, lives on.

And what of the recording's silence in response to Davy's question? In her chair, she smiles, sometimes nods, yawns.

She cocks her head to attention, or flicks it to the side when something is funny, or when she is making a joke. She slowly closes one eye and raises the other eyebrow when she jokes, too. She touches people she is near on the arm. A friend. A stranger. She cleans any hair or lint or stray artifact from their clothes.

This does not occur to me until the moment I get off the phone with them—they have to go, because they're due to stop by their afternoon musicians and hear a few songs and wouldn't want them to worry if they didn't show up—that all these years, Davy has been understanding the world through its sounds. Things make sense to him not through narrative, not through the stories people tell one another in direct conversation, but rather through what the sound of someone swaying beside a microphone as it records a folksinger might mean. What story *that* might tell. For the nearly three years that he has been telling me that he knows what my mom is saying, what she means, that even though she can no longer use any words he can translate her thoughts, I thought he was delusional, or, worse, lying. But maybe he's not. Maybe, just maybe, she is understood. And he is understood. And they're just somewhere else, outside language.

BEHIND THE NIGHT'S DRESS

Day 77 of 150

WORLD OF WONDERS
SEPTEMBER 2013

There had been fried flecks of potato suspended in their hair. Salt spread across their faces like the starry night sky. And I'd sat there, unmoving, brimming with inaction, and let their fight happen.

Right?

Or was it none of my goddamned business?

I thought about all the other times I'd taken this approach, sitting on the sidelines, lamenting the crisis but too afraid to actually do anything about it. The wilting ghost in the corner of the hospital room whose only action is to fade into white walls.

It was time to step a little closer. Get dirtier. I needed to learn a goddamned thing. Why the hell else was I there? Why would I stay?

Neither Cassie nor Short E speaks to the other for the rest of the night or the next day as we finish the drive or this morning as we begin setup. No one is actually talking much to anyone else until we hear this:

"What's up, fucks?" It's an unfamiliar voice, high and screechy, loud, calling from across our lot. We've just begun setup in Hutchinson, Kansas, where we're getting two new performers. I don't quite understand how staffing works, but there must be some careful tradeoffs the bosses work out behind the scenes, weighing, for example, seasoned performers and the kinds of acts they can do and when they can arrive, et cetera.

One of the newbies arrived the night before, a greenhorn bally girl named Lola Ambrosia. She is a burlesque dancer, wants to become a fire eater, and will stay with us for the rest of the season.

"It's really rare, unfortunately rare," Tommy says before he picks Lola up, "to have a nonwhite bally girl. A lot of the performers doing this kind of work look kind of the same—white, tattoos, piercings, kind of a fuck-you mentality."

"Well, for so many years, nonwhite folks were exploited in freak shows, right? All those ridiculous displays with Mexicans being dressed as cannibals from Polynesia, stuff like that," I say.

"Yeah, some were, and that was terrible. But many of them—most, even—made great livings. They got to see the country or the world, made a lot of money."

"Some of them were taken advantage of."

"Sure. But you tell me any business anywhere where that's not true," he says.

I try to find an answer but come up blank.

"It's weird," I say. "The freak show was supposedly about people who were different from you. About people who didn't fit in. But in reality, it was kind of a place where everyone fit in."

"Still is," Tommy says. "We have quite a mix here. And each season it's a new mix. Anyway, Lola's one of the only black bally girls I've come across in a long time. And she's good. And smoking hot."

"Well, don't leave her waiting too long or she might change her mind," I say, a little afraid that a new, skilled, hotter, fresher performer is already the favorite.

The other new performer, the yeller, is pale and wiry, with sharp cheekbones and a perfectly circular goatee on the very bottom

288

of his chin as if he had been dipped in paint. He is moving very quickly between assembling rides with one big duffel bag slung across his shoulder. He's not coming from the direction of the fairground's entrance. He seems to have appeared out of the dry brush lining the chain-link fence that surrounds the carnival grounds.

"Rash!" Tommy calls.

"Tommy!" He drops his bag and gives Tommy a hug. "Feels so good to be back," Rash says, hugging the other folks he knows. "This is where all the magic happens." He spreads his arms wide like he could hug the whole carnival lot. "FUCK YEAH!"

He talks quickly, in a torrent, and has freshly painted black fingernails and a thick headband that covers the top of his head and ponytail.

"How'd you get here?" Tommy asks. "I thought you were gonna call when you got in?"

"Missed my flight," Rash says. "Spent too long this morning imparting final wisdom to the offspring, so I had to hop another one. Took the bus after that. Then this hot chick offered to give me a ride to the fairgrounds, and I wasn't going to say no to that," he says, nudging Tommy in the ribs. Rash gives a quick laugh—an ear-splittingly loud, high-pitched cackle, the closest human sound to a hyena laugh I can imagine, with a hiccup between expulsions of air.

"Do you know why it's so good here?" Rash asks me a little while later.

I shake my head no.

"Anything can happen out here, and it does. The last season I was on the road with these fuckers, I had a threesome with two monkey trainers. I mean, come on. It can't get better than that."

He's getting into his clown costume as he tells me this, an outfit he has perfected over many years, he tells me, and prefers

289

to wear all day every day. He likes to stay in it after we close the show if we are heading to Walmart, for example. The only thing that keeps him from wearing it 100 percent of the time is that his face needs to breathe at night, so wiping away the white face paint is good. He wears yellow plaid pants, a collared shirt, a tie, a vest, and a dog collar around his neck. He has a red curly clown's wig that he's been working on for years, he explains, to dirty and give dreadlocks. His teeth seem especially yellow in contrast to his white face and neck. His eyes and mouth are lined with black thorny paint. Many people already think clowns are terrifying. Rash is, by all accounts, doing his best to be the *most* terrifying.

It is 101 muggy, stagnant degrees outside in the shade, 107 inside the metal truck. Hutchinson, Kansas, is full of salt mines. During World War II it housed German and Italian soldiers in POW labor camps to make up for the American labor force sent overseas. Think of them, all those men locked inside fences far from home and made to work incredibly difficult, physical jobs. Can a temporary carnival be haunted? Are there POW ghosts swinging hammers inside these carnies swinging hammers? The parallels are not parallel, of course. As a prisoner of war, you have not chosen to do the work you are doing. You may not leave. But, for the carnies from South Africa, if they break contract and leave before the season is over, for whatever reason, the company they have signed with will go after their families back home for money. For the American carnies, if you're a person with a criminal record, for instance, there are few other places you can find work. For migrant carnies—Mexicans, in particular—there are hundreds of others in line behind you to fill your spot should you complain about the seventy-, eighty-hour workweek, about the three hundred dollars for those hours.

The Kansas State Fair is the state's largest event of the year, according to the Kansas State Fair advertising. Three hundred and fifty thousand people from all 105 Kansas counties attend. There is the pedal pull state championship, which is a competition where little children pedal a toy tractor that has had heavy weights hooked up to the back, their small muscled legs straining and knobby like some farm animal learning to walk. There's mutton busting, where small kids clasp their bodies around an angry sheep whose torso is a bullet of dirty curled hair ten times as wide as the children's bodies. They clutch, are thrown, then trampled. There are obvious ties to the bull riding and wrangling that happens in the older crowds, but regardless of age, the task is epic: an ordinary human attempting to wrestle the beast.

I wake because I am drowning. I wake and will myself back to sleep and wake again until my sheets are so wet they stick to the mattress's plastic cover, which crinkles like disposable diapers with each movement, and sleep is no longer possible as a way to stave off reality. I have a fever, I'm in a hot tub, I've been propelled into the center of the sun. I open my eyes. The box fan is off. I must've kicked the cord that keeps it motoring, its square wedged perfectly into the foot of the bed, nearly the exact height and width of each bunk space. The only place to put the fan is on the bed itself, which then necessitates a bend in the sleeper's knees to give up foot space to the fan, a further bend if the sleeper wants real air to propel from the blades by collecting the air behind the fan and not propping it up against the plywood board at the foot of the bed that makes a half wall every six feet. The price of a breeze is bent knees all night. A special dampness at the bend in the leg where skin is forced to meet skin.

I plug the fan back in, but it is too late. We sleep in an enclosed metal box in the middle of an asphalt parking lot in Kansas. It is early September; none of fall's coolness has arrived. Each of us bought a fan on one of our 1:00 a.m. Walmart trips when the nights started heating up; they help a great deal, but there

291

is only so much they can do. It's just past sunrise, but I give up, gather my things, and head to the showers.

"Holy shit," Short E says later that afternoon. He walks past my chair and climbs down the metal stairs toward the hose outside. He swears with each stair he dismounts, the heat of the metal, and then I hear the water turn on. "Fuck fuck fuck fuck," he says. "This water is scalding hot."

My head is dizzy with heat, my vision a little blurry, and I lean back against the wall to steady myself between acts but immediately shoot straight back up, having forgotten that the metal walls, too, have been collecting heat all day. My shoulder, upper arm, and back where I touched the wall pulse with heat, and I wonder if they are red or will blister; at this moment I want them to blister and get infected and threaten my life, anything to force me out of this box.

We've just closed the show for the night. We've untied the slipknots at the base of the support beams, lowered the banners to their halfway point and rolled them up. We've closed the mummies' doors, counted out the cash we made that day, marked envelopes, made change, recounted, and sealed the money away.

I peel off the polka-dot tank top and sequined shorts, fishnets beneath those, note how horrible everything smells, how damp it all is with sweat, note the good idea to wash these things sometime soon, next time I go to the showers, which I am considering doing tonight, but now I hear Spif rustling around in his bunk beside mine, changing clothes, smoking. He's got more pep in his step than he should for midnight.

"Whatcha doing?" I call as he passes by.

"Heading into carnietown. Gonna play poker with the boys."

"Can I come?" I ask. Despite all the warnings against carnies, I've been disappointed by how separate our show has been from carnietown during the meat-grinders—and how I was too busy to even consider the kind of trouble I wanted.

"No," Spif says. "Not this time."

"Why?"

"Not this time."

"Next time?"

He sighs, exhales his smoke. "Fine. Next time. But you have to be cool."

"I'll be cool," I say coolly, being unsure what that might mean in carnietown.

The next night after the show closes at eleven, I ask Spif if it's carnietown night and he shakes his head no, sits down on the stage beside Lola.

"Soon," he says, "but not tonight."

"Why the fuck would you go hang out with a bunch of bigoted assholes who will try to feel you up every moment when you can stay right here with these much cooler cats?" Rash the Clown says, coming out of the shadows. "I can't think of a single reason you wouldn't just want to hang out here with these folks."

"I already know what you assholes are like," I say. "I want to see what those assholes are like, too."

Rash sits down beside me and begins drawing his fingernails across my bare thigh.

"Besides," I say, "they can't be so bad. I'm sure I get felt up over here a lot more than I'd get felt up over there."

"Probably true," Sunshine says, parting the curtains and coming out onto the stage. She has two big, stiff ropes draped in loose coils around her shoulder.

"Whips," she says very quietly as she walks past, down the stage's steps, and out the tent's front flap. We all stand up and follow her, a row of ducklings.

Outside, the bright moon casts shadows behind the stilled, sleeping rides, like time has stopped and all the machines are

293

just waiting to be woken up. Sunshine drops the whips onto the ground, though they look mostly like lassos.

"Move," she says, shooing us all far to the side as she picks up one of the whips. She brings her arm back, then throws it high in the air in front of her and cracks it. The sound is a gunshot, and the other folks on our crew are soon outside, too.

Tommy grabs the other whip and begins cracking. In front of him, behind him, to the sides. Sunshine wraps her body in the whip's coil, then undoes herself.

I'm overly eager. When Sunshine takes a short break to puff on her cigarette, I sidle up to her and casually say that this act, a Wild West whip act, is an act I'd sure like to learn.

"I'll teach you," Sunshine says. "Hold the handle firmly in your fist, like this." She picks up the whip and grips the long tape-wrapped handle. Standing with one foot in front of the other, she brings the whip handle in front of her, then behind, and then finally up and over her head before it cracks down in front of her. She demonstrates a few more times, popping the cracker each time with a snap that breaks the sound barrier.

"Stand behind me," she says, "and put your hands on my hips. I know this is weird, but it's how I was taught, too. Feel how my body moves beneath the whip."

I do, holding my hands around her hips as the rope of the whip makes a cage around us. It's hard to believe the whip doesn't cut into us in our center sanctuary, but it doesn't. I try to move with her as she is moving, to get a feel for the swings and speeds and flicks and twists.

"Give it a try," she says, handing me the whip. She keeps her hand on it, though, and presses herself against me from behind, guiding my body with hers as she connects the fluid motions of the stance to the arm's swing.

"Don't lean into it," Rash says. "Keep your body upright, let the whip do the work."

The noise has attracted some carnies from down the way, who lean against a ride beside our tent and, sipping their beers, watch us whip. Tommy has brought out a third whip and is practicing a ringmaster's move, and Sunshine is learning from Rash how to wrap the whip around a pole, and I have the third, a little ways away from the others, since the movement of my cracker, the end piece that makes the sound, is still relatively unpredictable. It can hurt. The carnival is powered off, no lights glowing from the rides themselves, but some streetlights behind the big wheel are on, and they cast long strange shadows onto our outdoor nighttime circus.

Whip acts in a sideshow come in a few forms. There's a solo act, where the performer will come onstage with the whip and perform a bunch of fancy cracks in rapid succession, wrapping herself up in the whip between sets, doing the whole thing in time with music so it looks like a dangerous dance. There's also a tandem whip act, where one performer will hold a newspaper or flower in his hands, between his legs as he bends over, in his teeth. The other performer will crack the whip and knock the item down. It's better to master the solo act before attempting the tandem, since an imprecise crack can be painful for your partner.

I do not improve immediately. It's not something like escaping from the handcuffs or turning the one-dollar bill into a five that you master as soon as you learn the mechanisms involved. There is progress to be made. There are techniques to learn. But I can tell already it's a much more likely prospect than getting a sword all the way down my throat. I feel powerful with the whip, like this could be an act that would actually amaze the audience. Within fifteen minutes, though, I've given myself a small cut on the cheek. It stings, is red and swollen, but doesn't bleed. I don't slow down.

"Wear your sunglasses when you practice," Sunshine says as we're wrapping up. "That way you're less likely to lose an eye."

The next night, after the fair closes at eleven, we blare Tom Waits inside the closed tent. Rash the Clown plays *Rain Dogs* on repeat, an album that sounds like the sound track to a demented circus in another universe. Though there had been some hangouts after hours with smaller clusters of people earlier on in the season, the last month hadn't provided much time for leisure. Here in Kansas, for the first time, the night hours become a circus of our own.

Though the midway's power is shut off each night, we have the stereo and one big cage light at the top of the tent's center pole plugged into our generator. The edges of the tent are shadowed, the Feejee Mermaid and Queen Kong barely visible in their nightdresses. But the music is loud and keeps getting turned up louder and louder.

Rash the Clown and Short E are throwing knives. They're playing some kind of knife poker–meets–darts, where playing cards are stapled to an old board and the knife you throw must land on a certain one. It's a little alarming how often they don't hit the target, considering most of the time a female body is standing in the way of any room for error.

Sunshine is teaching Lola a fire transfer from the tongue, and Spif is practicing a tarot card reading on himself. He cleansed his cards with the last full moon, he says, so now is a perfect time to reenergize the deck. Cassie has her practice sword out and is trying to get the metal down. Tommy has stretched a sheet of newspaper between two ladders, clipped them to the rungs, and I am cracking the whip to try to split the sheet in half. Mostly, I knock one side off the ladder rung, walk back to set it up, whip again, knock it, walk back. I'm determined to get better. Red is in his van, as usual, and Ben is in his bunk in the semi's cab, but the rest of us are here rehearsing for the acts we won't perform.

Once Tommy turns in for the night, each of us pauses to sip from the flask on the stage or pass one of the circling joints, some voices increasing their volume with each pass, others getting a little quieter. The official policy here is no substances, and though I'm sure Tommy knows what goes on, he seems fine turning a blind eye as long as people can hold themselves together.

There's something both playful and serious in the focus on learning new acts after hours. They are fun to do in and of themselves, but there is always also the small, distant tease of what might just possibly happen should you get very, very good at it. A TV appearance, maybe. A movie gig. Money. A role in one of the few other shows like the one in which Short E sometimes performed, where you had one gig a night in a bar full of excited, drunk enthusiasts, an inconceivable kind of luxury.

But anytime one of those possibilities was mentioned, people were quick to dismiss it. Too easy. Not hardcore. Shirking from tradition. There was something about lasting a season here that was a kind of rite of passage, though it was never clear to me what was on the other side. For me or for anyone else, really.

"Once you've performed with the World of Wonders," Rash the Clown had told me earlier in the day, "you can do anything. You are learning from the masters."

"Like, you can perform with any of those other shows?"

"Like, you can do anything."

⚡

I thought I could see the world, but it turned out I was only seeing the first layer. You cannot stop at the first layer. There are always worlds behind worlds, days inside days, the richness of any moment magnified by how open you are to what's happening, each person not just who they are in some interaction with you, but a whole world opening infinitely out from your expectations, from their experiences. What was set up, what appeared onstage, what the audience saw, what happened behind the curtain, what happened beyond.

The setup:

Inside Vickie Condor's chair, it reeks of mothballs. The

four-legged woman illusion requires a hollowed-out armchair, covered over by a seat and a back, upon which the outer Vickie sits. The inner Vickie must be small enough to squeeze her body within the very thin hollowed-out space inside the chair, must have bony enough thighs that they fit through the slit at the chair's front, covered by Vickie's skirt. The inner Vickie's body is pressed against old wood and a few springs and what-ever small, dry creatures hid themselves in the cracks while the chair was tucked away with other unnecessary props in the off-season.

Behind the curtain:

The turkey appears out of nowhere. Spif is walking from the main backstage area to his bunk to grab something, and when he comes back, a giant turkey leg is sitting on the steps at the stage door. It is wrapped in tinfoil and the size of a small cat.

"Somebody left a turkey leg out here," Spif says over his shoulder toward us.

Lola slowly raises her head from the book she is reading. "Oh," she says. "That's for me." She reaches her hand out toward Spif, slowly unfurling it like a tongue readying to coil the meat.

"You got somebody dropping off meat for you?" Spif asks as he hands her the wrapped leg.

"Maybe," she says.

"How'd you do that?" he asks.

"Spif," Sunshine says. "Guess."

"It's not fair, all the shit you get 'cause of your titties."

"It's not fair all the shit you get 'cause of your dick," Lola says.

She unwraps the tinfoil and the salty meat smell of roasted bird spreads through the whole container quickly.

At that moment, Sunshine and I simultaneously rise from our chairs backstage and walk behind the curtain to the side stage. It's time for us to become Vickie. We kick off our shoes,

298

climb, carefully, onto the rickety side stage, one of us holding the curtain for the other. There's an act taking place on the main stage, different acts in different orders at different fairs. This time, it's Short E's balancing act, with his loud voice and the crowd's loud cheers and the continuous noise of the carnival whirling through space all around, so there's no need for us to lower our voices as we prep.

"Damn, that smelled good," Sunshine says, "and I'm a vegetarian." She hands me a pair of Vickie socks.

"I don't know how they make those turkey legs so amazing," I say, putting on the socks, then the vest and skirt.

"It's especially nice after the smell of the bathrooms in this place. Did you go this morning?"

"Yeah, horrible."

"I can't even tell what that smell is," she says, lifting the cushioned back of the chair up and seat cushion out.

"Yeah, it's not really sewage smell," I say, taking the chair's back from her hands to hold up while she slides her body inside the chair.

"It almost smells like there's standing water in there. Like, rotting pools of water with shit in it." She's inside the chair now.

"It does smell like old, stagnant water," I say, lowering the back and seat cushion on top of her body as she turns her head to the side and tucks her arms in close. She's inside the chair now, in darkness, with the mothball smell. I sit down on top of her.

What the audience sees:

"Hello!" I say to the crowd as the talker on the main stage pulls the curtain aside.

"And how are you today, Ms. Vickie Condor?" the talker asks.

"Oh swell, just wonderful. Except for one of my cats, Pickles. He had a bit of a sneeze fit this morning," I say, or something

299

else I make up on the spot, because one way I've learned to survive the strange monotony of performing the same acts over and over and over is to keep my brain active by saying new things each time.

Sometimes people laugh a bit, humor me. Mostly they don't. They stare at my four legs, craning their necks around the person in front of them to see if there is a trapdoor beneath the chair that a person hides inside, or if someone is crouching behind the chair, or what could possibly make this dumb trick work.

We banter a minute, and then the music starts. I tap Sunshine's legs as if I'm counting time on my own legs, and at the agreed upon tap, we begin our dance routine. We alternate pairs of legs kicking together so the audience, the haters, the mugs, can see there are in fact four real human legs, four live limbs that can move independently of one another. This is when they really pay attention. I have a big smile and splay my fingers in jazz hands, but all the audience's eyes are on our legs, trying to work out how the illusion is done.

Behind the curtain:

"Actually, I think the smell is rotting pumpkin," Sunshine says as I lift the false back of the chair up once our act is through and the curtain has been closed.

"That's it! Rotting pumpkin and stagnant water," I say, lifting the seat off her and then offering her my hands. She grabs them.

"I heard some carnies in there talking about pumpkin as I walked in, and I didn't pay any attention, but now I know exactly what they meant." She's standing now, and we're peeling Vickie's socks off. A breeze blows inside the tent, starts to billow the velvet curtains around us. Sunshine reaches out her leg to pin the curtain to a pole with her foot, and I hold the curtain against the pole nearest me with one hand while the other finishes sliding my Vickie costume off.

"It's going to be hard for me to drink a pumpkin-flavored latte anytime soon," I say, and she laughs, folding both our sock pairs back together, laying them on Vickie's chair as I part the curtain in the back for her to pass through.

"I think those are nasty anyway," she says as we walk behind the stage curtain, back to our seats backstage, ready to head out for our next act in thirty seconds or four minutes. "Pumpkin-flavored stuff. What is that?"

Lola and Spif are still discussing the turkey leg.

I wonder if Lola recognizes the parts of the leg, if the tendons or bones mean more to her than they do to me. Story goes: she was premed as an undergrad, excelled in sciences. Wanted to help make people better. Her mom was so proud. And she'd started med school, learning about what the body could or could not withstand in textbooks and lectures, but something didn't feel right. She went to a burlesque show in town one night and saw the women onstage teaching the audience about what their bodies could or could not withstand. That was the kind of help she wanted to do. She dropped out of school and started dancing.

Behind the curtain and onstage:

Sometimes Sunshine's conversation isn't with me and it continues even once we're onstage. We perform our choreography together as we prep for the act, but instead of directing the nonstop stream of chatter to me, she holds a phone to her ear. She talks often to her boyfriend and mom and cousin, and I can hear her conversation continue inside the chair as I perform above, the soft vibrations and low tone of her voice beneath me, discussing their electricity bill or her mom's health or a hilarious thing her boyfriend's son had just done at the park, and I love that these two worlds are happening simultaneously, knowing that inside the magic of the illusion, the same kind of conversation is happening as happens everywhere—the particulars of what her mom is going to eat for dinner, about how

301

she bruised her foot. Knowing my body is a conduit between the two worlds.

Behind the curtain:

The next day, there is a container of fries on the step. And the next, Lola will come back from her break with an ice-cream cone. She's reaching past the world of our performers, making connections on the outside.

"You're fucking around with a foodie," Spif says when the fries arrive. "That's smart. They can get you things."

Lola doesn't say anything. She dips a fry in ketchup, inspects it, and puts it into her mouth.

Sunshine and I walk to the side stage, perform Vickie, and return.

"Who is it?" he asks.

She shrugs her shoulders and licks the salt off her fingers before she adjusts her thigh-highs, then goes back to her food.

I want to seem cool and uninterested in Lola's love life, but there is so little to do backstage between acts. I'd seen her talking to somebody a few nights before, a tall, pale guy who seemed like he would never meet Lola's cool quotient, but here was all this food. Physical evidence of love.

Sunshine and I walk to the side stage, perform Vickie, and return.

"So, you've been hanging around that guy?" I ask her quietly when it is just the two of us in the hallway doing makeup the next morning.

She smiles, just slightly, and shrugs.

"Is it good?" I ask, stretching the corner of my eye way out to the side to ready it for liquid liner.

"It's good," she says, and nothing more. That's the end of that.

Sunshine and I walk to the side stage, perform Vickie, and return. Again and again, what we appear to be doing remains the same, but the world inside and behind is always changing.

But it wasn't the end for Lola and the turkey-leg man. They kept in touch once we left that spot, which I knew because she'd give me updates on where his show was headed, and what disaster befell a kid on one of their rides somewhere down the road. And it wasn't the end, because when the season was over, Lola went to Florida instead of back to St. Louis. And it wasn't the end, because some months later, her Facebook status changed to engaged, and she and the man who had delivered her gifts of food on the steps were married. A backstage miracle brought in front of the curtain.

CHRISTMAS FISH

Eighteen years before the stroke

DECEMBER 1992

My mom decided we needed to eat like Jesus.

Story goes: it was Christmas, and she was walking around again after a mysterious illness that had kept her in the hospital for half the summer. Her spleen had died. Nobody knew why. My brother and I were shuttled between relatives and neighbors. We went on family camping trips with other families, played in our cousins' pool for weeks. We even shot a BB gun. We were allowed to shoot the gun because it looked like she might die. A reward for impending tragedy. But then, months later, she'd come home.

A small pile of figs sat on the kitchen counter beside matzo crackers, a plastic bear of honey, and peanuts. There were dates, too.

It wasn't about religion, my mom and Davy said. It was about history. They wanted us to feel the spirit of Christmas by pretending we were at its moment of origin.

"Jesus didn't have a dining table," my mom said as I readied to set the table. I was nine and had learned some incredible napkin-folding techniques in Girl Scouts.

"Jesus probably didn't have forks either. Or chairs," she said, pouring some honey from the plastic bear into a little bowl.

"Or napkins folded into lotus flowers. Put this on the coffee table," she said, handing me two big glasses of milk. "We're going to eat with our hands. We're going to sit on the floor."

My brother, five, screamed a few high-decibel notes, which meant joy. He loved the floor.

"We could use a little luck this year," Davy said, lighting some waxy pebbles in two small bowls. "Wise men brought frankincense and myrrh to baby Jesus," he said. "For ambiance."

We all sat down on the floor, the air quickly overpowered by the smell of pine resin wafting from the burning nuggets of sap.

"Well, isn't this nice?" my mom said, coughing. She smiled. Changed position on the floor. "I think historical Jesus would have wanted us to be comfortable," she said, grabbing pillows from the couch for her and Davy to sit on.

My dad's side was Catholic, and I'd been to church with my grandmother quite a bit, where there was also something we did that involved eating Jesus. What I knew of the Bible so far mostly had to do with eating, like the fish people had on their cars to mean Jesus, and also the PB&J sandwiches my grandmother and I made by the hundreds for homeless people. I thought it was all pretty great.

My mom reached out and took our hands, the four of us making a square around the table. "Thank you, historical Jesus, for letting us try your food," she said.

"And thank you for the health," Davy said. It had only been a few months since she was back. "And a wish for the coming year," my mom said. "For a trip to Italy."

Davy smiled at her, squeezing her hand tighter.

"You're going to Italy?" I asked.

"Yep. One day. We've got to wish it into the universe," she said, winking at Davy.

"Dear Universe," Davy said. "Thank you for the trip to Italy that we will take."

"Amen," my mom said. She looked at my brother and me, cleared her throat.

"Amen?" we said. She smiled.

We wanted to be good, all of us. We wanted to eat like historical Jesus so the Universe would bless us with things, so that the mysterious forces would take over. No more sicknesses. Money. Italy.

We chewed some dates, crunched crackers. We chugged a lot of milk. We dipped our fingers in honey and brought big gooey piles of it to our tongues, filling ourselves with amber.

The bowls of frankincense and myrrh smoked and billowed, and finally my mom said it stank too much and we opened the doors and windows to let the cold air rush in.

The fruit was gone, then the honey, the crackers, the milk.

"We're hungry," my brother and I said.

"Historical Jesus was just fine," my mom said.

"But *we* are starving," we said.

"Have more milk," she said, gesturing toward the fridge. We were still sitting on the floor, full only of history, and so my brother let out more high-decibel shrieks as he started spinning on his knees on a stuffed animal, and his foot kicked me as he spun, so I kicked him back, and his screaming became higher pitched and I told him to shut up and we knew, even without knowing much about Jesus, that Jesus would not have approved, but so, too, would he not have approved of a summer of sickness and an almost-gone mom, and so we kicked and slapped and screamed and finally my mom said, "FINE."

We stopped, waiting for our prize.

"I'll put in some fish sticks."

We sat silent and still in our victory.

"Historical Jesus probably had fish," Davy said to her back as she walked into the kitchen.

Maybe fish sticks would do the magic. Maybe money would rain down on us like fish. A whole entire house filling with money fish, no, health fish, those slippery bodies pouring down

306

from the ceiling, thwacking our foreheads and shoulders as they fell, no, a neighborhood of Italy fish, the whole California sky dumping them down, our arms wide and our heads thrown back to receive them.

DR. FRANKENSTEIN'S HUSHED BLOOD LOVE SONG

Day 84 of 150

WORLD OF WONDERS
SEPTEMBER 2013

The stage collects droplets of blood. He is already on it, waiting for them.

"I must concentrate absolutely," Dr. Frankenstein says. One hand is holding the mic. He speaks softly in a low, monotone voice.

"Now I am slowing my heart from seventy-eight to sixty beats per minute." He is quiet. Things are slowing. The rhythm of the last drips of rain falling from the eaves. "If I don't hit any veins or arteries, I won't bleed much."

He is Dr. Frankenstein for this act alone, afterward returning to Red, our sword swallower, our blockhead, our lover of cats. But for this one act, he becomes someone else.

"I don't work strong," Red had told me. "Learned the pincushion act, which I call Dr. Frankenstein, from Bill Hitch the Son of a Bitch. He always worked strong. He'd look for veins and arteries in his pincushion act and pierce right through them to make a bloody mess, to spray the audience. So they'd know it was real. Not me. I do deep muscle pierces. There's blood sometimes, but I perform this act so often, I can't do it strong. I'd bleed out and die."

Dr. Frankenstein is seated on a stool and his kilt drapes over his thighs, but his knees jut nakedly out and bend at perfect right angles, his feet braced against the stool's lowest rung. White athletic socks reach midcalf. His Velcro sandals are brown and grainy with fairground dust.

The audience sees the three-inch pins with the sharpened tips. Gleaming, they lie in a pile beside his stool. Can they look at that sort of instrument and not imagine it hammering into their own bodies, sliding through their skin and into the mysteries of what lies inside?

He takes one pin in his right hand, holds it against his forearm so the sharp tip is pressing against his skin and he continues talking in slow, soft, melodic sentences. This act happens in a small tent within the larger tent. Shoulder to shoulder the crowd stands, clutching their mouths or stomachs or each other in anticipation of seeing something they don't want to see but have just paid an extra dollar to see.

Quiet voice, slow voice.

"Now the other thing is the sensation of pain. That is nothing more than a simple meditation technique. I'm capable of shutting down that part of my brain by turning it off like a light switch."

The thick, hot air is heavy as a costume. Drip drip, lulling all the heads in the room into some partial sleep, some dream calm, some sleepy trust, and then midsentence, metal pin hovering against his forearm, the air slowing with his heart, he slaps the metal head.

Hard.

The pin jams into the meat of his forearm. The pin's head is flush with his skin and the rest of the metal is inside.

I never see this act, but I hear it every time. It has a separate PA system, which rests on its own small stage made of four rectangular pieces of steel and two pieces of wood. A separate stage, on a separate side of the tent, for a very different kind of act. Dr. Frankenstein refuses to share a stage with any

309

"illusions," because he doesn't want anyone even considering that he is not doing the thing it appears he is doing.

Before we open we take a soapy bucket and scrub the stages to release the mud and grass and blood. Mostly, we scrub to loosen the blood.

"Are you ready to see it?" Sunshine asks me three months into the season. I nod.

I am standing at the back of the crowd. It's not an act we can peek through a curtain to watch, because it's enclosed in its own tent and, more important, because Red wants nothing to break his concentration. I know that metal pieces will slide into Red's body, that he will become a human pincushion, but I have never been able to actually imagine the act. He isn't allowed to perform it everywhere, since not all fairs allow for dings—our extra moneymakers. But all these big fairs let us have the dings, and so every twenty minutes, his low, slow voice slides through the mic and a new kind of pain begins back there. I am nervous standing in his tent, like a child who has wandered in and doesn't know for sure whether Dr. Frankenstein will survive this act, like I don't know if Red, a person I see every single day, a person I have worked hard to make remember my name, a person I admire, will survive this and be able to perform it again.

"When I was young, I had the strangest way of cleaning my teeth," Dr. Frankenstein says. His low monotone picks up a little lilt at the end. A cue for a joke. "I liked to clean them from the outside. And I'd do that by lining this up right about here," he says, holding a metal pin—the kind used for upholstery or corsages—perpendicularly against his cheek. He opens his mouth wide, then slowly wiggles the pin into his cheek.

Dr. Frankenstein's tent within our tent is small—fifteen by fifteen feet—and intimate enough that I can see the wet, pink skin on the inside of his mouth push into a small mound before the silver glint of the pin peeks through. The head is sticking two inches out from the outside of his cheek, the sharp tip an inch inside his cheek.

310

This isn't an illusion. There is no trick. It isn't anything but exactly what it is: pain, mastered.

My breathing becomes shallow, and I have to keep looking away from the pins. I look back to Dr. Frankenstein, to Red, this man I have watched eat hamburgers and brush his long orange hair, and he slaps another pin into his flesh, and I'm worried that this might be the one to do him in. That after his forty-plus years in sideshows, this one pin will kill him.

I'm also jealous. This is an act the audience will never forget.

A few in the crowd have turned away from the stage or have closed their eyes or cast them to the dirt. When I sit backstage and listen to the sound of the voice, slow and low, a local radio station occasionally crossing frequencies and filling his silences with quiet staticky country music, there is an occasional other sound. The other sound is the violent rip of the two massive Velcroed curtains containing the tent within the tent as they tear apart, and when I am not too tired to peek my face out from behind my own curtain to make sure everything is okay enough, I see a pale face rushing between the Velcro flaps, out from Dr. Frankenstein, a face wet with perspiration.

Some barf. Some faint. Falling ovations, everyone calls them. At least one in each town. Compliments, all of them. High fives backstage sometimes, depending on the mood, depending on how much we hate each other at that hour. Sometimes high fives for everyone except the one whose fault it is that everything is bad that day, who sits alone off the back of the truck chain-smoking and typing furiously into their phone.

Next comes the pin through a large pinch of skin on his neck. There's a little blood. I take a deep breath, dig in. I want to watch pain happen without looking away, but I can't. I look away. Cover my eyes with my hands like a child in a scary movie. I thought, after all this time, that I'd be tough enough to see this act without flinching, but the truth of the moment is too powerful—a man, a coworker, a friend, even, harming his body right in front of my eyes, for my pleasure.

He leaves the pin in his neck for us to stare at. The part of a human most sensitive to hot and cold is the neck. As a fetus is developing, its heart is surrounded by a protective layer of dermis. As it grows larger, it sloughs off the dermis to the cranial/spinal connective growth area. That skin becomes a neck. Dr. Frankenstein's neck, through which a piece of metal pierces, once protected his heart.

In the torture arts, you are both the creator and recipient of your pain.

In most bodies, the more metal there is inside, the more the body is failing. Imagine: needles and staples and implants and knives and pins. I see the pins entering Dr. Frankenstein and think of all the medical metal that has pierced my mom these last three years. How she has taken it and taken it and taken it. How she has been the recipient of pain and then chosen to keep moving her mouth to make sound come out, to try physical therapy month after month after month, even when progress wasn't evident, how she is always practicing and working. And now she is in Italy, posing beside restaurant owners who love to give her free dessert.

Will this photo of her smiling above gelato be the last image I see of her alive?

This one with flushed cheeks and an empty glass of red wine beside her?

Dr. Frankenstein finishes his act, the sixth pin sliding into his skin, and tells the audience where they can find the exit. The air is thick and hot with more than weather. I can hear people whispering to one another, trying to pinpoint the secret. Even though he has told them, they don't understand the secret is that he can take it and take it and take it.

⚡

"All right, Tess," Spif says a few nights later. "I'm going to play poker in carnietown. You can come, if you want."

I jump up from the backstage chair I'd been slumped in and change into a black T-shirt and black pants, something that will make me look a bit tougher and cooler than I am. As we're walking out of the tent, Lola sees us and asks if she can come, too.

"Whatever, sure," he says. "Just, don't be offended, any of you. And keep your mouth closed if you are. These aren't fuckers you can disagree with."

We agree, and march into the night.

"Peace, love, and titty-fucking, who says that? Ho's a calling," a man is chanting at a picnic table. We've woven our way through a few layers of trailers and are in the heart of carnietown. There are a cluster of tables with lots of men all around, and scattered chairs and open beers on the table. Next to the tables is the carnie commissary, the first I've encountered, which sells everything from snacks to razors to laundry services, only for the carnies.

The man leading the chant stops when we get close and stands up to give Spif a hello handshake, then introduces himself as Jack to Lola and me. He's in a clean, crisp basketball jersey with a backward hat, gold chains stacked around his neck, and skin sunned to the color of graham crackers. His arms are covered in tattoos, with swastikas sprinkled through the naked women lounging across his forearms. *White Power* runs across his biceps.

"You look good, man," he says to Spif as he sits down at the table and pulls money out to buy into the poker game. "You got nice shoes. Gotta have nice shoes. When I was locked up, I knew the exact right kind of shoe polish to buy to keep my shoes shiny for visits. You gotta get an old oil rag, and you gotta buff your shoes with this polish, like in little circles, and that's how you keep them looking nice. You girls want a beer?" he asks Lola and me. "On the house."

"Sure," we say, cracking open the Budweisers one of the guys behind Jack hands us. We're the only females in sight.

313

It's hard not to stare at his swastika tattoos, because I keep thinking that they're something else. Maybe I've misinterpreted them. Stars, perhaps, or Chinese characters. Or that Sanskrit symbol for luck. But, no. They are swastikas. I wonder if I should walk back. I wonder if Lola wants to walk back. I wonder if it is more rude or less rude to ask her if she is okay here, if she wants to be here. She's twenty-two, and at twenty-two I was usually too uncomfortable to ever say I was uncomfortable. Even though I'm thirty, only eight years older, I feel oddly motherly toward her in this moment. Also, a little nervous. I lean over, quietly make small talk to try to gauge her comfort by the tone of her voice. She makes some snarky joke and takes a big lug of her beer, sits down. She's got more spine than I do. I take this as a decision to stay.

"Let me introduce you around," Jack says to us. He calls the names of each of the guys at the table, and as he turns his head I watch his long, straight ponytail sway against his jersey, notice the shaved sides of his head, his gold rings, and wonder what kind of friendship Spif has with him, and why.

"This is Beyoncé," Jack says, pointing to a big guy with penciled-in eyebrows and a spaghetti strap tank top whom I recognize from the carnietown food truck—not for fairgoers—from the day before, when Spif had brought me here to buy a walking taco: a small bag of Doritos split open on the side with ground beef, lettuce, and cheese on top of the chips. They're heaven. Beyoncé wriggles his fingers at Lola and me in a wave. Next we say hello to a guy who looks just like a young Dan Aykroyd, but with a smashed-in face and blond buzz cut, then a bunch of Juggalos gathered beside one another with Insane Clown Posse T-shirts and hats and tattoos. Spif whoop-whoops and they whoop-whoop back. One of them is, predictably, drinking Faygo. There's an older guy at the end of the table with wide plastic-frame glasses who says he's leaving next weekend to go get him some pussy, pussy pussy pussy pussy pusssssssssy, he says, rubbing his chest hair beneath his orange

T-shirt, and we smile politely, happy for him. There's a Latino marine with a spiderweb tattoo running down the length of his arm and a handsome guy next to him in a Ferrari T-shirt who never opens his mouth, and beside him, one black guy sitting in a lounge chair with a beer in his lap and another open in his hand, and he's providing a continual stream of commentary on everything that everyone says. Sitting beside Jack is a young white guy with a sweaty face who keeps sitting up and turning completely around to look at Lola and me. Staring, he starts to make some sounds, the beginnings of words, a gargle or a sort of hum, but never finishes any of the sounds, gives up, and turns back around. He has *RIP LUCY* written in huge cursive letters across the back of his neck, and when the conversation turns to a fair in Texas this crew plays that is just six miles from the Mexican border, this guy nods vigorously as Jack gestures with two full hands to the size of the bag of weed you can get for ten dollars, and this one special strip club where the girls don't speak any English and call everyone *Papi*.

Jack is a boss here, owns a bunch of the games, and just bought a house with his lady, he tells us. "You know why I love having kids?" he asks. "Because I get to watch cartoons and not have anybody look at me funny. Like *Madagascar*. It's so good. *Madagascar 2* is even better than *Madagascar 1*. You know why? Because it's in the circus. You fucks should like that," he says, offering Spif a cheers.

They begin a new game of poker. There's another guy at the table with a suitcase full of money. People hand him bills, and he hands them chips for the poker game. The marine with the spiderweb tattoo deals the cards, and I stay close to Lola, quietly chatting with her so it won't look like we don't want to talk to anyone, but keeping my ear to the conversation at all times, both fascinated and nervous about what I might hear. This is about as far from my childhood's twirling women with armpit hair as I can get.

Someone starts talking about a ride malfunction at the last

315

spot they played, and the man holding the briefcase slips Jack something under the table and the guy with the wide plastic-frame glasses says, "Hey, man. I saw that. You passing cards here?"

People get quiet.

"No, fucko," Jack says. "I dropped my card and he handed it back to me." Another guy at the table stands up, and he's huge and hovering above the game, and he starts pacing. A young pale guy beside him with rotting teeth and two fat pockets of eye gunk says, "This is supposed to be a clean game, don't worry, man," and he's trying to pat the big pacing guy on the arm as he passes, but the arm is just past his fingertip range. "It's cool, man," he says, pawing at the air.

The pile of chips in the center of the table is big. "Keep playing," Jack says to the other guys in the game, and they do, adding their bets or dropping out as they go around the table. "Sit down, brother," Jack says to the pacing guy. His tone is very even, but strong. That he is a boss here seems very, very clear.

"He passing you cards?" the pacing man asks, and the air seems to tighten as jaws clench all around. Eyes move sharply between Jack, who does not move from his seat, and the standing guy. The young guy keeps reaching out and trying to touch the angry man, but still can't make contact.

"Sit. Down," Jack says to the man. "Ante up or get out."

The angry man looks down at his shoes. Shakes his head. All the faces are turned toward him, Lola's and Spif's and mine as well, waiting to see if this will grow into a brawl we'll need to leave quickly. He calculates.

"All right. Fuck. Okay," he says, sitting back down.

"Rat crew won't cheat their own," Jack says, offering a shark's grin all around the table.

"Yeah," the man says.

Jack shows his hand. "See, man?" he says. "I don't have shit. I was just bluffing. Chill out," he says, laughing, slapping the guy on the back

316

The man in the thick-frame glasses wins and collects the pot.

"The thing is, man," Jack says, leaning back a bit to include us in what he's saying, "I used to have a lot of hate for a lot of different kinds of people. Like that. If some fuck tried to call me out, I'd teach him a lesson. A lot of hate. I did some bad things to them. Y'all know about that already." A few guys laugh. "But now I just don't have hate for anybody anymore. I love everyone. Everybody."

He pulls a T-shirt from a bag beside him and puts it on, covering up his jersey, and hiding the white power tattoo, along with most of the swastikas. With some of those hidden, what becomes clear is the huge cross surrounded by wings tattooed across the back of his neck. I'm not sure how much he's saying for our benefit—if he cares about us being there at all—but he does seem to want everyone here to have a good time.

"I'm just a love man," he says. "A love man trying to look good. You think I look good?" he asks, turning to face Lola.

She shifts in her seat, fake laughs once, and takes a sip of beer.

"Thought so," he says. "You know what I need, though? What's the freshest? A purple leisure suit. I'm serious. All purple, with one of those white Kangol hats and white shoes. Everything else all gold. Maybe a tie. That's what I'm gonna buy next. After my next come-up."

"That would be tight," Spif says, buying more chips. I try not to think about how each week I watch him get a draw on his next pay period before the week comes, how I hear him complain about child support for his baby daughter. Because it isn't my business. Not at all.

"Gonna get this fuck to come work for us next summer," Jack says, nodding toward Spif.

"Straight flush," Spif says at the end of the next game, throwing down his hand.

"Almost, man," Jack says, laying his cards down. "Royal flush. Tough shit," he says, pulling the pile of chips toward him. "But here, brother. Take these, and stay in the game," he says, sliding a few chips over to Spif. "Always stay in the game."

$$\lightning$$

"We have with us today the Pain-Proof Man," I say for the sixth time that morning, about a minute into the bed of nails act, after I've explained how sharp the nails are, how I've personally filed them to painful points. I don't realize I'm saying anything at all, don't even notice I'm onstage in front of an audience until a small girl, ten or eleven years old, in the front row shouts.

"Oh my god!" she says as Spif comes out. "Pain-proof?" She looks to her mom. She has on a pink Hello Kitty T-shirt, and when I ask the audience if we should add some weight on top of Spif after he's lain down on top of the bed of nails—a question that consistently draws cheers from the audience—the little girl screams.

"No!" she says, her hands flying to her face in case she needs to keep from witnessing the bloodshed.

I sit on him anyway, too tired to add much fanfare, and when I get to the autopilot section where I ask Spif how he feels, he answers, "Not great," his autopilot response in a comically pained voice. I tell the audience that he says he feels great, and the little girl screams again.

She pounds one flat hand onto the stage and looks me deep in the eye. "Not great," she says, insistent. "He said *not* great."

I wake up. It's easy to forget, after all the groans and eye rolls from the audience, that there are those who believe. There are audience members who think the headless woman illusion really is a headless woman, who trust in our deceit. And yet, the bed of nails act *isn't* deceit. Spif really does lie down on a bed of nails and I really do sit on top of him, but somehow, few people seem to think it is painful or dangerous or, really, very impressive at all.

318

But here are little brown eyes staring me down. Here I am, the monster, hurting someone, intentionally harming a person's body. How could I? And why?

I lower myself down onto him as I do every day, every twenty minutes, pressing into his back as his body presses into the bed of nails beneath him, and the girl, who has broken eye contact with me to look at Spif, to check on his well-being and monitor him for blood, suddenly darts her eyes back to mine.

The twenty or so other people in the audience are amused. She is not.

"You're a jerk," she says between my sentences.

The audience giggles.

I agree with her.

I think about the little girl later that day, how strange and delightful it was to be forced out of my stupor while performing. How odd to live inside a carnival and be here, thinking about how to do an act, but to have my brain elsewhere much of the time. Imagining what my parents are doing, or what it will be like to go back to California without them. What my brother and I will say to each other on the plane to collect them from Italy.

I enter the long, low, dimly lit buildings that house all the state fair competitions and walk slowly among the tables, repeating what I see in my head with the "Happy Birthday" melody I'd recently heard my mom hum when we talked on the phone, happy birthday a code, I was sure, for *Hello, I'm thinking of you*. It was nobody's birthday.

> *Duct tape apparel*
> *Lard-based cooking*
> *Yeast breads*
> *Fancy cakes*
> *Pickled goods*
> *Jams*

319

Jellies
Spam parent
Spam child
Novelties for a man
Flower arranging
Vegetable sculpture
Butter sculpture

I want to be present. Here, in this weird world. With tractors made of butter.

I read that to enter the miniature pony show, your pony must be shorter than thirty-four inches.

A woman outside the building, wearing a jeweled kerchief, is blow-drying her pony's tail and mane. She spritzes it with something, hairspray maybe, and then keeps blow-drying. The pony is cool and collected.

NORMALAPHOBIA

Day 88 of 150

A large and battered asphalt parking lot separates the gas pump where the van refuels from the Subway lunch destination. We're on a jump between Kansas and Arkansas. Short E lifts himself onto a skateboard and, using one gloved hand to balance his body on the board, uses the other to push against the rocky pavement toward the sandwiches. "I was a semipro skater for a while," he tells me, gliding atop the board with ease and speed. "I skated with Tony Hawk before the X Games made him a douche."

Inside Subway, a kid, three or four years old, is waiting for his mom to bring his food to the table and catches sight of Short E rolling across the asphalt toward the sandwich shop. He presses his face against the glass, mouth open and smeared on the window, his eyes never leaving the approaching man. Short E glides inside. The kid stares. The mother, a large woman with embroidered flowers on her pink T-shirt and a ruddy face, reaches her hand to her son's cheek as fast as she can get it there and turns it in another direction. She lets go, and he swivels right back around to Short E. The mom tries again, scolding her boy. *Don't stare*, she says in a loud whisper. *Stop staring*. Short E orders a turkey sandwich. The mom has given up, and she and the kid both stare. He doesn't get any vegetables. Extra mayo.

321

"Not even lettuce or something?" I ask. "Pickles?"

He shakes his head.

"How can you get all your vitamins?"

"Thanks for your concern, Mom," he says. Then, "Back in the day, I was sponsored and everything. Back when skateboarding was fun and full of punks."

The first famous "half boy" was Johnny Eck, who performed on the sideshow circuit for much of the twentieth century and died in 1991. Born in 1911 with a truncated torso due to sacral agenesis, Eck was walking on his hands at the age of one year, long before his twin brother could walk on his feet. As a kid, he often stood atop a small box when company was over and practiced his sermons, denouncing beer and sin. It was a big hit, until he passed around his collection plate.

Eck was an acrobat, painter, illusionist, musician, business owner, photographer, actor, and expert model-maker. He signed a management contract with a magician and went on the road with his brother. He was billed for years as the "half boy," or "the amazing half boy," and later as the "king of the freaks," and then finally, "the most remarkable man alive." For most of his career it was *boy*, though, not man. For many freak performers, there was a certain fear that ran alongside the audience's curiosity, and to stabilize some of that fear, the performers were emasculated. Presented not as men, but as boys. Or as part animals—Eck was cast as a bird-man in the *Tarzan* films. The relationship between sexuality and perceived monstrosity is complicated, and from what I saw on the road with Short E, involved both extreme attraction and repulsion. Some people left a wider berth around him than they might another person when they passed, but for many others, for many women we met on the road, the opposite was true. Short E met a lot of women. A. Lot. Of. Women. Many nights, one of their faces appeared like a little floating ghost in the darkness once the show closed. Short E would light a cigarette, put on his cowboy hat, and sit at the top of the steps, chatting with them. Often, within a few minutes, the woman and Short E would be gone. He'd appear the next morning with the chipper grin of a good night and indoor heating/plumbing.

"How the fuck you make that work, Short E?" Spif asked one morning just after Short E rolled in.

"Ha," Short E said. "You gotta learn some fucking lady skills, man. Plus, I can do things that you can't do. I can do things that no other man can do. Think about it," he said, lifting himself up on his hands and swinging his torso between his arms. He looked over at me, where I was obviously calculating some angles. "Tess, I can tell you're thinking about it. You wanna give it a test run? Free of charge."

"Very kind offer," I said. "I'll consider it."

"No customers are disappointed."

"That's a bold testimony."

"I do bold things," he said. "And whatever, man, you get pussy sometimes. I seen it," Short E said to Spif.

"Never as much as I could use," Spif said.

"Amen to that," said Short E.

In the Subway, Short E and I are sitting across from each other, eating our sandwiches. The little kid at the table next to us is sitting backward on his seat, still staring at Short E. Finally, his mom picks the kid up and they leave. Short E walks over to the soda machine and starts to reach up with one hand to refill his coke, but a teenager nearby asks if he can help.

"Nah, man, I got it," Short E says, filling up his cup. All eyes in the restaurant watch him doing this very boring thing. Me, too. I watch him. I watch him a lot. This is the hard part. I both recognize the ridiculousness and sometimes total insult of the way Short E is ogled all the time, and yet he is fascinating to watch. It's so simple— he's very good at getting around in the world in a way that most folks wouldn't know how to do.

"People treat me like they're wearing kid gloves," Short

E says. Last season, he tells me, a man in line behind him at McDonald's insisted on paying for Short E's meal, then handed him a twenty-dollar bill.

"Did you take it?" I ask, thinking of the injustice.

"Shit yeah, I did," he says. "People always hand me money. Pay for my meals in restaurants, or hand me tips. Like I'm my own charity. And I always take it. If they're going to be jackasses enough to just hand me their money, I'm going to take it. It takes away the insult. Then it's just another version of GTFM."

"GTFM," I parrot back.

"Does it bother you that you look so normal?" he asks. I ponder this, the years I spent trying to look as much like everyone around me as I could.

"Kind of."

"It would bother the shit out of me."

"People don't usually believe me when I say I'm with the show. They think I'm the stagehand or something," I say.

"You do have to do more work because of it."

"To prove myself, you mean?"

"No. You ever notice who always gets sent in to reserve rooms at hotels, or talk to bosses, that kind of shit?"

"Oh," I say. I hadn't considered why it was always me.

"People are comfortable around you, because you look like their dentist or their kid's teacher. You wear cardigans and shit. That's why you sell so many Bibles and turn so many people on the blade box. They trust you and your weirdly normal whitey female self."

"Shit's not fair."

"If only they could have seen you dumping their money out of your underwear backstage. You're as crooked as the rest of us," he says, giving me what I'm sure is a nod of approval.

⚡

324

It is evening, still an hour or two before the darkness that brings twinkling lights, still five hours until we'll close for the night. We are backstage at the Arkansas-Oklahoma combined state fairs. Moments between acts. I am staring out the truck's back end, pretending I'm inside a moment of peace and quiet when I hear Cassie say, "Well, Tessa's a shitty performer anyway."

This kind of playful teasing is usually easy to ignore, laugh away, stick my middle finger at, and move on from.

But not today. I have space for no humor inside me. I turn from my blank stare. Look the hunter right in the eyes.

"Fuck you," I say.

"I'm just kidding," she says, sighing like having to explain this is exhausting. But her knife is glinting as she picks her teeth with its blade. Her sword is sheathed against her side.

"Fuck you," I say again, not dropping her gaze. My hackles are raised.

"Chill out. Jesus," she says. "You know I'm kidding."

I do know, but my teeth are chiseling themselves inside my mouth. The idea is unbearable. That I am a shitty performer. That after these months, after this literal blood, sweat, and tears, I'm no good.

"Get over it, come here," she says, standing and starting toward me with her arms out wide.

"Don't come any closer to me," I tell her. I am coming unhinged. My organs might explode out of my body, because I'm suddenly so filled with anger. My head is rocketing straight to outer space.

"Come on, come here, baby," she says, stepping toward me.

"I'm serious." I do not want her love. I cannot bear a body forcing its love on me.

"Hug me, baby."

"Leave me alone," I snarl, and my mouth makes blood and calls for her blood and my skin is hot with the memory of stage lights and the burning possibility that I'm no good out there. I put a hand up as a stop sign to warn her to stay back.

"I'm hugging you," she says, and she is upon me. She is standing. I am still sitting in the chair, and her arms close around me like terrible shackles. I push them off, but she is stronger, and she leans down to bury her face in my shoulder, and I punch at her side, my eyes gone from my head, my face hot and throbbing, and she leans in even harder, grabs me tighter, trying to smother me with her love, and my mouth opens up on her shoulder. My teeth clamp into her skin. Bite down.

I feel her arms loosen. She stands up, laughing at first, and rubs at her shoulder.

"Teeth marks," she says, rubbing the skin on her shoulder and then looking at me, still laughing a little with surprise. But then the laughing stops. "Jesus Christ, Tessa. You bit me."

Let me start again.

Two months earlier, three fairs and four and a half weeks into the season, I turned thirty. On the morning of my thirtieth birthday, I found five different bags of Doritos on my bed. Big bags, not the kind you buy at the fair for walking tacos, but the giant air-stuffed bags, all with different flavors— Nacho, Cool Ranch, Taco, Pizza. I ripped into one immediately, first thing in the morning, tasted that salty chemical crunch and crumble in my mouth. It was the greatest luxury I could remember, something unattainable in this closed system. When I turned around, Cassie was standing in the hallway, beaming. She started jumping up and down and clapping her hands. "Do you love it? Do you love it? Do you love it?" she chanted, and I did, so deeply, hadn't even remembered telling her my birthday tradition, which was to give myself this gift once a year: unlimited Dorito-eating. This secret self-love nobody else had ever paid attention to before.

But she had, Cassie, and procured them by some unknowably complicated means, this pile of salty love, this unexpected kindness that nearly made me weep.

The part of my mouth that had tasted those Doritos and

then later had come down on her skin were the incisors, maybe a bit of the canines.

I don't apologize. Not right at first, still flushed with anger. But later in the evening, when my adrenaline cools, I start feeling sour in my stomach. I'd punched Cassie. Bitten her. Even if she'd initiated it, even if she hadn't stopped when I asked her to stop, the difference in our actions was huge. I'd never physically hurt anyone before, never had an eruption of violence. I hadn't been able to control myself. I couldn't stop thinking about that part. Some internal animal had taken over and hurt someone else and I had not stopped it. I had not wanted to stop it. What worried me was that the bite felt good. Like I was finally able to scratch an itch that had been bothering me for a long, long time.

I try to make it up to her. Leave a dumb apology note on her pillow. Give her space. Text her *sorry*. Try to chat here and there. No response. She walks away. And then, as I am blathering on to her four days later about some dumb idle thing, hoping that perhaps the best thing is to pretend as if nothing has happened, to sweep the whole thing under the rug, she spins toward me.

"I will not ever be your friend," she says. "You are an abusive person. I know about abusive people. I get to choose who I want to be around in my life, and I choose to have nothing to do with you."

I am struck silent.

The sickness in my stomach almost spews right out of me. I am an abuser. I am as bad as they come.

A month or so before, Cassie, slumped beside our bunks after another fight with one of the other performers, had told me about her life. She was on our truck's dirty ground in fishnets and a hoodie. We were closed for the night. She told me stories about her mother. Her ex-husband. I wasn't sure how often she shared these stories with people in her life, but they were tough stories about people who'd hurt her and things she'd come through, and I was grateful for her trust. It was hard to imagine these histories happening to the quick-witted, loud-mouthed talker on the bally stage who was always smiling. Remembering this made what I did—hurting her—feel a thousand times worse. That she had been through pain and I'd hurt her in a way that connected me to the worst people in her life.

Story goes: she'd moved far away from her home to start school. And one night two teenagers started to mug her and, unwilling to have this new safe city taken from her, she started screaming at the top of her lungs, flailing her arms, swearing and kicking at them, and, fearing a sick animal, they fled. She couldn't stop shaking. I've never felt safe again, she said.

She can't work a regular job, she says, but she's gotten really good at Dance Dance Revolution and she has been practicing her bally talking all off-season. What she really wants, though, is to be filled up with a baby.

"Tommy!" she calls to him often. "Please, just put a little baby right in here," pointing to her stomach and winking at him.

Three days after the bite, H-Town Hank—so named because as far as they could remember, nobody had seen him, in his thirty-five years in the business, not nodding off from heroin—appears at my side on the midway toward closing time. He and Cassie are friends.

"I heard you're crazy, lady," he says, laughing his deep, wet laugh, laughing hard, almost hysterically. He pats me on the shoulder. "I hear you're not one to mess with," he says, then is suddenly quiet. He raises his well-plucked eyebrows at me and walks away. I wish I could feel proud and tough, like I'd finally made a name for myself here as a person who shouldn't be screwed with. But the only thing I feel is shame.

There is no great moment of clarity arriving, by the way. No good answer to why or how it would be okay that I did this.

328

When I think of her, of betraying her trust, of the days and then weeks afterward, sharing a bunk with her when she wouldn't make eye contact with me, of how sad that made me, and then mad, and then embarrassed, I want to barf. *Who am I? Who am I?* I had a chance to de-escalate the situation, and I rejected it. Went, instead, for blood. Couldn't make blood happen. Just tooth marks.

I couldn't hack it.

A few days after the bite, in the van, Rash and I are alone while the rest of the crew runs a late-night errand. He turns to me from where he sits on the seat in front of me, still in full clown makeup, wearing his spiky dog-collar choker and big dirty matted red wig.

"The way you handled Cassie," he says, and the blood drains from my whole body. "That's how you get respect here. It was necessary. And great. You were being a pussy before. A pushover. Now you have asserted yourself. They'll respect you more."

"She hates me," I say.

"Maybe, but at least she notices you now. Before you were nobody. Now you are somebody. You pushed back."

"I hate me."

"Fine by me," he says, turning back around. "But I don't think you're so bad. Just needed some balls, that's all."

I cover my face with both hands, bury it against the seat.

"Sorry. Ovaries. You just needed stronger ovaries."

INVISIBILIA

Two years and eleven months after the stroke

DAY 51 OF THE TRIP
SEPTEMBER 2013

I stumbled onto a place which was invisible. It was a space where there seemed to be no space, Davy wrote from Italy. It was a story I'd heard before, a story he'd tell when he wanted to explain the pleasure of secret places, and his absolute devotion to the idea of traveling narrow and deep, as opposed to wide and quick.

I mean it was there, of course, but one's attention was taken elsewhere as you passed by.

My parents are in Rome. They've rented a little apartment and are staying for a few weeks. My brother and I get a few lines about the Vatican, a few about the fountain of Trevi. In one e-mail, the featured photo is a close-up on a Nutella and crepes advertisement, with a short paragraph about how deeply Davy loves Nutella, how he could eat a jar with a spoon without pausing for breath, how it takes all his restraint not to dive naked into a fountain of Nutella. *Sorry,* he writes. *I'm sure that's not an image you want in your head.*

This update begins with some photographs of the Spanish Steps, then quickly moves elsewhere.

45 years ago, Davy writes, *in 1968, my family visited Rome and in the evenings I would sometimes wander off from the hotel to do a little exploring.* One night while strolling above the Spanish Steps, he found a place where two roads diverged, leaving a little wedge of land in between. *I followed the wall back to the street which headed down the hill. I found myself under some arches with vines or something hanging down.*

There, he writes, he lit up a joint and sat in the shadows, watching the city pass by. Nobody could see him. *Being in a swirl of people and not being seen. I always remembered that little place. It was my secret in an ancient city.*

There's a photograph of my mom, hand shielding her eyes as she looks down a little strip of grassy land flanked by old, crumbling bricks and a few flaking pillars. She's in Bubbles, the wheelchair with the off-roading tires, and in the next photograph she's beside an old, dried fountain, assessing the ruin. Bulges of stone protrude from the fountain's central pillar. After forty-five years, Davy had not only remembered this place, but was able to recall where it was, and how to get there. He'd been talking about it as they were planning their trip because he wanted to share his secret place with his wife.

Why was this fountain here? Davy writes. *Had it played an important role in someone's life? Who designed it? Was he coerced into building it? What were those growths on the side of the fountain?*

His questions continue, a whole list, a translation of an inner monologue I almost never saw anymore, this kind of focus on something other than my mom, or emergency, pills, wounds, pain.

But they were in a different kind of life right now. The life that was dictated by emergencies, pills, wounds, and pain was there, but it was the internal architecture of their day instead of the external. Their eyes were directed outside.

There they were, far away, wandering some old, forgotten road and finding a place that was entirely theirs, something that felt like a secret, a place that allowed them to invent stories

331

about other lives and the marks other people left on the world. And what might theirs be?

Even with the story Davy writes about finding this special place years later, and wondering about the history, and remembering his teenage trip, and seeing the photos, even with all that, the pictures and the descriptions are glimpses into a world my mom and Davy have found that my brother and I are not a part of. For the first time, I imagine what it would be like to have a child going off into the world, making her own life with her own experiences, and how I would feel happy for her, and excited, and also quite sad that I was no longer a necessary part of it.

BLOODLUST

Day 97 of 150

WORLD OF WONDERS
SEPTEMBER 2013

"His eyeball was sinking," Dale says, "so the socket's probably smashed. Both his cheekbones are shattered, that's for sure." Dale is a massive game jock with thick hoops sagging from his ears.

I wrap my mouth around a giant turkey leg and peel off a chunk of meat. Nod.

"Fucker," he says. "I mean, I stay out of it."

"What happened?" I ask, wiping grease from my lips with the back of my hand. The midway's asphalt is growing hot beneath our feet. Dale unfurls his game's canvas awning, pins a few stuffed bulldogs, whose brown cigars sag limp from their felt teeth, to the corners. The fair will open in forty minutes, and by then Dale will be calling marks into his game, I will be in fishnets with no head, and the high school band now rehearsing the national anthem in the rodeo ring will figure out how to hit those high notes.

"You know, same dumb shit," he says, and I nod, but I do not know, not much. It's what I'm hoping I'll learn tonight. Tonight there's a carnie jamboree.

What I know so far is that the carnie with the sinking eyeball was a game jock, and after some minor conflict exploded, the ongoing ride vs. game jock rivalry unfolded in a brutal beat-down. This was the way of the carnival. A manic buzz always broiling that could be neither created nor destroyed, but spun on in little hurricanes of violence and excess. I'd finally seen it erupt in me, and was ready to witness it elsewhere.

"I'm gonna buy a ranch after this season," Dale says. "Get some sheep, steer. Nothing too big." The September sun shines off his bald head, heat as consistent as the always-humming milk factory across the street.

"Maybe Wyoming," he says, rubbing the cuts across his knuckles.

The stereotype of the American carnie as rough and lawless, toothless and tweaking, had proved both true and untrue, as stereotypes go. We were showpeople, a category I was often reminded was separate from carnies, but I'd heard people on all sides call themselves freaks. The carnival is a kingdom of self-identified outsiders. But what beat on everywhere, unwavering, was the threat of violence, a heavy breath on the back of the neck. Teeth ready to clamp. Which is why events like what would be taking place tonight were scheduled—an opportunity to blow off steam, or, as I'd heard someone joke, a chance for a contained explosion. It had just been our bad luck, Sunshine had told me, that none of the carnivals we'd been performing with had held a jamboree while we were with them. Well, bad luck and good luck, she explained. They could be fun, and wild, but it's also often where things got out of hand, where the hundreds of carnies with a collective excuse to get drunk and high inside the fairgrounds boiled over into violence. Where women should walk with not one but two men back to their bunks, where drinks were cheap and expectations high.

And here, tonight, our luck, good or bad, is about to change: a jamboree looms.

The party begins once the front gates are locked.

Rides across the midway that usually hold a few workers

334

repairing a bucket seat or scrubbing barf are empty, though the bunkhouses behind our tent are full of carnies laughing and whooping, draping one another in togas. Usually this manic energy pulsed through the kids with mouthfuls of cotton candy, wisps hardening in little red crystals around their mouths as they flailed off the scrambler, but not tonight. Tonight, that buzz broils everywhere. I will be on the front lines of unbridled wildness.

The good attitude I'd arrived with, my smiley willingness to help, was fading over time. Or toughening. Adapting. Dale yells, "Marry me, Ms. Hollywood," every time I pass by.

"I would, but I think your wife would be mad," I say, pointing to John, the wiry carnie in the balloon dart game beside him whose hand, I'd just heard, had been rebroken the night before.

This, our ninth fair in the three months we've been on the road, is a combined state fair for both Oklahoma and Arkansas, and the corn dogs and funnel cakes and frozen bananas are now all too familiar, but because this is the season's first carnie jamboree, I'm primed for chaos. Imagining an orgy with face splintering, circling meth pipes, destruction. Now that I'm an insider, I'm ready to come face-to- face with the blood and bones.

What does not occur to me at the moment of this bloodlust, will not occur to me until later, is that I am actively *seeking* the violence. I want to witness the worst. Why? For the story I'll tell about it later, sure, but there's something else. Something uglier.

Earlier in the evening, a few of the lot men closed one of the bumper car rides early and carried the cars one by one out of the pen. The detached cars formed a long row behind the ride, glittering red and green and gold ovals ringed with rubber. The bumper pen was filled instead with tables holding huge trays of ribs, chicken, potato salad, green beans, and macaroni.

Up front were auction items: leather work gloves, tool sets, an electric kettle, and ten or fifteen different kinds of liquor in decorative bottles with attached shot glasses. Red donated one of the swords he frequently deep-throats.

In the bathroom, women spritz cotton-candy body spray across their chests, vanilla surprise into their hair. About 20 percent of the carnies are women. "Want some?" one asks as I pass.

"Yes, please," I say, grateful, and hoping to cover some of what sweating through the Arkansas heat in full costume smells like.

Our sideshow crew rolls into the jamboree, and immediately Short E returns from some dark corner with a baggie of Jell-O shots dangling from his teeth.

"It's time," he says, passing me a plastic cup. I start to squeeze it, but he grabs the shot out of my hand.

"Not like that," he sighs. "Watch this." He wedges the tip of his tongue between the Jell-O and the plastic, then wriggles the tip and twists the cup in a full circle.

"Did the strippers teach you that?" I ask.

He raises his eyebrows, gives me a thin smile, and begins tonguing another. "They taught me a whole lot more than that," he says, swallowing and then twerking against my leg before heading off in search of more.

I sit down and wait for something to happen. Something nasty. All around, people are talking and laughing and sipping, but I stay put. I have an idea that if I can get my face right up against one of the tent-pole beatdowns I've heard about, or directly beside John's rebroken hand—now full of sores and boils from wrapping it in dirty pieces of cloth for so many months—then maybe I will have some way of measuring the vague darkness of this place.

Here's the worst thing that happened, I'll be able to report. *This is how close I was to it.*

Of course, what I actually see are carnies sipping Budweisers and grinding and occasionally disappearing past the reach of the lights.

A man with clean clothes and a tucked-in shirt sits beside me. He has a full set of teeth and not much of a tan. Clearly a boss. Without looking up from his plate of food, he asks if I know why Red used to be called Lizard Red.

I do not.

"For years, Lizard Red ran our reptile show," he says. "One night, I woke up to a pounding on my door at three a.m. The rain was pouring and thunder was booming. 'Get up,' Lizard Red yelled. 'The storm broke our sixteen-foot python's cage and she's somewhere down the midway.' " The boss chuckles as he bites into his BBQ sandwich, a lightness in his voice like he's telling his favorite joke. "I wasn't wearing any clothes," he says, "and my first thought was—what do you put on to chase a giant python in the middle of a huge storm? I panicked and put on all the clothes I could find. By the time I waddled out of my trailer, Lizard Red was walking down the center of the midway in the pouring rain with the giant snake wrapped around his body."

"What did you do?" I ask the boss.

"Nothing," he says. "We put the snake in its cage and opened for business the next morning."

"I thought that story was going to end with something terrible happening," I say.

"That's our business. Steering clear of disaster."

All week, the thick smell of BBQ smoke has wafted over the Mirror Maze and Alpine Bob's from carnietown, where Merlin, whose job it is to dispose of all the carnival tickets at the end of each day, lit them on fire and cooked ribs.

"Had to find something to do with the tickets," he said, holding a plate of ribs inside our big red-and-blue circus tent earlier that day, grease pooling in small orange rivulets across the Styrofoam. With more than 135,000 visitors to this fair each year, thousands of tickets pass from tellers to riders each day and make their way into the sweaty palms of kids in line for the Crazy Mouse roller coaster they're finally tall enough to ride. And then they make meat. Merlin keeps coming to our tent because he likes Cassie, and he brings her plates of ticket meat.

He stands across the bumper car ring and I smile, wave. He glares back.

The auction, which funds some carnie charity, is jovial, so I duck out toward the bathrooms on the far side of the fairground to see if teeth are snarling elsewhere. The carnival is empty, dark. The boats bob silently in their pool, a half-moon reflected on the water. Carousel horses stall midprance. Though I can still hear shouts from the jamboree, there is also now the soft chirp of cicadas in the low trees around the fair, the factory whirring and motoring on through the night, and a baby inside a trailer, crying.

I avoid the upturned pile of funnel cake beside the pickle on a stick. The carnival buzzes on elsewhere, somewhere. Here I am in the center of it, but somehow always outside of it, too.

You'll never believe what I saw, I start composing in my head, my eyes searching wildly across the grounds. They land on a mirror outside the Mirror Maze that shrinks my head, doubles my feet. Too obvious. And yet, I feel like a distorted version of myself, the kind of person who bites a friend. A vulnerable friend. And likes it.

The country-rap remix of the summer blares from the bumper car's speakers. A toothless, bone-skinny woman charges me from head on, then apologizes profusely and walks off. *Take me with you*, I want to say. Instead, I see Dale.

Dale's silver hoops jiggle as he laughs and slaps the back of the carnie he's talking to. I begin to walk over, a snarky joke readied, but he joins another group and they all turn to walk off into the fairgrounds.

"Dale!" I call, and he spins back to me.

"What about horses on the ranch?" I ask him.

"Sure," he says. "Hell yeah."

"When the season's over?"

"Yeah," he says. Then, "Well, if I can save up enough. If not, then next year. Definitely next year."

"Next year," I echo.

"Night, Hollywood," he says, walking toward the low moon.

The two honky-tonk bars down the road are closed and, despite Fort Smith being the town where Elvis received his first military haircut, no rock 'n' roll music blares from anywhere off the fairground. A few carnies form a semicircle around Short E and ask him how he shits and if he can fuck. Same questions he gets everywhere. I want to say here that a fire starts or a massive fight breaks out, something to commemorate the end of the night, but the jamboree just trails off into a tray of leftover ribs being scraped into a garbage bag for someone to take back to their bunkhouse.

Two people remain. Despite a booming dubstep remix, the couple sways slowly, gently, a hint of vanilla mist as I pass.

The whoops and hollers continue in the distance, the night's electricity, true to the second law, neither created nor destroyed but still glowing somewhere farther away than I know how to reach. The couple wraps their arms around each other's shoulders and walks into the darkness.

⚡

After months of negotiation, Tommy agrees to let me leave for three days. This, I was reminded, was unprecedented. People don't leave. Or, people don't leave and then come back.

"My grandfather died two seasons ago," Tommy says in the van to Walmart. We're in Georgia. Honey Boo Boo saw the show earlier that day. "I didn't go home for the funeral."

"I didn't leave when one of my best friends died," Sunshine says.

"I wouldn't leave for anything," Spif says. "When you're here, you're here. The rest of the world is dead."

I watch Tommy in front of me, one hand loosely on the steering wheel. He has a metal bar as thick as a finger pierced through the back of his neck and a puzzle-piece tattoo on the inside of his wrist that I can see when he turns the wheel. The silence in the van is just as full of meaning as the words had been. There are the kinds of people for whom the rest of the world is dead while they are here, and there are the other kinds. The kinds who probably can't hack it.

The puzzle piece is just an outline of a puzzle piece, connected to nothing.

Truth is, I was nervous about leaving. Very, very nervous. I'd been around this crew for four months, day and night, and I couldn't imagine being away. But there was my other life, dangling just past the edge of my vision. A good friend of mine was getting married out in California, an old friend, and she'd asked me to be in the wedding, and I'd accepted, thrilled, months before I'd decided to join the show. It was at a fancy vineyard south of San Francisco, and fancy college friends of mine who had jobs in things like finance and PR and veterinary medicine would be there, and they'd have that bland skin smell of living indoors with plumbing, the smell of whatever nice perfume they'd wear and not this deep dirt stink from so many months in the truck.

I couldn't sleep the night before I left, I was so buzzed with excitement. And when I caught the bus to the airport, my legs wouldn't stop jiggling and my heart was racing. I was thrilled. I was thrilled and something else. Something hard to place.

I took a plane all the way back west. It was the first time I was in California when my parents weren't. But there wasn't much time to think about that. There was time only to drive down to the wedding rehearsal, to pull up to a giant chateau on top of a hillside, I mean straight up fairy-tale castle, and lather myself in deodorant. I thought about wiping it on my neck and the backs

340

of my knees, but the bride pulled up. I gave her hugs. And the bridesmaids piled out of the car and I gave them hugs, too, and I thought, See? I'm just like them, and we're all here and we have nice enough hair and I can laugh just like everybody else can.

We practiced walking the aisle, and then we moved on to drinking. And eating, too, a little later. That's when the trouble began.

"So what are you doing these days?" one of my college friends asked.

"Well, I know this sounds a little weird, but I'm performing with a traveling sideshow."

"Ha ha ha," he said.

"I know. But, actually, I am."

"Wait, what? Doing what?"

"Depends on the day. Fire eating, snake charming. Talking a contortion act."

"Holy shit. Why?"

We were eating shrimp and drinking some nice white, I mean, we had little pink tails in our hands, and while I didn't have an immediate answer ready, the long-winded story I'd use to talk around the question was one I was sure he didn't want to hear.

"I don't know, really. For fun?"

"Is it fun?"

"Sometimes."

"Weren't you, like, the student speaker at college graduation or something like that?"

"Yeah, something like that."

"And now you're eating fire."

"Now I'm eating fire."

The night went on, and then the next day with the hair and makeup and wedding and dancing and toasts and it all was fine, lovely, I mean, but a little like something I was spying on from another room. Even though I'd scrubbed and scrubbed in the shower, I still thought I smelled different, I had cuts and calluses on my hands, my shoulders were the deep brown of outside labor, and I don't mean to say I was somehow suddenly tough and nobody there was, but I couldn't stop thinking about all my showpeople friends, working and working and working. I hated it. I thought about them and thought about them and chided myself for thinking about them, reminded myself not to text them pictures of flowers woven into hearts because I was here and having so much fun so how could I be thinking about them, and besides, the sideshow was tiring, so exhausting, and I'd turned into a beast out there, an aggressor, something so far outside of the kind of person I thought I was, and then I thought about them more. I wondered how the show was going. How big the audience was. If the person who had been pooping in the shared bathroom's shower stall had stopped.

But I danced around, doing my best to fake it. That, I was very good at. Playing my part. Well, pretty good at. Though not the dancing part so much. I was limping my whole trip, my hip throbbing with each step from something I'd done to it in setup a week or two before. I'd tweaked it pretty badly on top of the ladder as I'd been hanging lights. So I was limp-dancing and keeping a smile on my face and reapplying deodorant every time I went to the bathroom just to be sure—by the end of the night I had a white crust under there— and feeling more sure each moment that I didn't belong here.

I was to fly out the next night. I had a few hours to spend roaming the city with Devin, and when he rounded the corner to meet me at a café, I almost lost it. I wasn't sure he'd be able to recognize me, if how I was changing internally could be seen externally as well.

"Jesus, kid," he said once we started walking. He was concerned. My arm was hooked into the crook of his elbow to help with my limp, and my skin was still very tan and I was cussing like a sailor. I did not talk about the sideshow, because it seemed like any words I could say about it would be too small, too insignificant.

I bought candies for the performers I'd return to, sweets and

342

cookies and chips and toys and little gifts that I felt I needed to give them in order to atone for leaving.

I didn't look around and think about the fact that this city might not see my parents again. I did touch the jar of kimchi in the market, thinking a little wish-prayer for my mom.

"You don't have to go back," Devin said as I was getting ready to head to the airport. "You can stay on my couch for as long as you need, you can find a job here, you can let this hip heal, whatever."

I thought about that, letting my body feel for a moment the sensations of living indoors, of walking through cities alone, my city, of erasing who I'd become out there. My loyal, lovely friend, trying to help.

"I know that's a possibility," I said.

"So? Do it."

"You know I can't."

"Why?"

"I can't let them down."

"Tessa. The show will go on without you."

"Yeah," I said, and it was true. They'd be fine. The show would go on. They'd finish the season and be no worse off, except that for a little while they'd be a person short and would each have to pick up a little bit of the slack. Except that I'd leave the show without having learned every single act, without having an act that I know wows each person watching each time: the electric chair. And except for the fact that someone would take that permanent marker and write on the inside of the truck, *TESSA: Couldn't hack it*.

The only way through it is through it. There is no trick.

"I gotta go," I said, hugging Devin.

"All right," he said, shaking his head. "Don't kill yourself out there."

So I went back to the show.

Nobody will look me in the eye.

Tommy picks me up from the airport, sweet, sweet Tommy,

343

and says he missed me, says the show wasn't the same without me, and I want to cry in gratitude for his white lies. When we arrive at the lot where setup has begun at the Pensacola Interstate Fair in Florida, I climb out of the van, pull on my work gloves, and am ready for a stream of hellos, how was your trip, how we've missed yous. But there is work to be done. And we are the workers. Nobody even really notices me. So I weave myself back in the best I know how, feeling like an alien, like a deserter, limping between tent poles, trying to work doubly hard to win some affection.

It doesn't feel good, exactly, to be back, but it doesn't feel bad either. I feel tired, immediately, and dirty, and guilty for having left. My bunk is still here, having housed the temporary performer—someone I'd recruited from Alabama with promise of adventure for a few days—who kindly replaced me while I was gone, and it looks the same. The snakes still coil around each other for warmth in their box. The banner-line crew, setting up the lights and flags that attach to the very top of the tallest poles out front, are managing just fine on their own, it seems, though when I offer help, Spif silently climbs off the ladder and motions for me to climb to the top. That's my job. That's what I know how to do. I mount the ladder, ascend to the top so my feet are near the highest rung, and I lean from there to attach items to the poles, slide in the flags, plug in the flashers, I do exactly what I know a person should not do for ladder safety, I reach farther out than I usually do during setup, work a little bit faster, because somehow I know, with the feeling of a rock in my stomach, that I don't want to be here, and I do want to be here, and I didn't miss it at all, and I missed it like crazy. I know that this place is inevitably, inexorably, but oh so temporarily, my home.

THE HEROES
Day 126 of 150

We are at the Pensacola Interstate Fair, and summer is ending. Even the leaves in Florida, the land of perpetual flip-flops, are turning gold and orange. The front-of-the-store Walmart displays have gone from Fourth of July to summer BBQs to back-to-school to Halloween, and the Halloween items will soon be discounted.

Marking a day when the boundary between the worlds of the living and dead is especially blurry, Halloween for us Americans in our costumes is a moment to become someone else. I feel like I've been doing some iteration of this for the entirety of the sideshow season, but this is a night to make that slippery identity explicit for everyone.

The fair bosses decide to throw a Halloween Jamboree. Halloween proper is still a few days away, but it's a great excuse for a party. The last jamboree, thrown by another carnival company, was only a few weeks ago, but now we're practiced in the art of Jell-O shots. We already have costumes, of course, but none of them seem like costumes anymore, since they are just our daily work clothes. Yet our fellow performers' costumes are still costumes, and so we trade around. Cassie takes my bumblebee costume, I take her sailor suit. She's become tolerant of

345

me, though distanced, and I take whatever I can get. Big, Big Ben wears a sequined suit coat, and Spif found a sailor costume at some thrift shop nearby. The rest of the crew already have costumes, and once the gates close jamboree night, the marks locked out and us locked inside, the party begins.

It starts off like the other one. Drinks. An auction. Trays of food. But this time, almost everyone is in disguise. There are fake policemen and monsters and men in business suits with two-foot-long inflatable dicks sticking out of their pants and superheroes and pirates and naughty nurses and serial killers, and something about costumes changes the rules. Who can touch whom, and when, and how much. And the amount of booze that should go inside a person in order to make them feel a little bit better about the ostrich they are riding.

You did what you had to do.

That's what everyone said after I told them the story of the Halloween jamboree night.

You did what anyone would have done.

That's what everyone said after I told them the story of the last few years of my life, about how much I wanted to move back to help, about how I kept not doing it.

But none of us have to do anything. We make choices. I made choices.

We pass a trailer full of skeletons.

It is three or four in the morning, the auction is over, and Captain America asks Spif and me if we want to head back to his bunk where the other Avengers are having beers and passing some joints around. We do. We wave goodnight to the skeletons, to a man in a bear suit curling up under the Octopus. The Hulk is pouring ice on a cooler of beers outside their trailer, and Thor is smashing his hammer into the ground, yelling something about ultimate power. I settle into a camp chair between Spif and Captain America, and the other heroes throw a few of their trailer's pillows into a small fire, and all is fine in costumed idle chitchat until a new group of faces emerges from the darkness.

"Hey," a man's voice says. "You work at Geoffrey's pizza joint?"

"Yep," Captain America says. "Who wants to know?"

"Your boss has been fucking with my girl," the voice says.

"What the fuck?"

"He's a piece of shit."

"Who the fuck are you?" the Hulk says.

"Tell your boss—" the voice starts, but the rest of the sentence never arrives, because Captain America, who had been sitting beside me, throws a punch that travels right beside my face and lands on the nose of the stranger, who had walked up behind me. The stranger's face takes the punch, but it hadn't landed all that well, and he immediately cocks his fist to return the blow, and suddenly my head is being jerked but it isn't by the force of a fist, which is a force I had tensed for, since I am seated between the two punchers, but instead I am being pulled by my hair. I have two braids beneath my sailor cap, and one is in a hand that is throwing me down to the ground and then yanking me out of the dog pile of superheroes and strangers forming where I had just been, as if their bodies were required to fill up the vacuum of space like water rushing in. There is the hard echo of a head hitting concrete, Thor's head, and the superheroes might be wishing they could really split the earth in half and shoot lightning from the ground back up into the sky.

Spif eventually lets go of my hair and grabs me by the hand instead, and off we go, rounding the corner of the bunkhouse and running on. I ask him what's going on, if he understands what is happening and he half laughs, half snorts. "Just two dumb groups of dudes needing to work out their feelings," he says. And I ask if we should tell someone, or find help, and he says no, that everything's fine, that it's two seemingly evenly matched groups and those things always work out naturally

347

and settle what needs to be settled, and we are running still, holding hands, past the other bunkhouses with carnies here and there still outside in their costumes and past the Zipper and funhouse and other darkened rides, and we finally round a corner closer to our tent and that's when we see it.

A circle of men.

I have to stare.

Some are bent over. There are things in their hands. I am staring, because I'm afraid that what I'm seeing is too tinted with what we'd just run from.

The things in their hands are long and thin. Metal. Metal pipes.

In the middle of the circle is a man. He is on the ground. He is on his knees with his head down on the ground in front of him, his hands wrapping his head, and then he is on the ground on his side. This is the moment. I take a step forward, toward them, the great carnie hero that I am, and Spif, who has just done so much work to drag me by the hair from the last fight, grabs my shoulder and throws me back into the Honey Bucket we are standing beside.

"Are you fucking nuts?" Spif says.

"Are they killing that man?" I ask, my chest heaving, breathing jagged.

"Maybe," he says.

"We have to stop them," I say.

"Yeah?" he says. "You want to be in the middle of that?"

We are in the shadows of our tent, but the men who make up the circle can certainly see us. Nobody seems to care. There's nothing to hide. There are rules here and I don't know them and I probably never will. But there is a human on the ground. Getting beaten. Badly.

"We could call the cops," I say. My brain is rattling, desperate.

"Ha. You think they'd come?"

"They might."

348

He swings his face over to me.

"The reason the guy is probably getting the shit kicked out of him is for calling the cops," he says. "It's not our business."

"But—"

"No."

"Spif—"

"Do you want to get us killed?"

I close my mouth. Watch the man on the ground.

"What do you think he did?" I ask quietly.

"Who knows," Spif says. "But he probably deserves it."

I lean against the Porta-Potty and watch the metal come down on the bones and organs and hair and unrecognizable black costume of the man on the ground, for five, ten more seconds. It's their business.

"This isn't safe," Spif says. "Go get in our tent, now, and don't come out until tomorrow."

And I do. Just like that.

I never knew if the man lived or died.

I stood there, watching. And then I left.

The next morning, I walk over to the spot to check the grass for evidence, but the grass has already moved on. There is a tight squeeze around my throat, a hot guilt, a shame, like I am searching for the spot where I'd let a man die.

When I get back to our tent, Captain America is there with an apology slice of pepperoni pizza.

"Sorry you had to see our fight," he says, handing me the pizza and a Coke.

"You guys okay?" I ask. "Everyone's fine. Was just some drunk bullshit. It's all sorted out now. But we didn't mean for you guys to be in the middle of that. Didn't want you getting hurt. You didn't, did you?"

"No, we ran away pretty quickly," I say, "and ran right into another fight. An uglier fight. I didn't stop it."

"Why would you have stopped it?"

"They were hurting some guy pretty badly."

"The less you know about this world, the better," he says. "There are systems in place here that have been working for many, many years. You can't change that."

"What about all the Germans who turned a blind eye when the Nazis started terrorizing innocent people? Didn't they have a responsibility to step in?"

He laughs. "So the carnies are Nazis here? Come on, now. I just brought you a piece of pizza and a soda. Fresh pizza. Straight from the oven."

I look out our door to one of the kiddie rides down the mid-way, where a lanky carnie with a long brown ponytail is helping a little boy into the airplane ride. I think about Leo at the first fair, who'd delivered me iced tea when it was hot and who only wanted to talk about orchids. About Dale and the dream of his ranch. And then about the posture of the man's body on the ground as he stretched his limbs over his most fragile parts like children are taught to do in earthquake drills in California schools. And I wonder how a person could not feel concern for someone else who is clearly so afraid that his neck will be broken. I do. I feel it. But I didn't do anything about it.

You did what you had to do.

New worlds call for new yous.

350

ELECTRICITY

Day 130 of 150

A day passes, two, three, more. The show carries on in its regular irregular swing, and I try not to think about the man on the ground, about my teeth marks on Cassie's skin, but those are not easy weights to lift. I'm surprised by this darkness inside myself. My whole life I have tried to be good. And nice. To act right. I thought being out with the sideshow would present clearer moral grounds than the gray area I'd been inside for so long with my mom. I thought I could be here, do the job right, be good, and that'd be it.

The electric woman is not nice.

"Can I be Electra?" I asked Sunshine during setup a few spots back.

I'd spent a long time watching the electric chair from afar. I'd remained quiet when Sunshine cast the acts for each new fair, waiting, patiently, until she thought I might be ready. She didn't ask. I stopped waiting.

"Sure," she said. "You're the new Electra."

It was that easy.

For the first two months, I had been a bally girl on the teaser stage, and then a month as an inside performer, mostly box

351

jumper and mic talker, and then, suddenly, miraculously, I am the electric woman.

Electra the Electric Woman is not a good girl. She's not a girl at all. The electric woman plays dangerously and loves it.

"It's entirely safe," Tommy said as he showed me the electric chair the day before I was to perform it. "You won't feel a thing. We used to have the girl light a cigarette off her body, and you won't even have to do that. Health nuts these days hate cigarettes."

I nodded confidently, always working on my fearlessness.

"The only problem with the electric chair," Tommy said, "is when it's raining outside."

"What happens then?" I asked.

"Usually nothing," he said. "If it's flooding, we'll cut the electric chair act. If it's just raining, there can be some small surprises."

"Shocks?"

"Little ones. But they don't feel like you think they would. They're soft."

I am standing behind the curtain as Red finishes his block-head act, thinking through Tommy's warning, listening to the dim plops of rain hitting the vinyl tent. Red says, "This next act will also take place on this stage, where you see this fine and most unique piece of furniture." His storytelling is so rehearsed after years on this stage, he almost sounds like a recording. Words blur together. "Every prisoner on every death row affectionately calls this thing Sparky."

I take the final steps up to the stage as I hear, "Let's welcome Ms. Electra," and part the curtain like this moment is my nineteenth rebirth of the day.

Scattered applause.

The vinyl curtain falls closed behind me, and now I stand beside Red, forty or so people looking back and forth between us. Over eight million bolts of lightning strike the earth each day. There's so much wattage out there. Currents buzz beneath

352

each leaf, inside all the open mouths. Red talks to the crowd and I stand with my hands on my hips, let them try to guess whether I feel any fear, what kind of person I am. The face I put on is confident, this half smile, this squinty-eyed woman who knows what kind of wattage she can withstand.

"Do you know who invented the electric chair?" Red asks the audience. Silence. "Thomas Alva Edison. Do you know how many are still in use? Forty-seven."

This chair is not one of them. We want them to assume it is.

I know this game. I know they know that I am about to be filled with something that can kill me. Why does this turn them on? I stand with my legs parted.

"I wonder," I'd asked Tommy when he first showed me the chair, "if there's any chance the electricity might stay inside you?"

"You won't become electric," he said.

The woman who knows how much wattage she can withstand, and then takes more.

What was better, to be safe or to be alight?

"Let's flip the juice," Red says. I step forward, swinging my hips, wink, take four sideways steps, hinge, and sit down on the electric chair, my bottom on top of my flattened palm. I adjust my angle so I lean back just a bit, casual. Unworried. My palm's skin against the metal plate beneath me. A direct conduit for the electricity. New audience members duck into the tent and shake their wet umbrellas into the grass. Rub their eyes like cartoons. Red reaches behind the chair with a small drop of clear snot about to leak from the nostril that has just been filled with metal. The rain continues outside.

He flips the switch. I'm electric.

"Now watch Ms. Electra illuminate this bulb with the very tippy top of her little head," Red says as he brushes the glass across my forehead. My face grows goose bumps as the bulb slides across the skin. It's as if the electricity demands that each

353

pore stand at attention. Not pain, exactly, but a sharp flick that translates internally instead of externally, a pinch that makes me feel very awake and sit up a little straighter.

I sit down firmer against my hand. I want to be sure each finger and my full flat palm are connecting with the metal plate, soaking up as many electrons the Tesla coil produces as I can so I can conduct it without disruption. I only feel the electricity move through my body— light pinpricks, like when your foot is just waking up after having been asleep—when I don't get enough. When it can't easily pass all the way through. And when it rains.

I've been performing this act for two weeks. One light summer storm brought sprinkles, and it made the electricity feel alive inside me. Lighting up wasn't just something I knew was happening by watching the audience's delighted faces. I felt it move inside me. I knew I was part of something larger, something stronger, something that spans the earth.

Red walks across the stage, a child screams outside, and I put the light bulb I'd been hiding in my shorts into my mouth. Press my tongue against the ceramic insulator, around the base, my teeth clamping around the fuse. Would it be so bad to become all the way electric? I know this may not make sense, but the rules of physics and fantasy were performed away on those stages. Can you hear a story about yourself as an electric woman over and over and not believe the story a little, too?

My tongue connects to the base of the bulb and my mouth fills with static and my teeth shiver in their skin clamps and a small pool of blood, no, water, grows from the side of the tent onto the stage. I hold the bulb in place and Red comes over to touch it with his finger and I light up. He completes the circuit. There's a glowing miracle between my teeth. I can feel the tickle of something great passing through me. Cameras are out and clicking at us.

I feel dangerous. Amazing.

Full of electricity, I am, for the first time, inside my own world of wonder. It's an act I imagine performing in front of my mom, something to echo her surfing routine. Two strong, poised women channeling a force from the earth, two women choosing how to be awake in the world.

A beach at dusk, cold wind, reeds bending sideways. A girl, me—age eight or nine—sitting on a picnic blanket beside her mother. The mother is facing the ocean. Her face is turned up to the sky where the purples are moving in, eyes closed, making herself into a painting that she might re-create later. There is electricity brewing in the sky, potential energy collecting behind the purple clouds. This is sixteen or seventeen years before the mother's brain will be flooded with blood and she will no longer be able to walk or talk or, for a while, demonstrate that she even knows the daughter anymore. Does she know the daughter anymore? Of course she must. The ocean has trails of thin white foam like fat through a steak and the sand lifts with small gusts of wind.

"Do you feel that?" the mother asks, her eyes closed and facing the water. "Close your eyes. You can feel more."

I close my eyes. Wait to feel more. Wait. Peek over at her, and there is some sort of private smile across her mouth I've never seen before and it scares me a little. I close my eyes and try again, but I must be doing it wrong.

She is right beside me, we are in the same wind and our skin is stung by the same sand and she is also elsewhere, feeling more. I wonder for the first time what it means if you can't feel what another person is feeling.

The seagulls walk in slow circles on the beach and move toward us like predators, and the mother thinks nothing of being wrapped in torn, old down coats that smell of sweat and campfire, thinks nothing of peeing mostly in view, waving and smiling as she walk away from where I sit. She winks at me and then walks off alone down the beach, turns to wave once, but then walks farther and farther until her size is halved and halved again, a retreating body meeting the last light on the ocean. What I'm saying is that she already knew how to travel away. I had already lost her. I never had her.

The evening drops its yellow ball straight ahead. Dim stars behind. The cold wind and the cold salt smell. I imagine that the mother sees herself swimming to the next coast. How it would feel to be inside that Pacific water for days or weeks. How far she would go.

When she comes back, she tells the story again of herself as a little girl, a swimmer, how nobody could ever get her out of the water, nobody, and how it's just impossible for her to believe she has babies who aren't water babies, aren't interested in the submersion, not even a little. I mean, really.

What I'm saying is, of all the things that happened later, there was this moment of unattainable beauty, of a person whom I did not possess, who did not possess me, walking slowly down the cold beach, touching things I couldn't see on the sand. I only knew her a little at that moment. I wasn't part of the multitude she was experiencing—her ocean, her sand, her crabs, her shells, her memories of a time before I was born, her fears, all that electricity humming its perfect, separate self.

My mom is plugged in and her eyes are closed.

It has been three months since her stroke.

I am leaving the hospital for the day and kiss her arm goodbye because I can't kiss her face because there's too much machinery. Because her brain is still bleeding despite four surgeries, despite a pump that sucks liquid out of her skull, carries it down her neck, and deposits it into her stomach. She is her own machine.

I am not allowed to kiss her face and I am not actually supposed to be touching her skin at all right now. She has sepsis. She's in a white-starched bed in a white-walled room sealed within another room, and everyone coming in or out must be covered head to toe in plastic protectant, eye guard, mask, and mine is down and I hear a rap on the window from a nurse in the quarantine station:

PUT ON YOUR MASK.

What kind of prayers? What last rites would you like for her? the hospital priest had asked Davy and then kept asking as the days and then weeks of emergency turned into months. *What kind of life will she have now?* the doctors asked, we asked, and *Is it our job to decide if it goes on?*

There are tubes that go into her hand. The crook of her elbow. Her forearm. One that pumps right into her heart. I kiss her arm and my nose catches on one of them. I jerk my head up, startled, and it pulls the skin taut under the tape holding a needle in and there is a shrill cry of emergency on top of the wheezing of the accordion putting air into her mouth from a fat tube. The machines alarm. Flashing and buzzing. What I need to do is keep breathing, but how can I as the nurses rush in to check and reset the machines and see if I've killed her. Her eyes are still closed.

The nurses in their germ-free spacesuits touch their fingers to buttons that reset her circuits. They tell me she is fine.

I am waiting for her to be fine.

To open her eyes. To say, *Babygirl*.

There's so much wattage that performs the wonder of keeping her alive. This electric woman.

I smile and wave for the audience, keep the other hand beneath me against the metal plates of the electric chair. They cannot hear the blood roiling in my temples, the nerves, they cannot feel my hammering heart. From the corner of my eye, I can see the water pool beneath the chair. I choose to remain seated. To flare my fingers, angle my wrists, press as firmly into the chair as I can so the bulb burns brightly. The possibility of getting hurt—which I'd thought a lot about earlier in the season—is secondary. What matters now are the bright stage lights on my skin. I will keep one hand beneath me, the bulb glowing from my mouth, the other hand up, up, up toward the sky, that kind of woman, directing attention toward what's bright.

357

BY SHIP INTO THE SEA

Three years after the stroke

I get an e-mail from Davy. They've recently boarded the ship that will bring them back to the States. Before that, though, in Florence, they were staying in an apartment with a window that looked out over a busy pedestrian street. Every morning, he says, in their pajamas, they have their coffee while they sit all scooted up against the window, setting the cup on the sill while they watch the world go by outside. There are a few photographs of my mom here. You can see only her back, her softest skin in the world beneath a nightie or a camisole, her silver hair wild and messy from sleep. She is in shadow because of the brightness of the window she's looking out, a bright white building with turquoise shutters across the street, cars and motorbikes parked and in motion below, and people in light jackets walking every direction.

How does the recycling work here? Davy wants to know. There are these bins and it looks like they empty underground, but how could that be? How do the trucks pick them up? He posts photographs of the Italian police, the Carabinieri, writing parking tickets to a line of scooters. And the bakery that opens each morning with fresh hot bread. And the street artist setting up his paintings in the morning beside the used-book man opening his tarp top, and a photo of the two of them having one of their discussions they seem to have each day. I'd spent two weeks in Italy just after high school, so I wanted to imagine myself watching the daily street life with them, but I couldn't. They were on their own journey.

Another e-mail from Davy follows just after, letting me know that their travel plans were messed up, delayed ships and work on the train tracks that they'd need to take back across the country. That they were panicked and didn't know how all the timing for getting home would work out now, that the plans we all had to reconvene in California on Thanksgiving the day after we all ended our respective journeys might have to be tweaked.

I didn't pay a lot of attention to the details in what he said, because I was too transfixed by the idea that they were returning at all. I had never asked, but they had actually made the plans to return, and were following through, boarding ships that needed to be boarded. The idea was miraculous.

TWINKLERS

Day 136 of 150

WORLD OF WONDERS
NOVEMBER 2013

We're headed deeper into the swamp.

For the season's last gig, we're playing the Volusia County Fair in DeLand, Florida. Three days of set up, ten days of performing, a day of teardown, and the season will be over. What does that even mean?

A bed in a room with a door. Clean sheets. Blankets. Toilets that flush. That fancy Trader Joe's hand soap that I would lather my whole body in, rinse with hot water. And then sleep for weeks.

My muscles are sinewy and strong. My skin a deep bronze. My hair very blond. All the clothes I'd purchased on the road, a very few, all at Walmart, are black. I am tough. Dirty. Grizzled. I have never been more exhausted. My mother is on the open sea. I am falling apart.

We'd had a week stopover in Gibtown to appear on the reality TV show *Freakshow*. TV pays better than carnivals, so the bosses were game. Rash the Clown was delighted, and tried to be in as many shots as possible. Terrifying yet talented clowns are great for TV. Sunshine had a fire-eating nemesis to compete with, who turned out to be disappointingly nice. Spif was annoyed with how much more work we had to do than the TV cast. Tommy was happy for the money.

One night, to pass the time before filming started, we went to the Showmen's Club. The big flat building is a private club for members of the International Independent Showmen's Association, more than 4,500 people. Because we were with Tommy and Red, we went in with no hassle even though we were not all members. Ward's and Chris's pictures hung on the wall. They're royalty here. We posted up at the carousel bar because there were only a few other people in the whole club. Red sidled up beside me, asked what I was drinking, and bought me one.

"This girl here is going to be a doctor," he said to the bartender as he ordered our drinks. I had no idea he'd been paying attention to conversations I'd had with other folks about my plans for after the season—more grad school. Didn't know he cared.

"I like when I see you reading," he said, handing me the drink. "Good to have that kind of a mind. Ever read the mystics?"

We chatted for a while, about books first, then his plans to spend Christmas with his mom, who had even more kittens now, about the value of social media for reconnecting long-lost family. We toasted to my lack of sword-swallowing skills—I'd practiced here and there over the last few months with little progress, more seduced by the flashy whip acts. There were some people who took a few years to get it. Others just never did.

Eventually I sat beside Tommy at the bar. Tommy, who doesn't drink, and me, who had a few. Tommy, the great road boss, the young sword swallower who figured out, at twenty-one, that this was the life for him and hasn't left. Tommy, who works as a piano mover in New Jersey in the off-season, who performed as an amateur wrestler for a few years, who was infinitely patient with my screwups on the road, with the snake bringing me to tears, with the gasoline headaches, who called me Tessy right away as if I already belonged.

"I just want you to know," I said to him. "You're the greatest boss I've had. In any kind of job."

"Oh, stop, Tessy," he said.

"I mean it. You are kind and patient, but firm and tough when you need to be. And you're doing this hard thing, keeping this show alive, struggling each year to make sure it happens. I admire you. You're such a good person."

"That's not true."

"Of course it is."

"I keep the show alive because it's fun. That's why I do it. I like it."

"Well, thank you for doing it. For liking it."

I finished another drink, feeling good. Feeling hopeful, though Cassie and I hadn't made eye contact at the bar and still weren't talking much. I felt buzzed and happy to be a shitty sword swallower, a mediocre fire eater, for transforming into the electric woman, for being of medium strength, of sometimes sour moods, for all the good reasons I'd had to leave the show but had chosen instead to stay.

$$\lightning$$

We haul Queen Kong from the back end for the very last time.

We're in DeLand, Florida, at the season's last fair, our twelfth. Unroll the tent walls once more. All these actions that have finally, finally, become so ingrained in my muscles that it takes almost no thought to put up the show anymore.

"Hey, girl," a familiar voice calls as I head down the midway before opening on the second day the fair is open. I grab her arm in response, squeeze the sinewy bicep as a greeting. It's Tanya, operator of the Smash the Beer Bottle game.

"Wanna play?" she asks, her permed blond bangs standing at attention. "No charge."

The rows of empty beer bottles shine green and brown with morning sun, the smell of old beer and the warm Indian summer dust in the air.

"Come on," Tanya says, leaning in close. The scent of beer

362

is replaced by cotton-candy body spray, and I wonder if the grandchildren she keeps telling me about think of this smell when they think of her, sweet and thick and edible. They wait up all night for her when she finishes the season, she tells me, the little faces sleeping on the trailer's couch right against the front window that looks out onto the street so they can be ready for her to pull into the driveway well after midnight, their sweet-smelling granny with a face whose deep brown lines offer a map of where she's been that they can't quite read.

"Sure," I say. It isn't often I have an extra moment on the midway, but I do, and I like Tanya. I hold the giant softball in my hand. Lined up in front of me are dozens of empty glass beer bottles. Row after row at the far end of the game. The point is to smash them. Send the glass, shattered, flying. It reminds me of a relaxation chamber I'd heard about once, a place in Japan where you could pay to go into a room full of breakable things. You were handed a bat. It was a way to unwind.

She leans in close to my ear. I can smell the spritz. It's the same one she has shared with me a few mornings when I've run into her in the portable bathrooms in carnietown. We can't agree whether the bathrooms smell like old mildew or diarrhea. It's both, somehow, and so strong that many of the carnies have taken to peeing in the woods instead. Tanya is dating one of the bosses, who is also her ex-husband, and has been on the road with some fair or another for almost thirty years.

"You're my alarm clock, honey," she said, coming into the bathroom one morning. I'd seen her head pop up from the bed of a pickup truck when I'd walked by, and she smiled at me vaguely and looked away quickly, off into the kudzu and jungle trees stretching as far as we can see on all sides of the fairground, with caution, hunting grounds signs nailed to the tree trunks. Carnietown is set up in the small jungle clearing. "When I see you trotting by, I know it's time to get my ass up."

"Here's the trick," Tanya says. She leans her temple right up against mine and points at one of the bottles at the end. "Think

363

about your boyfriends. Think about one of them who's done you wrong. There's his face right there."

I look at the empty old Budweiser. The bottle is just a bottle. Brown, dusty. The light from behind, sunshine and the red vinyl backdrop, gives the bottle an amber glow, just a little, just from the right angle. The bottle is also a face.

I step away from her, plant one foot in front of me, and take the ball into two hands. Crank one arm back and let the ball loose, imagining a face there, though not a boyfriend's face. The ball sails through the air and lands on the ground, just short of the first row of bottles.

"Not to worry, my friend. Give it another go," she says, handing me another softball.

"Imagine his eyes right there, where the label should go. Imagine his smug little asshole smile," she says, patting me on the shoulder.

I squint at the bottle, take in the light, and transform it into eyes. Blur my vision so the bottom lip of the bottle becomes a tight-lipped grimace. Take a deep breath. Pick my front foot up as I lean back for force, then let the ball go once again toward the rows of bottles. Big white moon charging for the brown and green stars. Bullet.

The ball flies between two rows of bottles but doesn't graze anything.

"Look, sweetie," she says. "I'll give you three more balls for five dollars. Because you're with it." *With it* is a term that carnies and showpeople used to mean "with the carnival." It was a way of shutting up other carnies who tried to sell you things when you walked by.

"Thanks, Tanya. That was fun. I gotta go, but I'll come back later to try again."

The trouble was, the only face I could imagine on the bottle was my own.

⚡

364

When I come onstage for the electric chair act later that day, I see in the audience a carnie I've chatted with a few times. He is standing in the back row and has a huge wide grin on his face. I try not to stare. His blue uniform shirt is wrinkled, and he moves his fingers up to spread them wide across his mouth, a side smile behind the hand, openmouthed, and I know that just past those fingers is a tangle of crisscrossed teeth.

Who are you? he'd asked me a couple of days in a row as I'd walked by his joint.

I feel good about that pink mouth, those yellow teeth. The tenderness of people with a little contained mess. His handsomeness.

He claps like mad when the act is done.

That night, once the show closes, our crew chats out in front of the tent while we wait for the big wheel to shut off so we can fold up the banners and quit for the evening. Everyone cheats their bodies toward the wheel like a flock of seagulls facing the first light each morning. I am also cheating my body toward the balloon dart game where the handsome snaggletoothed carnie is folding it in on itself.

Across from our stage, the man who works the goldfish joint reaches to the ground and gathers four or five white Ping-Pong balls in each hand and tosses them into plastic baskets that line the wooden counter around his game. He does not feed the fish all season except to add some of the chemical they put into the tanks to keep the fish from needing to eat so they don't have to buy food, he'd told me the day before, when I'd asked to feed the fish.

We wait. Snapping his fingers, Spif presses his butt into my crotch, bends over and pops his hips. His face is tilted slightly to the side so he can keep his eyes on the wheel. He jiggles his ass, shimmying it back and forth across my hips.

"You're a beautiful dancer," I tell him, hoping the carnie isn't seeing this and getting the wrong impression.

365

"Mine's thick. Like a Red Bull can," he says, eyes on the wheel. "Give me a reach-around and feel it, just to see if you agree," but before I can come up with a snarky response, he screams, "Wheel's off!" the moment the orange and red and yellow flashing lights stop chasing one another, the moment the wheel becomes dark bones. Within seconds, the rest of the rides across the midway cut their lights and sounds and the darkness kills the lights from one end of the fairground to the other, *swoosh*, silence, *swoosh*, silence, the darkness chasing everything out.

We work.

When the final banner is tied, I look up, and standing in front of me is the carnie.

"Roelof," he says, extending his hand to shake mine. Then he hands me a slip of paper with his phone number. "There's a flea market outside the fairgrounds in the morning, before we open tomorrow. Do you want to go with me?" he asks. I do, I say.

Roelof and I are walking down the rows of Florida's best used goods in the parking-lot flea market, and he slips his hand in mine right away. It feels extraordinarily nice. He asks about the show, tells me about his passion for distance running, what it feels like to run up mountains and watch the ocean for hours, tells me stories about teenage antics, makes jokes about cats. I ask about his game, where they've been this season. His family.

"My dad is dead, actually," he says.

"I'm so sorry. How young were you when it happened?"

"It's been nearly eight weeks now."

All the words jam up inside my mouth. Eight weeks. The loss is so fresh. It would have happened while he was on the road. I start to say sorry and change the subject, but I remember how much I appreciated people wanting to know more about my mom when I told them she was sick. Not that sharing information shares the grief, just that it spreads the network of care.

"Did you get to see him before he died? Or go home for the funeral?"

"No, we can't leave once we've signed these contracts for the season."

"That's insane."

"Yeah, well, it's the system. I mean, I could have, but then they would have come after my mom for money, and she's got enough on her plate right now."

We are in front of a young woman in a tight pink sweatsuit who is looking eagerly back and forth between our faces. In front of her, every imaginable baby item lies spread on a giant blue tarp, clothes and used books and monitors and bright plastic toys and teething rings and car seats and swaddling blankets.

"Really good prices," she says, pointing to a swing.

"What was he like?"

"Tough. Wonderful. An inspiration, but tough."

"I wish I knew something better to say than *sorry*."

"Me, too," he says, smiles, and kisses me on my knuckles.

I feel a kinship to him. Another person figuring out how to get through this new world.

"Can I see you a little later?" he asks. "After the show? Can we take a walk or something?"

"Sure," I say, trying to sound very cool. Nearly giddy.

Roelof and I meet just after banners are over and walk the dark midway rows, laughing and chatting. He tells me story after story and then asks about my life, my stories. It has been a long time since I've wanted to share my stories, since someone wanted to know them.

We end up near the main stage, at an open area filled with picnic tables. There are giant weeping willows above, all strung with small white glittering lights. The wind rustles the leaves and the night birds are calling. It's strange, hearing the sounds of nature doing its regular work after so many months of human-made sounds. The Cuckoo House behind where we sit, for example, which blares German technopop sixteen hours a day and invites you inside with a mirror maze on the ground floor and vibrating, twisting metal plates up top that you have to jump between like lily pads on a pond. Roelof tells me that carnie women bring men up there sometimes to have sex on the vibration plates.

Behind the twinkling lights in the trees, the stars are twinkling, and Roelof has one of my hands in his hands, and he is inventing stories about each of my fingers. And then he kisses me. It is the middle of the night, in the middle of the fairgrounds, beneath low-hanging trees. He kisses me and I kiss him back and we sit like that for a long time.

"Shall we get a hotel room?" he asks softly, blushing a bit, kissing my knuckles.

"I hear there are bedbugs in all the nearby hotels," I say, which is true, from a story about waking up covered in bites I'd heard from Tanya at the break-the-bottle game, but also an irrefutable excuse.

"Right," he says. "Darn."

"There's a quick romance-killer."

"Nothing like bedbugs to really foil a guy's dreams."

We stay beneath that tree for another hour, telling jokes, recounting dramas from the season, sharing stories about our families. I hadn't thought much about romance in so long, hadn't met anyone who sparked anything in me. But here it is. Maybe just for a moment, or a few days, a week at most. Here it is.

The next morning, a mother and her young daughter are sitting on a bench beside a food joint, eating a hot dog. They are sitting side by side, facing a plastic table, and the little girl's feet, which don't reach far beyond the edge of the bench, are bouncing slightly. The hot dog has ketchup on it and a very light yellow line of mustard, and the mother is holding it in one hand, bringing it to the little girl's mouth and waiting for her small lips to part. The girl takes a bite and begins chewing, looking around her at the rides, which are in final preparation to open for the day. Maybe they know someone here, or the mother works here. Regular marks can't get in early. Maybe they have a prizewinning steer. The mother takes a bite next, looks off another direction to assess these wild territories, and, after the little girl has swallowed, brings the hot dog back to her lips.

I'm watching this from two benches over, sipping some coffee, wanting a little space outside the truck. I can't take my eyes off this pair, this young mother with dark hair and her small child, and the way they are sharing this food, how easy it seems, how smooth and regular, and I'm overwhelmed with the size of my heart, swelling and swelling in some slanted joy for witnessing this little miracle.

THE GREAT REVEAL

Day 145 of 150

I am in the middle of talking the blade box act.

There is a girl in the front row, seven or eight years old, a small skinny thing I've brought around to the back of the box we've just stuck sixteen blades through while Sunshine twists her body inside. This is part of the act—getting an audience member to confirm for the rest of the crowd that our contortionist, a Romanian born with yellow elasticity in her joints, I say, is indeed twisted around those blades. The girl stands staring at the contortionist with a big O'ed mouth, a really giant gape between her lips like she's never seen anything so astonishing. It is pure gold, wonderful GTFM lubricant.

"Is Miss Sunshine REALLY inside that box?" I ask her and bring the mic to her lips as I always do to the volunteer, hope she'll speak with a tone of pure awe and reverence, but the little girl doesn't say anything. She hasn't taken her eyes off the contortionist twisted between those blades. She just nods and nods, her head moving in overly dramatic sweeps between chest and sky. I thank her and ask her to come around front to rejoin her family, but she stays, eyes on the contortionist, mouth open wide enough to take the strangeness and amazement of the whole entire world inside. I thank her again and

370

move the mic away from our mouths and ask if she's okay and she keeps nodding and I start walking around to the front of the box, hoping she'll follow, but she stays and stays, this little girl without a front tooth, her arms tucked inside a Green Bay Packers jersey, staring at what amazes her.

Finally, I reach out my arm and offer it to the little girl. It breaks the spell. We walk back in front of the audience and they clap and she drops my arm and her mom reaches toward her. "What's the trick?" the mother wants to know. "Is she really doing it?" Her hands run up and down the girl's arms, and the girl nods yes, yes, yes. What have you seen and what is the story you'll tell about it?

And when I look back out to the audience, scanning the crowd to estimate what kind of turn I might have, thinking how I can best leverage her astonishment, I see them.

A flash of light on metal.

Not a sword.

Not a tent stake.

A flash of light on the metal frame of a wheelchair.

I see him first. Davy.

He is behind the chair, pushing it, and looking right at me. And then I see her, my mom, sitting in the chair. I see her eyes sliding across the objects of this world, the freaks in their cases, the stage, the lights, the tent, the audience watching me to see how I will try to amaze them next. Her head grazes left to right, up and down. Her eyes don't seem to land on anything.

Nothing in the world has ever been as beautiful as her wild silver hair in the orange glow of the circus tent, like she is made of the moon and the sun both, and also that rare.

There are no words in my mouth. There are only worlds, breaking open.

I swallow, and try to find something to say. There are dozens of eyes on me, staring. I choke back the whole season of grief, the years of it. I look to the astonished little girl who is still staring at the blade box and use her wonder for strength.

I start talking. Put word after word to finish the act, look out at the audience and then back to my parents, checking to see if they are a mirage, if this is one of my daydreams, but there they both are each time. And my mom finds me with her eyes. She locks in on me. I can hear her softly singing in the back of the crowd, *na na na na, na na naaaaa*.

I turn as much of the audience as I can and my parents line up, too, getting closer and closer with each dollar I take until, finally, they are right in front of me, alive, completely alive, the strangest thing of all. The most beautiful, tender, impossible thing of all.

I dive down to my mom, throwing both arms around her shoulders, pressing my cheek up against her cheek. The softest skin of any person in the world. I feel the ledge of her skull, and inside, know that her brain contains universes. Travels between them, even.

Davy has tears in the corners of his eyes, more gray in his hair, but he is smiling. I stand to hug him, a huge, deep, grateful hug. I hadn't given him a lot of those, even though he'd been around almost my entire life. Even though he has stuck around, and stuck around, and stuck around.

He looks exhausted but also brilliantly, brilliantly alive.

Not knowing what to say, and needing to begin the next act, I direct them behind the blade box so they can see Sunshine contorted inside. Davy pushes my mom across the uneven grass, the big wheels on Bubbles bumping over the knots and clumps, and we go on with the show.

I sneak into the tent to stand beside them in the audience once I have a few minutes between acts, pull them into the far corner.

How could a person believe that a thing like this was happening?

A miracle, right inside this very tent.

Turns out, their ship had arrived in Orlando, Florida, which was just a few hours from the fair, and the train they were supposed to immediately board had been delayed a few days for repairs. They'd rented a car and driven over and would stay a night before they went back to board the train and head across the country to California. To home.

"After all, what is adventure but inconvenience, properly regarded?" Davy quotes. It's his favorite new phrase, one that now accompanies every e-mail he sends. My mom agrees with a hum.

They stay for two rounds of the show, see me as the headless woman, see me talk the bed of nails act, and see me, best of all, as the electric woman.

I sit on the metal plate, connect myself to the grid. The bulb is in my mouth. Davy is snapping photos on his phone, and behind that, I can see his wide smile. My mom is watching, too. Carefully. Tracking me exactly, even when Red is talking and gesturing beside me. She is watching a moment of this adventure in the glowing mouth-light, and I am watching an afterglow of her adventure emanating off every part of her body, a body I did not think would ever recover, did not think was recovered when they left for the trip, and am seeing here, finally, finally seeing here, and knowing that eventually, recovery is beside the point.

Her body right now is alive, full of light.

An hour later, they tell me they are pretty worn-out, ready to get a little sleep. I can't even imagine what has happened to their understanding of fatigue, their sense of what is possible, to their relationship in the months they've been away, or, really, what it means to them to be back on this continent.

My mom hums, holding her palm against my cheek. I don't know if this has happened during their trip, or if I'm just noticing it for the first time, but her eyes are back to green. A shade of pear, and bright, with flecks of orange, the same as they were before she had the stroke. It seems impossible, but there they are.

She presses the side of her face into mine. The sound of her song gets softer and softer until it is just a quiet sort of whisper for a child. The kind you make to reassure her that everything's all right.

OUT OF THE MIST

Day 146 of 150

WORLD OF WONDERS
NOVEMBER 2013

It is lightly raining and very gray. Up and down the midway rows, carnies in their bright blue polyester shirts are hanging new tigers and Martians from their games and stacking milk bottles and sweeping broken glass and blowing up flaccid balloons to tack on the board.

My mom and Davy come to the fair early the next morning, before it officially opens. There is only a little bit of time before they have to get back into their rental car and drive to Orlando, to rest a bit before getting on the train that will complete their journey to where they began, though I wonder if it will look or feel like the same place.

I see them approaching from the end of one of the rows, two people appearing from the mist. They might have looked like this on a street in Florence, discussing what they'd see that day or which café to visit for espresso.

Something dumb strikes me. They are in this mist, getting closer to me, but I see them more clearly than I have in a long, long time.

Story goes: once there was a girl who kept her parents in a fog in her mind. There, it was easier to keep the sick safe and distant. And then one day, the girl saw that actually, while she thought they were napping in the fog, they'd been riding goddamned dragons in there.

It is a ridiculous and obvious metaphor, but I feel it happen, these two clear whole people walking out of something, and I can see them as people who are not first and foremost my parents, who are adventurers. I try to imagine meeting them somewhere on their journey, in the audience of the opera, maybe. How much I'd like them. How incredible I'd think their trip was. How ballsy.

We sit together at the same little table where I'd watched the mom sit and share her hot dog with her little girl. We try to ask each other questions about the last five months. It's hard to know where to begin, or even the right kinds of questions to ask.

I tell them about walking tacos.

They tell me about fettuccini.

I show them the lump on my hand from where the tent stake barreled down on me.

My mom shows me the earrings and necklace she's wearing, modeled after a pair Queen Mary once had, that she'd bought on the ship because of extra onboard credit. Then they show me some of her bruises.

"But even that bad stuff was still good," Davy says. My mom nods her head. She seems to understand everything he is saying, everything I am saying, which is not something I was ever sure of before she left. Does this mean that she'd understood when I'd told her I loved her as she was going into one of her brain surgeries, when I hugged her goodbye for this trip?

"We found a closeness we never knew possible," Davy says.

"What do you mean?" I ask.

I look over to my mom and she is looking at him. She pulls her hand up from the coffee she'd been holding and runs it through the back of his hair. She breathes out softly, a kind of breath I'm not sure I've noticed before, a calm release of air. Not a sigh exactly, there is more sweetness to it, and a sound in it, subtle, a faint tone with the breath. She is saying something.

"I think your mom and I are pretty positive people," Davy says. "We knew we would be able to work through whatever happened. At least we weren't shrinking into a little dark hole someplace. So many people just stay in their home and start smelling like urine. Being old wasn't something I wanted for us."

I laugh. My mom does, too. It sounds so simple like that—choosing not to accept the kind of life that's expected of you.

She understood. She understands. And she is still here.

"We became so incredibly close along the way. I don't know, it wasn't something I was expecting, being able to communicate nonverbally. But we have no artifice between us now. No secrets. Everything that happened, happened to both of us. You kind of merge a little. In the hospital, everything is built around pain and progress. When you're out and you're trying to decide what to eat, do you like that painting, how about that statue of the David, that's much more broad and unstructured, and it builds you together in a different way. It led to a kind of enrichment that the show me where your pain is on this scale just doesn't have."

It is almost time for me to go, to get into costume and perform a few last days on the stage before it is all over. It is almost time for them to go catch their train.

My mom reaches out her hand to my hand and pulls me close. She exhales slowly, letting out that same soft note. She runs her fingertips over the calluses on my hands, over my hangnails. I run mine over her necklace, through her hair. There is no hesitation in her movement. What is there left for her to fear?

I give them both big hugs, and, just as I'm running back toward my tent, Davy yells for me to wait.

"They got any fried ravioli here?" he asks. I point them in the right direction.

And then they're gone.

The last few days of performing are a blur as everyone makes their final travel plans and we start packing and fixing what needs to be packed and fixed backstage between acts. There is no time on the final day for tears or reflection, because, like every closing day, the work starts early and hard and never ceases, the day of performing sliding into the night of teardown, folding and unpinning and stacking and rolling and hauling and heaving, working on and on into the night and only occasionally remembering, as we load Queen Kong into the back of the truck, that this is the last time I'll ever do that particular thing.

Roelof runs to our truck after teardown, 9:00 a.m., morning light streaming in. His crew is leaving in fifteen minutes. Driving the trucks to Orlando, spending the night in a motel there and getting on a plane the next morning for South Africa. But he runs to our truck before he leaves, grabs my face in both his hands. He is panting, sweating. We'd spent eight days of this fair, when my parents weren't here, together. He brings his face close to mine and looks at it up close, keeps his bright blue eyes on mine, and then kisses me.

"Goodbye," he says. He turns around and runs, quickly, away from the truck.

There are some romances that last until death. Some that start in childhood. David and Teresa. For Roelof and me, it was just for the time the carnival was in town. It was finding a kindred spirit who was trying to find his way through the arc of grief while still living, and it was bright, and sweet, and sexy, and funny, and I was smacked in the face with the simple, obvious idea that the world isn't all about what has been lost. There is so much still here, to be found.

I imagined my mom out in that field again, the one where the author of that book on strokes, and all the other people who'd recovered, had left her. And she was still there, partially, and there were little blue and yellow and white flowers everywhere, but she wasn't alone. There were animals out there, talking to each other. There were all the other people from all over the world who had to figure out new ways of communicating with each other. And Davy was out there, too, somehow he'd found a way to her. He was whittling a stick and sitting beside my mom as she arranged the bright petals into some complicated, beautiful pattern on the dirt. I didn't need to shoot everyone who tried to enter in case they might hurt her. I didn't need to be skulking on the edges or gnashing my teeth for violence. I needed to go into the goddamned field myself. To sit beside her.

The crew drops me off with all my bags at a discount car rental office in a strip mall in the Florida suburbs. Most of the other performers are flying home the same night or the next day. One is heading to the bus station. They're dropping me off first, quickly, on the way.

Before we'd left the carnival fairgrounds, I'd walked over to Red, who was sitting on the ground and had just been delivered a Styrofoam container of Chinese food by some old-time carnie friend, and waved goodbye.

"Thank you," I said, giving him a bit of a bow. He set the food down and, in a few stiff maneuvers, got to his feet. He wrapped his arms around me.

"I wasn't sure about you at first, Tess," he said. He let go and kept his face close to mine. I could see all his human pincushion divots. "But I want to know about all the things you do next," he said. He had never asked if I'd be back for another season, but he knew. "You've got it, girl," he said. I had no idea what it was for Red, but I wanted to tell him that I'd do everything I could, really, forever, to try to keep having it.

Instead, I squeezed his forearm. "It has been a great, great honor to work with you, sir," I said. He made a fart noise and sat back down to his Chinese food.

There's a rush as I get out of the van, haul out my bags, and give quick hugs. I was hoping for some sort of wrap-up conversation, or parting words of wisdom, something, anything,

379

but all the goodbyes happen fast and then everyone is back in the van, ready for the next destination.

I hug Tommy last, and as I do, he whispers, "MVP," into my ear. I laugh. It's something he's taken to calling me, and even though it's probably a lie, I feel a glow at even the suggestion that what I did out here was useful, and maybe even, dare I dream it, significant. "Keep in touch, Tex," he says.

It's hard to believe that this van is about to drive away and permanently separate me from the crew. Their lives will carry on, maybe back in this van in seven months, maybe not, but I won't be here. It's hard to believe that I'm headed to see dear friends in Tallahassee for a few days, and then home to California to meet my parents—I'll arrive the day before Thanksgiving, two days after they get back, and we've decided we'll eat together—probably something Chinese, my mom, Davy, Sam, and I. It's hard to believe that time even exists past this moment, because the last five months have felt like five years, so packed full, so many days inside days inside days. Maybe time is starting over again.

I don't cry. I've wondered about this last moment of the season so many times, about what I'd do first once I had control over where I could go and what I could do, whether I'd weep. But I don't do anything except stand there in the rental car parking lot, struck still.

Tommy drives the van away. I watch it go, the big white beast. Those fuzzy dice still dangling from the rearview mirror. Our lost comrade's teeth still rattling in that cup. All their sounds traveling farther and farther from me.

"Last time I'll sign this thing," Sunshine said right before we began teardown on closing night. It was the final moment the back end of our truck—our home, our backstage area, our living room for twelve fairs and a week of TV filming, the epicenter of five months of our lives—would be empty. In just a few moments, we'd begin the careful stacking and strapping, stuffing it full again for another winter.

"Still think it's the last time you'll come out?" I asked.

"Yes, if I can help it," Sunshine said. She handed me the Sharpie. "But who knows," she said. "I mean, if they're desperate, I'll come help."

I looked at the semi's wall, where she'd written 2013, the seventh year recorded beneath her name. It was hard to picture the show without her.

Spread across the wall were other names I recognized, Red and Rash the Clown and Short E and Cassie and Tommy and Big, Big Ben and Spif and Lola Ambrosia and Pipscy, and interspersed between the names I knew, there was a whole world of names I didn't know, people who had come before me for a season, maybe two, maybe ten. Names that stretched back the full twenty years that the show had had this semi container, and then, of course, names that stretched across other walls before that, on older trucks and trains, people who knew what fire felt like in their mouths and swords in their throats, who knew how to transcend the limits of their fragile human bodies twenty-five, thirty times a day.

I opened the pen. Found a spot on the wall, and signed my name. Signed the year.

There was nothing to write below it. I had hacked it.

My name was indistinguishable from the rest as I walked out of the truck and looked back once more, just one smear on the wall among many who'd said yes, I am alive, and I am not afraid to show you how.

EPILOGUE

Where You Will Float Electric

JULY 2016

My mom and Davy leave for another trip two and a half years later. This time, a few months into their adventure, my brother and I fly to Greece, to the island of Rhodes, to meet them. We spend five days there all together under that bright sun.

On the last day, we help my mom into Bubbles. We search for a beach with the most gentle slope into the ocean, and, through the crowds tanning outside their resort, wheel her to the water's edge. We inch the chair in. Slide her off the side. Her body lies across Davy's arms, my brother's arms, my arms. She is swimming. This is her first time in the ocean since her stroke. We wade farther out, the three of us with our feet on the ocean floor, her body floating between us. Then she is just in Davy's arms. She is beaming. She is looking up at the sky and then her eyes close and her skin glows and she is just singing and singing and singing. The sun is on her face and the ocean is very blue and we all watch her there, smiling at her, at each other.

A few days later, after my brother and I say goodbye, she has another stroke on board a ship in the Mediterranean. She dies a few hours later. Out in the blue, blue water, under that bright hot sun, singing.

ACKNOWLEDGMENTS

There are so many people who helped make this book possible.

Thank you to my agent, Ellen Levine, for believing this story was worth telling, and to my brilliant, patient editor at FSG, Jenna Johnson, who pointed out enough bad sentences to make the story worth reading. FSG was my dream press, and the whole team there has been wonderful.

I am lucky, lucky, lucky to have a network of amazing writers and friends in my life who have been invaluable readers. My deep gratitude to my writer crews in Salt Lake City and Tuscaloosa who helped train me toward precision and beauty: Susannah Nevison, Cori Winrock, Noam Dorr, Alex Distler, Catie Crabtree, Laura Bylenok, Sarah Eliza Johnson, Adam Weinstein, Danilo Thomas, Betsy Seymour, Dara Ewing, Jess Richardson, Tom Cotsonas, Kevin Weidner, Annie Agnone, and my sister-friend and bright anchor, AB Gorham. Katie Robertson, Alexis Hyatt, Cricket Kovatch, you loves. Nadja Durbach for reading an early draft. To my dear friend, my first reader, the brilliant rogue cowboy Devin Gribbons: thanks for calling me on my shit.

I wrote most of this book sitting at home in my pajamas and mainlining coffee, but I had the opportunity to attend a few conferences and residencies through generous fellowships that gave me great energy, and to them I am grateful: Writing by Writers at Tomales Bay, the University of Utah's Taft-Nicholson Center, and the Fine Arts Work Center in Provincetown's summer session.

I've had some extraordinary teachers and mentors who have guided me along the way. First and foremost, my deepest gratitude to Melanie Rae Thon, a lantern through the night, and also to Kellie Wells and Michael Mejia, true guides, and to the splendid Lance Olsen, Wendy Rawlings, Michael Martone, Joel Brouwer, Lidia Yuknavitch, Paul Lisicky, Jerald Walker, and my fifth-grade teacher, Katie Rasmussen, who let me turn in poems for extra credit.

Dear Family: this book is yours. Thank you for the love and support and ideas about who should play who in the movie. Dad, thanks for having my back and publishing a chapbook of my dramatic yet sincere poems when I was seventeen. Nico, the trick is there is no trick—pure magic. Davy and Sam, thanks for letting me share this joyful, hard, bad-joke ridden road with you. I'm so much better for it.

And for Jeremy, my adventure partner, thanks for giving me my own great love story.

Dear World of Wonders Crew: I'll never find the right way to say thanks for letting me be part of your wonderful, weird world for a season. The full story would take a thousand volumes to fill. Chris Christ, Ward Hall, Tommy, Red, Short E, Sunshine, Spif, Pipscy, Cassie, Ben, Hermie, Francine, Rachel, Rash, Snickers—you will forever hold my wonder.

Thank you to all the great storytellers I met along the way, and to some books I found especially helpful for reference: *Freaks* by Leslie Fiedler, *The Arts of Deception* by James W. Cook, *Struggles and Triumphs* by P.T. Barnum, *Circus and Carnival Ballyhoo* by A.W. Stencell, *A Cabinet of Medical Curiosities* by Jan Bondeson, *Phantoms in the Brain* by V.S. Ramachandran and Sandra Blakeslee, *My Stroke of Insight* by

Jill Bolte Taylor, and the great sideshow novel *Geek Love* by Katherine Dunn.

Want to see a great show? Follow the World of Wonders on Facebook to learn where this carnival season will take them: facebook.com/world.of.wonders.show

Portions of this book originally appeared, in earlier versions, in the following fine publications:

Hayden's Ferry Review, 2016 (Winner 2016 AWP Intro Journals Award, Nonfiction): "Dispatch from the Carnival: And the Low Sky Opens"
Autre magazine, May 26, 2016: "The Electric Woman"
The Rumpus, December 2015 (nominated for a Pushcart Prize, 2015): "Dispatch from the Carnival: Instructions for Losing Your Head"
The Rumpus, June 2015 (nominated for a Pushcart Prize, 2015): "Dispatch from the Carnival: Taking in the Sword"
The Rumpus, April 2014: "Dispatch from the Carnival: Bloodlust"
The Rumpus, November 2013: "Notes from the Road: The Snake Charmer"
The Rumpus, July 2013: "The Trick Is There Is No Trick"